101 Careers
in Social Work

ABOUT THE AUTHORS

Jessica A. Ritter, BSW, MSSW, PhD, is Assistant Professor and Director of Field Education at Pacific University in Forest Grove, Oregon. Jessica has 15 years of experience as a social worker. She earned a BSW, MSSW, and Ph.D. in Social Work at the University of Texas at Austin. Her career as a social worker and academic has been dedicated to political advocacy, child welfare, and children's rights. Over the course of her career, she has held a variety of positions at both the micro and macro levels—from working as a caseworker at Children's Protective Services to working in an administrative capacity in child welfare to conducting research. Today, her passion includes teaching policy and macro level social work courses with the goal of getting undergraduate social work students excited about social policy, demystifying the political process, increasing their levels of political efficacy, and inspiring them to be engaged politically. She is currently the chair of the Legislative Committee for NASW Oregon.

Halaevalu F. Ofahengaue Vakalahi, MSW, PhD, is Associate Professor and Director of the MSW Program at George Mason University in Arlington, Virginia. She is a Pacific Islander woman, born in Tonga and raised in Hawaii. Her areas of teaching include human behavior and the social environment and social policy. Her research interests include Pacific Islander culture and community, and the experiences of women of color in the academy. She received a PhD in social work from University of Utah, an MSW from the University of Hawaii, a master's in educational administration from the University of Utah, and a BS in business management from BYU-Hawaii. Prior to George Mason University, she was an Accreditation Specialist at the Council on Social Work Education and served on the faculty at San Francisco State University, BYU-Hawaii, and New Mexico State University.

Mary Kiernan-Stern, MSW, LCSW, is an Instructor and the Director of MSW Field Education in the Social Work Department at George Mason University in Arlington, Virginia.

Mary is an experienced social worker with over 20 years of practice in the areas of medical and mental health and multicultural and spirituality issues. A graduate of the University of Pittsburgh, she has an MSW degree in Community Organization with a specialization in Employee Assistance Programs. Mary has been at George Mason University since 2002.

101 Careers
in Social Work

JESSICA A. RITTER, BSW, MSSW, PhD

HALAEVALU F. O. VAKALAHI, MSW, PhD

MARY KIERNAN-STERN, MSW, LCSW

SPRINGER PUBLISHING COMPANY
New York

Springer Publishing Company, LLC
11 West 42nd Street
New York, NY 10036–8002
www.springerpub.com

Acquisitions Editor: Jennifer Perillo
Project Manager: Cindy Fullerton
Cover Design: YAY! Design
Composition: Aptara Inc.

11 12/ 5 4

Library of Congress Cataloging-in-Publication Data

Ritter, Jessica A.
    101 careers in social work / Jessica A. Ritter, Halaevalu F.O. Vakalahi, Mary Kiernan-Stern.
        p.   cm.
    ISBN 978-0-8261-5405-7 (alk. paper)
    1. Social service—Vocational guidance—United States.   2. Vocational guidance—United States.   3. Job hunting—United States.   I. Vakalahi, Halaevalu F. Ofahengaue.   II. Kiernan-Stern, Mary.   III. Title.   IV. Title: One hundred one careers in social work.   V. Title: One oh one careers in social work.

HV10.5.R58   2009
361.3023′73–dc22   2008040791

Printed in the U.S. by Offset Paperback Manufacturing.

This book is dedicated to my wonderful and amazing family who never stop believing in me: my mother, Christina Ritter, for teaching me the meaning of love and compassion and the art of listening; my father, Clinton Ritter, for inspiring my love of politics and the fight for the underdog; and my sister, Alissa Ritter, for being my best friend in this life.
—JR

To my son Tuihakavalu, the light of my life; and my parents Moana and Faleola Ofahengaue who inspired me to think and live outside the box in order to achieve my passion in social work.
—HFOV

I would like to thank my best friend and husband, Lew, for 33 years of love and support, and my family Ethan and Kaytee Stern, and Anna Jean and Peter Shirley for giving me such great happiness, and much laughter.
—MKS

Contents

PART II: CAREERS IN SOCIAL WORK   29

4   Careers in Child Welfare   31

5   School-Based and School-Linked Services   57

Preface

We were extremely motivated to write this book because there has never been a greater need for smart, competent, and compassionate social workers than right now. There are many pressing social problems at home and around the world. In the past few years, we have witnessed the war in Iraq and Afghanistan the home mortgage crisis, rising income inequality, Hurricane Katrina and other natural disasters around the world, and a heated political debate surrounding illegal immigration. We know that social workers will continue to be in demand as the aging population grows and as we grapple with the millions of Americans who are without healthcare and are struggling to adjust to the ever increasing cost of food and gasoline. Social workers will also be needed to aid returning American soldiers and their families, many of whom will need medical and mental health services for years to come.

However, despite these challenges, there is hope; many Americans have been galvanized by these issues and want to have their voices heard. There is talk of ending the war in Iraq, having national health care, and improving public education. These are exciting times—and especially for social workers!

After reading this book, we hope that readers will understand the mission and values of the social work profession and will use this book as a guide to help them assess which field(s) of social work practice might be a good fit for them. We hope they will be inspired by the real stories of social workers from all across the country who are doing exciting and interesting things (see the "Social Worker Spotlights" in each chapter).

Finally, we wrote this book because we are troubled by the idea that very few people "get" the social work profession. The general public has a fairly limited view of what social workers do across this country every day. Many people are familiar with the clinical or direct services work carried out by social workers, but have no idea that there is a "big picture" side to the social work profession and that the mission of the social work profession includes a commitment to social justice. Most do not realize that social workers work with organizations, communities, and in the political and international arenas. They do not know that social workers are filmmakers and artists and politicians and community activists. We want to educate people about the countless array of options out there for social workers with an earned bachelor's, master's, or doctorate in social work and inspire them to be very creative in designing their career based on their own unique skills and passions. We hope that after reading this book, you will realize that there is no "typical social worker"—and no "typical" social work career.

Acknowledgment

We would like to acknowledge our wonderfully gifted and supportive editor, Jennifer Perillo. We could not have done this without you—heartfelt thanks to you, Jennifer!

We would also like to acknowledge the following social workers who shared their inspiring stories with us for the Social Worker Spotlight sections of this book:

Elizabeth Alex, MSW
Joel T. Andrade, MSW, LICSW, Doctoral Candidate
Marilyn Peterson Armour, MSW, PhD
Marleine Bastien, BSW, MSW, LCSW
Sheryl Bruno, MSW
Ali Cusick, MSW Candidate
Lori Delagrammatikas, MSW/PhD Candidate
Odis Dolton, MSSW
Maya Doyle, LCSW
Anne Driscoll, LCSW
Magda Flores, MSSW
Richard B. Joelson, DSW, LCSW
Robert Klekar, LCSW, LCDC
Amy Krings-Barnes, BSW, MSW
Brandy Macaluso, BSW, CVP
Purnima Mane, MSW, PhD
Sue Matorin, MS, ACSW
Murali D. Nair, PhD
Elliott Naishtat, MSSW, JD
Kristin Noel Ludwig, MSW
Mary Jane O'Rourke, MSW
Simon Paquette, LCSW, RC
Juliane Ramic, MSW

Brian Rivers, BSW, LSW
Greg Shufeldt, BSW, MSW
Trina Scordo, MSW student
Shana Seidenberg, MSW, LSW
Lyn K. Slater, MA, MSW, PhD
Laura Elmore Smith, LMSW
Erica Solway, MSW, MPH
Cindy Southworth, MSW
Agnes Zarcaro, LCSW

The Profession of Social Work

1 What is Social Work?

In these times of difficulty, we Americans everywhere must and shall choose the path of social justice, the path of faith, the path of hope and the path of love toward our fellow man. *—Franklin Delano Roosevelt, October 2, 1932*

Congratulations! By picking up this book, you are taking an important step in exploring a career in social work. Perhaps, we are a little biased, but we believe that social work is a career for an extraordinary life. This book will help you assess whether social work is for you. Or, if you have already decided to be a professional social worker, this book will help you decide which specific fields of social work practice are a good fit for you based on your interests, skills, preferences, personality, and of course, your passions! In fact, this book profiles 101 different career options for social workers—including the classic or traditional social work vocations, emerging ones, and a few that are somewhat unconventional.

People find their way to social work in many different ways. Some of you may have a close friend or family member who is a social worker, so you are somewhat familiar with the kinds of things social workers do. Many of you have probably seen social workers portrayed in movies, such as *I Am Sam* or *White Oleander*, or television shows, such as *ER* or *Judging Amy*. (Unfortunately, many portrayals of social workers in the media are not always accurate or very positive depictions.) Others find their way to social work because they know they want to help others or improve society but are not sure what path they want to go down exactly—perhaps teaching, or counseling, or psychology, or nursing, or law, or public policy, or maybe social work? In social work programs, you will find a wide range of students, from those young, traditional college students, to those who are not so traditional, such as mid-career changers who want to do something completely different in the second phase of their lives.

The variety of options available to those with a social work degree is extremely impressive and is one of the many reasons students choose to pursue a social work degree. If you are looking for a career that is meaningful and challenging, and never boring, social work might be the one for you. A degree in social work will enable you to create your own unique career path—one full of exciting possibilities.

SEPARATING THE FACTS FROM THE FICTION

Some say social work is a science, and some say it is an art. We would argue that it is both. However, once you become a practicing social worker, you quickly learn that most people have a fairly narrow conception of what social workers do and the kinds of jobs they hold. There are also a number of myths about the social work profession. If you want to try an interesting experiment, ask people you know the following question: "What do social workers do?" One of the following responses is fairly typical: Social workers "help people"; they "work with troubled children and families"; they "work with poor people who are on welfare." While these answers are technically accurate, they barely skim the surface in terms of the options that are available to those interested in a career in social work and the knowledge and skills required to do this job.

Top 7 Myths about the Social Work Profession

Myth #1: Most social workers are employed by the government.

Fact: The majority of social workers work in the private sector—in non-profit organizations, for-profit settings, faith-based organizations, and many are self-employed.

Myth #2: All social workers are poorly paid.

Fact: While it is true that some social workers receive salaries that are lower than they should be, many social workers are well paid, particularly those who move into administrative or supervisory positions (see individual career chapters for more information about specific salary ranges).

Myth #3: All social workers have stressful jobs.

Fact: Though some social workers, such as child protection caseworkers, have very stressful jobs, many social workers have jobs that would rate low on the stress scale. However, an important skill for a social worker is self-care in order to avoid burnout.

Myth #4: Anyone who has a job where they help others can be called a social worker.

Fact: Only those who have earned a degree in social work can call themselves a social worker. In some states, you must also be licensed to use this title.

Myth #5: To do therapy or counseling, you need a degree in psychology or psychiatry.

Fact: Many social workers work as mental health providers. Some choose to have a private practice while others work in a counseling center or other setting.

Myth #6: Social workers "enable" their clients by solving their problems for them.

Fact: Social workers empower others by providing them with the skills and resources they need to solve their own problems.

Myth #7: Social work is "easy" since you are dealing with "touchy-feely" stuff.

Fact: Though social workers are caring and compassionate individuals, they also need to be intelligent and have strong critical thinking skills in order to understand research, policy, and the various theories that guide social work practice.

According to the Code of Ethics of the National Association of Social Workers (1999), the primary mission of the social work profession is:

"to enhance human well-being and help meet the basic human needs of all people, with particular attention to the needs and empowerment of people who are vulnerable, oppressed, and living in poverty. A historic and defining feature of social work is the profession's focus on individual well-being in a social context and the well-being of society. Fundamental to social work is attention to the environmental forces that create, contribute to, and address problems in living."

One very simple definition of social work is that it is the study of social problems and human behavior. Thus, social workers address any number of important social problems in this country and around the world, including, but not limited to:

- poverty and homelessness;
- child abuse, neglect, and exploitation;
- severe mental illness;
- teen pregnancy, suicide, and other problems facing youth;
- family problems such as poor communication, divorce, and domestic violence;
- sexual assault;
- depression, anxiety, and other mental health problems;
- community problems such as crime, substandard schools, violence, lack of transportation, jobs, and childcare;
- supporting older adults and those with disabilities;
- assisting immigrants and refugees;
- working with individuals diagnosed with AIDS and other chronic or terminal illnesses;
- discrimination against women, people of color, and sexual minorities;
- substance abuse; and
- natural disasters.

Social workers are change agents who work with a wide variety of client populations in a vast array of settings. We work in schools; domestic violence shelters; adoption agencies; courts and prisons; hospitals; treatment centers; in government agencies; for profit, non-profit, and faith based organizations; counseling centers; nursing homes and long-term care facilities; homeless shelters; international organizations; and in the military. We are community organizers, counselors and therapists, caseworkers, activists, researchers, academics, and human service administrators. We also work in the political arena as lobbyists and legislative aides. And the best part is that we can work with one client population for a number of years and then decide to switch to another arena for an exciting new challenge. Have we hooked you yet?

HOW IS SOCIAL WORK DIFFERENT FROM OTHER RELATED PROFESSIONS/DISCIPLINES?

Many people are confused about how social work is different from other related professions, such as sociology and psychology, or various degrees in counseling, so we will help sort this out for you. There are a number of unique features that define the social work profession and set it apart from other disciplines. One of the most important distinctions is that social workers engage in both *micro and macro practice*. This means that we work directly with individuals and families, but we are also concerned with social change and working to address social problems at the community, national, and international levels. We are concerned about addressing social problems such as discrimination, oppression, and human rights violations, and we work to achieve *social and economic justice*. We care about the problems of poverty and violence in our communities and the fact that millions of Americans do not have health insurance. Social workers not only help individuals function better within their environment, but also work on changing the environment so it works better for individuals and families. This is what we call social work's *person-in-environment* perspective.

Table 1.1 shows some of the differences in educational requirements, course work, and focus between social work and related disciplines.

The social work profession has a number of core values that help define and guide our practice. Many of these core values are outlined in the National Association of Social Worker's (NASW) Code of Ethics. Social workers value *diversity* and are trained to be *culturally competent*. In social work, diversity is broadly defined and encompasses race, culture, religion, gender, age, sexual orientation, and socioeconomic status. When we work with individuals, families, groups, and communities, we operate from a *strengths perspective*. We use interventions that *empower* others to solve their own problems. We respect an individual's *right to determine their own course of treatment* and to make their own decisions, except in cases when they are at risk of hurting themselves or others. We believe that people are *resilient* and *can change* when they have the will and the necessary knowledge and resources.

Social workers who earn their bachelor's degree in social work (BSW) are trained to be generalist social work practitioners, which means they have the skills required to work with individuals, families, groups, communities, and organizations in a variety of social work and host settings. Earning a master's degree in social work (MSW) allows social workers to

Table 1.1

SOCIAL WORK AND RELATED FIELDS

	SOCIAL WORK	PSYCHOLOGY	SOCIOLOGY	COUNSELING PROGRAMS
Education	Can practice with a bachelor's degree; however, a master's degree is preferred by many employers	PhD required to earn title of psychologist	PhD required to work as a researcher or university professor; variety of potential settings for those with a master's degree in sociology	Master's degree needed; some programs have a special focus such as school counseling, substance abuse, marriage and family, pastoral counseling, etc.
Course Work	Liberal arts perspective; required coursework will include policy, human behavior and the social environment (HBSE), research, and clinical courses	Specialty areas: clinical psychology, cognition, developmental, neuroscience, social, and personality. Heavy focus on research	Courses may include: criminology, demography, race and gender inequality, religion, social organizations, research, and family structures	Education and training focused on assessment, counseling theory, and in-dividual/group interventions
Primary Focus	Micro and macro practice; help people with problems of daily living that may require direct intervention or referral; also concerned with social justice and helping clients who are oppressed and living in poverty	Heavy focus on psychological testing, diagnosing client disorders, and providing psychotherapy	Study of human behavior and interactions at the group level; also, the social structure and institutions that humans create; tends to be more of an academic, rather than an "applied," profession	Helping people through individual, couples, family or group therapy

develop advanced skills and to concentrate or specialize in a specific area of interest. Social workers who earn their doctorate pursue careers in research or work as university professors. For more information on social work education and licensure, please refer to chapter 3.

HOW DID SOCIAL WORK BEGIN?

Social work has a rich and colorful history. In 1898, Columbia University became the first school of social work in the United States, marking the beginning of the social work profession. However, there were many individuals who did what we now identify as "social work" before social work was professionalized. Perhaps the most famous example of one of these early social workers is Jane Addams, a remarkable woman who founded Hull House in Chicago. Hull House was a settlement home that provided a wide range of services (e.g., literacy classes, health clinics, daycare, art appreciation, social and hobby clubs) to immigrants in Chicago who were facing serious problems such as exploitation on the job, living in over-crowded tenement buildings, discrimination, juvenile delinquency, in-adequate schools, and insufficient sanitation. The women who worked at Hull House lived in the community where they worked instead of return-ing to their middle class communities, which was more typical at the time. They also advocated for these individuals and families to pressure city leaders to improve the living and working conditions in this community.

A Brief History of the Social Work Profession in the United States

1877 American Charity Organization: First organized attempt to help people with severe social problems.

1886 Settlement House movement begins, the most famous being Hull House in Chicago led by Jane Addams. These settlement homes provided a wide range of services to immigrants and the poor.

1898 Columbia University becomes the first school of social work in the United States.

1916 Social worker Jeannette Rankin becomes the first woman elected to Congress.

1931 Social work pioneer Jane Addams receives the Nobel Peace Prize.

1935 Franklin D. Roosevelt's New Deal: Social Security Act passed, which created a number of important social welfare programs (e.g., social security, unemployment compensation, public assistance) and a safety net for the poor. Social worker Frances Perkins served as Secretary of Labor.

1952 Council on Social Work Education (CSWE) is formed.

1955 National Association of Social Workers (NASW) is formed.

1965 Lyndon B. Johnson's Great Society and War on Poverty, Head Start, Medicare, and Medicaid programs created.

1998 Social work profession celebrates its centennial!

The philosophy behind the settlement home movement included many of the hallmarks of the social work profession, including a respect for ethnic diversity and customs, the value of community members taking care of each other, a belief in the inherent *dignity and worth of all individuals*, the importance of political advocacy, and the recognition that poverty and lack of opportunity are often the greatest barriers to success—not a flaw in one's character.

The social work profession was greatly expanded and legitimized by the presidencies of Franklin Delano Roosevelt (New Deal) and Lyndon Johnson (Great Society) when they significantly expanded the role of the federal government in providing for the social welfare of its citizens. Frances Perkins, a social worker, was the first woman to be appointed to the cabinet of a U.S. President. As President Franklin D. Roosevelt's Secretary of Labor, Perkins drafted much of the New Deal legislation in the 1940s. In 1955, the National Association of Social Workers (NASW) was founded, and in 1998, the social work profession celebrated its 100th birthday!

WHAT IS THE FUTURE OUTLOOK FOR SOCIAL WORKERS?

The job outlook for professional social workers is very good. Unfortunately, because individuals and families will continue to face personal

Table 1.2

EMPLOYMENT BY TYPE OF SOCIAL WORKER	
Child, family, and school social workers	282,000
Medical and public health social workers	124,000
Mental health and substance abuse social workers	122,000
Social workers, all other	66,000

(*Source:* Bureau of Labor Statistics, http://www.bls.gov/oco/pdf/ocos060.pdf)

problems and challenges, and because social problems such as poverty, illness, substance abuse, and family violence continue to persist, social workers will be needed. In fact, certain demographic trends—like the growing number of older Americans and the continuing influx of immigrant populations, many of whom will need social services and support—mean that social workers will be in higher demand than ever.

According to the U.S. Department of Labor, the employment of social workers is expected to increase faster than the average for all occupations through 2016. The employment of social workers is projected to increase 22% between 2006 and 2016, particularly for those working with older adults, children and families, substance abuse, and in medical/mental health settings. The growth of medical and public health social workers is expected to be 24%, while mental health/substance abuse social workers will grow by 30%, much faster than the average. According to the U.S. Department of Labor, social workers held about 595,000 jobs in 2006. Table 1.2 provides a break down by type of social worker.

Individuals with an earned degree in social work are very marketable because employers know that they are trained to be excellent communicators, are skilled in crisis intervention, are creative problem solvers, have good "people skills," and have a valuable skill set that is transferable to many settings.

Social work is a dynamic profession that is constantly evolving and growing. The profession has a colorful history and continues to be relevant and vital to many individuals, families, and communities across the country and globally. It is a noble profession—one that is dedicated to service and social justice. Social workers have a unique mission and value system to serve people in need, many of whom are forgotten or invisible to the general public.

One of the most appealing features of the social work profession is that there are so many diverse career options—this book will profile over 101 career paths for professional social workers, including a fun checklist in each career chapter to help you assess which ones might be a good fit for you. Social work is a wonderful career, but it is not for everyone. Chapter 2 will help you assess whether it might be for you. Good luck!

REFERENCES

Code of Ethics of the National Association of Social Workers, (1999). Approved by the 1996 NASW Delegate Assembly and revised by the 1999 NASW Delegate Assembly. Retrieved May 13, 2008, from http://www.socialworkers.org/pubs/code/default.asp

U.S. Department of Labor, Bureau of Labor Statistics. *Social Workers*. Retrieved June 13, 2008, from http://www.bls.gov/oco/pdf/ocos060.pdf

2 Got Social Work?

Social work is an extraordinary profession, but it is not for everyone. One of the goals of this book is to help you figure out whether a career in social work is a good fit. A part of the self-assessment process discussed below is determining whether you have the values, ethics, qualities, knowledge, and practice skills necessary for a successful career in social work. For a start, completing a degree in social work will provide you with a foundation of knowledge and practice.

IS SOCIAL WORK FOR YOU?

Social work is a demanding but highly rewarding field for those who are willing to accept the call to restore, maintain, and enhance the social functioning of individuals, families, groups, and communities from diverse cultural and economic backgrounds.

In assessing your interest in and suitability for social work, consider the following general issues and questions (Morales, Sheafor, & Scott, 2006):

- Commitment to humanity: Are you passionate about social change and social justice? Are you concerned about social problems such as poverty, racism, and inequality? Are you committed to working with people from diverse backgrounds to enhance their social functioning and thus contribute to the betterment of humanity as a whole? Are you resilient and committed to cultivating resilience in others? Do you possess empathy for others? Do you genuinely care about people? Are you willing to advocate for the most vulnerable members of our society and connect them to resources necessary for a better life?

- Self-awareness: Are you able or willing to acknowledge and examine your own biases as well as other hindering personal issues and maintain an open mind towards working with people from diverse backgrounds?

- Adherence to professional values and ethics: Are you willing to adhere to the National Association of Social Worker's (NASW) Code of Ethics and demonstrate commitment to these values and ethics in working with individuals, families, groups, organizations, and communities from diverse backgrounds? Do you possess or are willing to develop the quality of professionalism, being nonjudgmental and acceptance of others? Do you believe in the worth and dignity of every human being? Are you willing to grapple with and resolve ethical dilemmas?

- Commitment to diversity in all its forms: Are you accepting of differences and diversity by race/ethnicity, family background, social economic status, sexual orientation, national origin, immigration status, age, class, disability, gender, and religion?

- Commitment to confidentiality: Are you committed to confidentiality and showing respect for other's rights to privacy? Are you committed to building relationships of trust with others?

- Superior interpersonal skills: Do you have or are willing to develop and employ problem solving and decision making skills? Are you willing to make hard decisions and follow through with them? Do you have or are willing to develop superior leadership, networking, and teamwork skills that are necessary for effective social work?

- Excellent analytical and communication skills: Are you willing to develop excellent analytical, organizational, and communications skills to utilize in your practice with individuals, families, groups, organizations, and communities? Do you have or are willing to develop strong listening and interviewing skills as well as other skills such as confrontation, support, limit setting, and self-disclosure? Do you have strong problem solving skills?

■ Flexibility and balance: Are you willing to work at unorthodox hours yet able to maintain a healthy balance between your professional and personal lives? Are you able or willing to undertake multiple tasks and assume awesome responsibilities?

■ Lifelong learning: Are you committed to engagement in lifelong learning, keeping abreast of current literature, evaluating your own practice, and contributing knowledge to the profession? Are you willing to accept criticism and utilize it for self-improvement and continuous professional growth?

BENEFITS OF A CAREER IN SOCIAL WORK

There are many benefits of a career in social work, which are reflected on various levels, individually and collectively. A few major benefits are highlighted in the subsequent text. For instance, one of the greatest benefits of a career in social work is the extensiveness of the field in terms of career paths and opportunities. In 2006, the *Wall Street Journal* identified social work as one of the eight best careers (*Wall Street Journal*, 2006). Social workers provide services in a large variety of areas, including both private and public settings, such as schools, corrections, health care, and child welfare systems, to social services and mental health facilities, among individuals, families, groups, and communities, to name a few.

Furthermore, the profession of social work has historically served as a vehicle for enhancing and maintaining better lives, functional systems, and thriving communities. Fundamental to the profession and among its professionals is a greater sense of social justice, equality and equity, and building human capacity and communities. Unlike other careers, social work provides endless opportunities to advocate for social change and build individual, family, and community capacities.

In addition, a career in social work provides opportunities for personal and professional growth; working in a community of committed and inspired social workers; gratification in helping others; lifelong learning, including learning to critically think about human behavior and complex social problems; using creativity in working and building rewarding relationships with clients and other professionals from diverse backgrounds; and career advancement, including supervisory and administration level positions. A career in social work is an opportunity to engage in important and meaningful work that is always exciting, interesting, challenging, and never boring!

CHALLENGES OF A CAREER IN SOCIAL WORK

Similar to other professions, social work careers also have their share of challenges. In fact, the characteristics that reflect the benefits of social work can be its greatest challenges. For example, the very nature of the work and interaction with human beings and multiple systems can make a career in this profession challenging. Whether a social worker is working with individuals, families, groups, or communities, helping people with complicated and complex psychological, health, social, or financial problems is part of his/her day. This investment in helping people, at the same time dealing with the system in which they work, can be emotionally draining and sometimes result in disappointments with oneself and/or clients. The stressful nature of the job emphasizes the absolute importance of self-care and living a balanced personal and professional life. Likewise, working with people who are troubled or unstable also speaks to safety as a critical issue that must be taken seriously. Dealing with ethical dilemmas associated with helping people can also be particularly difficult.

Moreover, the ever-changing nature of social work demands that a social worker keep abreast of the existing literature in relation to current knowledge, skills, policies, and programs in order to be effective. This requires additional time and effort in education, training, and other professional development endeavors. However, you must be careful not to be trapped in the "perfect social worker" syndrome. There is no perfect social worker—we all make mistakes from which we learn to be better. Likewise, it can also be challenging when a social worker has to specialize in a particular area, knowing that people experience concurrent problems.

As in other helping professions, such as teaching and nursing, social work continues to advocate for respect as a profession and equity in compensation. Because such changes are slow at times, it is necessary to be patient and continue to press forward.

THE SOCIAL WORK OATH

Social work is a profession built on professional education, accreditation of social work schools, licensure, ethics, and competencies. This combination contributes rigor to the development and training of new, as well as seasoned and effective, social workers. To this end, social workers adhere to the NASW Code of Ethics (National Association of Social Workers, 1999) and the Standards for Cultural Competence in Social Work Practice (National Association of Social Workers, 2001), to name a few of the core documents that guide the profession of social work.

The NASW Code of Ethics provides the core values, ethical principles, and ethical standards that guide the conduct of social workers. The core values upon which the social work profession is grounded include service, social justice, dignity and worth of the person, importance of human relationships, integrity, and competence. From these core values are ethical principles, which state that social workers help people address social problems, challenge social injustice, promote respect for the inherent dignity and worth of the person, recognize the centrality of human relations, behave in a trustworthy manner, and practice within their areas of competence and continue developing their expertise. Based on these core values and ethics are the standards that guide the professional activities of all social workers. These standards articulate all social workers' ethical responsibilities in practice settings to clients and colleagues, ethical responsibilities as professionals, and ethical responsibilities to the social work profession and to the broader society.

In addition, to meet the constant changes in demographics in the United States and affirm the ethical responsibility of social workers to be culturally competent in serving diverse populations, the NASW also issued the Standards for Cultural Competence in Social Work Practice. These standards define the meaning of cultural competence in social work practice and provide indicators for achievement of such standards through the articulation of social workers' ethics and values, self-awareness, cross-cultural knowledge, cross-cultural skills, service delivery methods, empowerment and advocacy, promotion of diverse workforce, professional education, importance of language diversity, and cross-cultural leadership.

AN INVITATION TO YOU

Because life is complex and complicated, yet precious, there is always a need for dedicated and effective social workers. Social workers are needed by individuals, families, and communities from diverse walks of life. In the words of Lynch and Vernon (2001):

You'll need a Social Worker. . . when you come into the world too soon; when you can't find anyone to play with; when you are left home alone; when you hate the new baby; when you don't think your teacher likes you; when you are bullied; when you don't want mommy and daddy to divorce; when you miss your big brother; when you don't like how the neighbor touches you; when you get into fights at school; when you don't make the team; when your best friend moves away; when you get poor grades; when you always fight with your siblings; when your friends pressure you to get high; when you can't adjust to the move; when you can't talk to your parents; when you want to quit school; when your friends don't like you anymore; when you didn't want this baby; when you feel like running away; when your friend swallows an overdose; when you are the only one that thinks you're fat; when you can't find someone who speaks your language; when you can't forget the assault; when you can't decide on a career; when your family pressures you to marry; when your boss is hitting on you; when you can't stick to a budget; when you want to adopt; when you wonder if you are drinking too much; when you think you are neglecting your kids; when you are hated because of who you are; when you lose your baby; when your community has gang problems; when your kids want to live with your ex; when your partner is unfaithful; when you want to meet your birthparent; when your disabled child needs friends; when your step-kids hate you; when your mother won't speak to you; when you just can't face moving again; when your spouse wants a divorce; when you want to be a foster parent; when your city officials don't respond; when your best friend has panic attacks; when you find drugs in your son's room; when your job is eliminated; when your mother-in-law wants to move in; when your neighborhood needs a community center; when you find there is no joy in your life; when your car accident destroys your career; when you sponsor a refugee family; when your legislature passes a bad law; when your brother won't help care for dad; when your partner has a mid life crisis; when you are stressed by menopause; when you are caring for parents and children; when you want to change careers; when you lose your home in a fire; when you are angry all the time; when your nest really empties; when your partner insists you retire; when you can't afford respite care; when you can't find a job and you're sixty; when your kids demand you move in with them; when your daughter suddenly dies; when you are scared about living alone; when you can't drive anymore; when your children ignore your medical decisions; when your retirement check won't pay the bills; when you learn you have a terminal illness; when you need a nursing home.

If you are ready for a challenging and extraordinary professional life, we invite you to consider a career in social work. For most of us, it is a passion and we have never looked back!

REFERENCES

Lynch, D., & Vernon, R. (2001). *Life's challenges–Social workers are there for you.* Retrieved May 28, 2007, from http://www.belmont.edu/socwork/about_us/youll_need_a_social_worker_when....html

Morales, A. T., Sheafor, B. W., & Scott, M. E. (2006). *Social work: A profession of many faces* (11th ed.). Needham Heights, MA: Allyn & Bacon.

National Association of Social Workers. (1999). *Code of Ethics.* Washington, DC: Author.

National Association of Social Workers, National Committee on Racial and Ethnic Diversity. (2001). *Standards for Cultural Competence in Social Work Practice.* Washington, DC: Author.

Wall Street Journal. (2006). *2006 Best Careers: The Results are In.* Wall Street Journal CareerJournal. Retrieved June 18, 2008, from http://online.wsj.com/article/C60711INTRO.html?mod=Careers

3 The Yellow Brick Road: Education and Licensure for Social Workers

One thing is certain in pursuing a career in social work—you will be taking a clear path of adventure and challenge in completing your professional education toward this goal. In reviewing what your educational options are, you will realize that there is more than one entry point into the social work profession. To give you a clearer picture of what we mean, let us share with you how we came to be social workers.

■ Valu began her career by studying business administration as an undergraduate. After working for a while with this degree, she decided to pursue a master's degree in education (*MEd*). Valu found that she loved working in the educational system and that her business background was very helpful in her administrative role. Yet, somehow, this work was not focused enough on what Valu's real passion was—helping others in more direct ways. So, it wasn't too long before Valu returned to graduate school to earn a master's degree in social work (*MSW*). Employed as a professional social worker and also as an educator, Valu later made a career decision to earn a doctorate in social work (*PhD*) in order to teach and conduct research in university settings. This way, she would be able to use all of her practical experience to contribute to the development of knowledge and skills in the social work profession.

■ Mary started down a different road to becoming a social worker. She knew she enjoyed learning about people and how they behaved when individuals formed a group. Mary was also interested in understanding people from different ethnic, cultural, and religious backgrounds. In college, she earned a bachelor's of arts degree in sociology (*BA*). After working for a few years as a crisis counselor in a hospital clinic, Mary was encouraged by her supervisor, who was also a social worker, to return to school and obtain an MSW. The MSW degree would offer further opportunities in Mary's career, and her first job after graduating was as director of a social work department in a hospital.

■ Jessica always knew she wanted to be a social worker. As an undergraduate, the college Jessica attended offered a bachelor's degree in social work (*BSW*) and she was able to begin working in Child Protective Services (*micro practice*) shortly after graduation. Jessica soon realized she wanted to learn the skills needed to make changes within in larger child welfare systems at the *macro* level. She returned to graduate school and completed her MSW very quickly as an *advanced standing* student, since having a BSW degree allowed her to skip the first year of the 2-year master's program.

A BSW degree prepares an individual to go out into the workforce as a professional with the general knowledge and skills to assist individuals, families, groups, and communities in coping with basic day to day problems in living. Earning an MSW degree provides you with more advanced and specialized knowledge and skills. Most often, a person who pursues a doctoral degree in social work has worked in the field for a couple of years. A career path toward the PhD will provide opportunities in research for the causes and solutions of various social problems as well as in teaching in higher education.

For example, a BSW prepared worker in a family service agency would be able to assist clients with finding housing or health insurance, make referrals to appropriate community resources, or facilitate a support group for persons returning to employment. An MSW might be the health provider clients of this agency are referred to, or the supervisor or executive director of the agency. A person with a doctorate will be researching the causes of homelessness or health disparities, providing information to help solve present conditions and prevent these problems in the future.

The Council on Social Work Education Web site (www.cswe.org) has a link where you can search all of the accredited colleges and universities that have undergraduate (BSW) and graduate (MSW, advanced standing, and PhD) programs. Several universities also offer *dual degree* programs that allow you to receive the benefit of earning two graduate degrees, one in social work and the other in a related area such as law, public health, nursing, or pastoral counseling. You may be very lucky and have a social work program close to where you live.

The Baccalaureate Program Directors Web site (www.bpdonline.org) includes many links regarding social work educational programs, student resources, and professional issues.

The Group for the Advancement of Doctoral Education in Social Work (www.gadephd.org) includes links to doctoral programs and information regarding social work research.

WHO QUALIFIES AS A SOCIAL WORKER?

According to the U.S. Department of Labor, every state currently has some licensing or certification requirement for social workers. However, not every state agrees on the definition or requirements for the occupational job title "social worker."

Our profession defines a professional social worker to be a person who holds a BSW or an MSW from a college or university program that has been accredited by the Council on Social Work Education (CSWE). The CSWE sets the educational standards (EPAS) that all educational social work programs must meet in order to be accredited.

In general, the National Association of Social Workers (NASW) is our professional membership organization, and the NASW Code of Ethics is the universally accepted standard of professional social work behavior. Many states and professional social work organizations have used the NASW Code of Ethics as their guide in writing certification and licensing requirements. The regulation and establishment of licensing standards for many professional occupations is the responsibility of state governments. All states, including the District of Columbia, have some form of licensing or certification of social work practice.

WHAT DO I NEED TO KNOW ABOUT SOCIAL WORK LICENSING?

The Association of Social Work Boards (ASWB) is the professional organization that sets the national standards for licensing examinations. "The purpose of licensing and certification in social work is to assist the public through the identification of standards for the safe professional practice of social work. Each jurisdiction defines by law what is required for each level of social work licensure" (Association of Social Work Boards, 2005).

There are four categories of practice that states may regulate:

- Bachelor's level exam: To qualify to take this exam, you must have a BSW degree and in some cases you may also need to have post-BSW work experience.
- Master's level exam: An MSW degree is required to apply for this examination, and you are eligible to take this exam right after graduation.
- Advanced generalist level exam: An MSW degree is required as well as 2 years of post-master's work experience. Your work experience only qualifies if you have been supervised by a social work professional that is licensed at this level or higher.
- Clinical level exam: An MSW degree is required with 2 years of post-master's work experience in direct clinical social work, providing assessment, diagnosis and treatment of mental, emotional, and behavioral disorders, conditions, and addictions. You must also have been supervised by a licensed clinical social worker for your work experience to qualify.

All licensing boards only recognize BSW and MSW degrees from accredited CSWE programs. The ASWB has written a Model Law that many states have adopted as the "best practice" guide in determining the minimum standards to set in protecting the consumer from incompetent practitioners. The ASWB offers, for a fee, a practice study guide with sample questions for each examination level (see www.aswb.org).

IS LICENSING REALLY NECESSARY FOR THE SOCIAL WORK PROFESSION?

The licensing exams created by the ASWB ask questions in all areas of social work practice in direct service, administration, social policy, and research. The exams set the minimum competency standards every social worker should meet regarding social work knowledge and skills, as well as values and ethics.

Many NASW state chapters support the licensing of all social workers to protect the title of "social worker" to mean a person who has graduated with a BSW or MSW degree from an accredited program. This is to ensure that state and local governments and human service agencies cannot hire nonprofessional social workers without our specialized training.

The state has a fundamental interest in protecting the consumer. Having licensed professional social workers at all levels of practice enhances the public's trust of state and local governments, as well as raises the profession's value to society.

DO ALL SOCIAL WORK JOBS REQUIRE GETTING A LICENSE?

Not all social work positions require a license. In many states, there are "exempted from licensure" settings such as hospitals, community mental health centers, and state agencies. However, there are many social work professional organizations, such as the ASWB, that are advocating all social work positions have some level of licensure. Under the ASWB's Model Law, there are no exempted job settings because this organization believes no consumer should be less protected than another.

Your employer will know what regulations to follow and will be able to advise you as to whether you need a license and at what level. A clinical license is always required in any state if you decide to treat people for a mental health condition through the use of psychotherapy as an intervention.

IF I AM LICENSED IN ONE STATE WILL I BE ABLE TO USE THIS LICENSE IN A DIFFERENT STATE IF I RELOCATE FOR A JOB?

Currently, there is no "reciprocity" between state jurisdictions. If your new job in another state requires a license, you will need to apply to the state board of health or state board of professional occupations. The state board will have all the required information for you.

If you would like to research the requirements in a particular state before you relocate, there is an easy way to do this. The ASWB has complete contact information and a hyperlink to every state licensing board where you can find what you need. The ASWB also has a *"National Registry"* that, for a small fee, will allow you to register all of your professional information for each license you hold, making it very convenient to apply for a license in a new jurisdiction. More information is available at www.aswb.org/registry.shtml.

WHAT IS THE DIFFERENCE BETWEEN A LICENSE, A CERTIFICATION AND A CREDENTIAL?

- A license is the legal authority to practice an occupation or to operate a business.
- Certification typically means that a person has received approved training required for a particular occupation.
- To be licensed as a professional, you must have a credential such as a BSW or MSW degree. Having additional credentials beyond the BSW or MSW degree is not required in any state to be licensed as a professional social worker.

AFTER GRADUATION FROM MY UNIVERSITY'S SOCIAL WORK PROGRAM WILL I BE ABLE TO OBTAIN A LICENSE?

In most regional jurisdictions, graduates from accredited MSW programs will have satisfied the basic academic requirements for a license. In addition to your degree, you may need to meet other requirements, such as work experience providing direct services to individuals, families, and groups.

After graduation, you will need to check with the licensing board of the jurisdiction or state in which you are employed to see if a license is required.

WHERE CAN I LEARN MORE ABOUT THE REQUIREMENTS FOR THE SOCIAL WORK PROFESSION, SUPERVISION, AND LICENSING?

The following organizations can provide you with specific guidance for their jurisdiction. If the information you obtain from their Web site is not clear, please contact the licensing board and request assistance from a social work licensing specialist.

Association of Social Work Boards: www.aswb.org

National Association of Social Workers: www.socialworkers.org

Council on Social Work Education: www.cswe.org

The Institute for the Advancement of Social Work Research: www. iaswr.org

POSTSCRIPT

Information and regulations are always subject to change, so ultimately it is each person's responsibility to obtain the information they need for their specific circumstance.

REFERENCE

Association of Social Work Boards. (2005). *Mission.* [Online]. Retrieved August 13, 2008, from www.aswb.org

Careers in Social Work

4　Careers in Child Welfare

When you ask social work students what they want to do after they graduate, one of the most popular replies is, "I want to work with children and families." According to the U.S. Department of Labor, almost half of all social workers (47%) are child, family, and school social workers. Most of these social workers will choose to work in programs and agencies that are dedicated to ensuring that families have their basic needs met and that they have access to crucial medical and mental health services. Working in the field of child welfare also includes ensuring that children are safe and protected, helping them thrive at school and at home, and helping families through a crisis.

If you are interested in working with children and families, the good news is that you will have a wide range of options! You can work as a counselor or therapist, a case manager or caseworker, an advocate, as well as a program manager or administrator. One thing to keep in mind when working with families as a social worker is that there is no "typical" family structure—you will work with many types of families, including single parent homes; two-parent homes; homes with foster or adoptive children; families headed by parents who are gay or lesbian; children raised by grandparents or other family members; blended families (remarriages); immigrant families; and families of diverse racial, cultural, and religious backgrounds.

This chapter will highlight a number of popular fields of practice for social workers who want to work with children such as child protection, social work in private or nonprofit agencies, child welfare research, careers with the government, child advocacy, adoption, and foster care. However, many other chapters in this book include careers that involve working with children and families (e.g., mental health, medical social work, social work with older adults, criminal justice, school social work), so read on!

CHILD PROTECTION CASEWORKER

Child Protective Services (CPS) caseworkers usually come to mind when people think about various jobs performed by social workers. For obvious reasons, this job is not for everyone. CPS work has a reputation for high rates of burnout, due to the intensity of the job and the high caseloads carried by many caseworkers. Nonetheless, it is an extremely important and rewarding career for a social worker. Many dedicated child advocates spend their entire careers working in this system that assists families and protects vulnerable children.

CPS caseworkers, who are employed by the state or local government, are charged with protecting children and making decisions that are in the "best interest of the child." It is important to note that CPS workers will not only work with children, but they may also work with parents or caregivers of the child who may be the source of abuse or neglect. CPS agencies have a dual mission: focusing on protecting children and child safety, while at the same time focusing on family preservation and reunifying children with their parents whenever possible. With the passage of the 1997 Adoption and Safe Families Act, there is a much stronger focus on child safety and quickly finding safe, permanent homes for children to prevent them from languishing in the foster care system. As a result, parents have a much shorter timeframe (typically 12 to 18 months) to work toward having their child(ren) returned to their care and custody.

The CPS investigator, who comes knocking on the door and has the authority to intervene and take someone's child away in very serious cases of abuse and neglect, is the most commonly cited type of CPS caseworker. However, in most CPS offices around the country (with the exception of rural areas), caseworker positions are very specialized, as there are a range of responses that may take place before and after removing children from their home. Examples of CPS caseworker positions are as follows.

Social Worker Spotlight: Jessica A. Ritter, BSW, MSSW, PhD Children's Protective Services, Austin, Texas

After graduating with my BSW from the University of Texas at Austin, I accepted a position as a caseworker at CPS. In my first position as a practicing social worker, I worked with the most severe cases of child abuse and neglect, since cases were transferred to me after a child was removed from the home by the CPS Investigator. It was my job to work with the family and to make attempts to reunify the family if possible. I would set up services for the parents such as parenting classes, substance abuse treatment, and individual counseling. It was also my job to find a temporary placement for the child, usually with a foster family or relative. I would also arrange therapeutic services, if they were needed, for children. I supervised visits between the child and the parents and would get to know everyone in the family very well. I went to court frequently to update the judge on how the case was progressing. When children were not able to be returned home to their parents, I was charged with finding another permanent home for them. The best option was that the child would be adopted by a relative or into a new loving family.

What I really loved about my job at CPS as a substitute care caseworker was spending time with the kids on my caseload—trips to McDonald's for ice cream, driving them to appointments, and visiting them in their foster homes. I realized right away how important I was in their lives. I was their link to their families, and I would have major input into deciding where they would end up living permanently. This was a heavy responsibility, and I took it very seriously. I built special relationships with a number of children on my caseload, and I still think about them today and wonder how they are doing. This job was very stressful at times, but I will never regret starting my career at CPS. I learned and grew so much in those years. Not only did I learn about the dynamics of child abuse, I learned about domestic violence, severe mental illness, poverty, substance abuse, the challenges of parenting, and how the court system works. I could go on and on. What an amazing experience for a beginning social worker!

INTAKE WORKER

Intake workers are charged with taking reports of the abuse, neglect, and exploitation of children, as well as determining if a report meets the legal criteria for child abuse and whether it warrants investigation by a caseworker. In some areas, the intake department is set up in a large room, like a hotline, and caseworkers take calls from individuals around the state who are reporting the abuse, neglect, or exploitation of a child. Calls to report child abuse and neglect are typically routed through the state agency's 1-800 telephone number.

CPS INVESTIGATOR

Investigators talk with the child, parents, and anyone else who may have information about the family in order to make an informed assessment about the family's functioning, the risk to the child, and to determine whether the child was abused or neglected. It is important to note that children are only removed when there is a reasonable cause to believe there is an immediate danger to their physical health or safety and there is no other way to ensure their safety. CPS investigators often work with families, referring them to community services. They may also refer the case to the family preservation unit at CPS if they are eligible.

FAMILY PRESERVATION CASEWORKER

Family preservation caseworkers provide needed child abuse prevention services to a family to prevent a child from being removed from the home. The services may include counseling for parents and/or the children, parent education, home visits, financial planning, substance abuse treatment, and referrals to other community resources. The relationship with the family is less adversarial, and the family often views the family preservation caseworker as helpful and supportive, instead of "the bad guy" who wants to take their child away. Some critics of the CPS system believe that CPS should offer more prevention services to families in order to keep families together and prevent children from entering the custody of the state.

SUBSTITUTE CARE CASEWORKER

Substitute care caseworkers work with families when a child has been removed from the home. After the child is removed by the CPS investigator, the case is transferred to a substitute care caseworker. These caseworkers attempt to reunify the family by providing parents with needed services in the hope that they can be rehabilitated. They are also charged with finding a temporary placement for the child (e.g., foster home, relative, group home, residential treatment center) and ensuring that the educational, medical, recreational, and therapeutic needs of the child are met. If family reunification is not possible, the caseworker will find another permanent plan for the child. This plan for permanency may include permanent placement with a relative or family friend, or terminating parental rights and placing the child for adoption.

FOSTER CARE AND ADOPTION CASEWORKER

Foster care and adoption caseworkers are charged with recruiting, training, and supporting individuals who foster and adopt children. Depending on how the responsibilities are defined, they may also be responsible for matching children with families and preparing children for adoption. A recent trend is that an increasing number of relatives are adopting children or becoming their legal guardian, thus new programs have been developed to serve these "kinship care" families. Witnessing a happy ending for a child to be wanted and placed in a home for adoption is certainly an upside of this work. These jobs are discussed in more detail later in this chapter.

As you can see from these descriptions, career planning and development is possible as caseworkers are able to transition from one position to another utilizing their skills and knowledge base. Some common duties of all CPS caseworkers include case assessment and documentation, supervising visits between parents and children, arranging needed services for children and parents, examining children for abuse and neglect, making home visits, transporting children and parents to needed services and appointments, attending court hearings, working with other professionals on a case (e.g., service providers, psychologists, therapists, attorneys, community volunteers, foster parents), keeping supervisors informed of case progress, and case planning for children and parents.

CAREERS WITH PRIVATE OR NONPROFIT AGENCIES

There are a number of child welfare related jobs that are located outside of the formal child welfare system. Many of these jobs are with private or nonprofit agencies that contract with CPS to provide services to children and families. Some social workers work in Children's Advocacy Centers, which are charged with conducting forensic interviews of children who have been sexually or physically abused. Social workers are also employed by Court Appointed Special Advocates (CASA), a national organization (with many state and local chapters) that trains members of the community to be advocates for children in CPS custody. Furthermore, social workers are employed in emergency shelters, residential treatment centers, or private foster care agencies where children are placed after they have been taken into custody by CPS. Social workers can also be found in organizations that provide transitional housing or other independent living programs that serve youth who will be emancipated from the foster care system when they graduate from high school.

CAREERS IN CHILD WELFARE RESEARCH

Some social workers with a strong interest in child welfare choose to work at the macro level by conducting research. They enjoy doing research so that we can better understand the root causes of child abuse and the best way to intervene with children and families. This is how we ensure that the interventions that we use with clients are "evidence based." A few of the many questions that can be answered through research include: Why do people abuse/neglect their children? What types of children and families are most vulnerable to experiencing child abuse? What types of interventions are most effective when treating abusive parents? Why are children of color overrepresented in the foster care system? How many children experience adoption disruptions? What are the long-term outcomes for youth who emancipate from the foster care system in the United States?

Social workers interested in conducting research typically work for universities, the government, or nonprofit research organizations.

Prominent organizations that conduct research in child welfare include the Children's Bureau/Administration for Children and Families, the Child Welfare League of America, Casey Family Programs, Chapin Hall Center for Children (at the University of Chicago), Prevent Child Abuse America, and the American Humane Association.

CAREERS WITH THE GOVERNMENT

Some child welfare social workers who become recognized as experts in their field find themselves working for the government (city, county, state, or federal) after having many years of direct experience in the field. Many states have a Department of Children and Family Services that employs social workers to engage in the important administrative work required to run successful child protection programs. For those interested in working at the federal level, there is the Administration for Children and Families, the Administration on Children, Youth, and Families, and the Children's Bureau, all under the auspices of the U.S. Department of Health and Human Services. Most of these jobs include working in policy, program planning, or program evaluation. The upside of working in a high-level government job is that it includes good benefits, regular working hours, and often higher salaries because you are recognized as an expert in your field.

CHILD WELFARE ADVOCATE

After gaining a number of years of experience at the micro level, some child welfare social workers choose to move into an advocacy or policy making role. Social workers interested in advocacy are charged with educating the public about children's issues and influencing legislators to pass legislation at the local and national level that would benefit children and families. In recent years, child welfare advocates have been successful in getting funding for grandparents raising grandchildren, children who emancipate from the child welfare system, and adoption subsidies for parents who adopt children with special needs. They also urge lawmakers to appropriate more funding to state child welfare systems that tend to be understaffed and underfunded. Social workers interested in this type of work might work for a legislator or an advocacy organization such as the National Court Appointed Special Advocates (CASA), the Child Welfare League of America (CWLA), Every Child Matters, Prevent Child Abuse America, or the Children's Defense Fund.

Core Competencies and Skills

- Excellent risk assessment and decision-making skills.
- Sensitive to parents as well as children.
- Strong interviewing skills and ability to ask sensitive questions.
- Assertiveness/firmness/ability to confront others when necessary.
- Strong writing skills (e.g., court reports, case documentation, case plans).
- Comfortable dealing with conflict and working in an adversarial environment.
- Strong rapport with youth of all ages.
- Ability to prioritize and multitask.
- Strong crisis management and problem-solving skills.
- Ability to maintain a balance of objectivity and empathic understanding in dealing with families living in stressful and crisis situations.
- Self-care, as this job can be emotionally draining.
- Strong verbal communication skills (e.g., meetings with clients, court testimony).
- High degree of cultural sensitivity; can respect various cultural practices of diverse families.

Educational and Licensing Requirements

Social workers can be employed at CPS with a bachelor's degree in social work (BSW) or a master's degree in social work (MSW). Many social work education programs across the country receive federal funding to place BSW and MSW students in CPS field placements. This varies by university, but students are usually provided with a generous stipend as well as reimbursement for tuition and fees. In return, students sign an agreement to work at CPS for a certain time period after graduation (at full pay). Likewise, some social work programs receive federal funding that allows current CPS employees to earn their MSW while being employed full-time. Again, they will sign an agreement to return to work at CPS for a certain time period after graduation (at full pay).

Unfortunately, because CPS workers around the country are in such high demand, many caseworkers are hired without social work degrees.

Because this job requires a high degree of knowledge, skill, and training, candidates with a social work degree or related degree are preferred, and many efforts are being made to increase the number of caseworkers with social work degrees. Having a professional degree ensures that you will be well qualified upon graduation for the demands of such work.

Best Aspects of this Job

- Working with children of all ages from infants to young adults.
- Learning about the dynamics of child abuse and neglect as well as a range of other social problems that often contribute to the abuse/neglect of a child (e.g., poverty and homelessness, domestic violence, juvenile justice, substance abuse, mental health issues, severe mental illness).
- Opportunity to work with many types of professionals (e.g., judges, attorneys, therapists, psychologists) and the community resources available to help solve problems.
- Extensive learning about children and families; a wonderful job to launch a career in social work. One can do anything after this job!
- Playing an important role in the lives of the children on your caseload.
- Being a significant influence on the outcomes of your cases and working in the area of prevention.
- Being a witness to many happy endings, (e.g., seeing parents make enough progress so that reunification can occur or watching a child get adopted into a wonderful new family).
- Every single day is different; never a boring moment in this job!

Challenging Aspects of this Job

- Seeing the effects of abuse and neglect on children is not easy.
- Being caught in a catch 22—CPS divisions are often criticized in the media for either intruding into the lives of families too much or for not intervening promptly enough.
- Dealing with criticism and conflict every day can be stressful.
- The heavy burden of being responsible for making decisions that affect the safety of children.
- Working with involuntary clients can be challenging.
- Because CPS cases often involve volatile or crisis-driven situations in which the child may be taken away, caseworkers must be careful

to assess and guard their own safety. Safety precautions include bringing another caseworker or a police officer with you when you visit someone's home and having your cell phone with you at all times.

■ Some CPS agencies are understaffed (though this varies by location). Because CPS agencies are funded by the government, they are at the mercy of legislators who decide how much funding they will receive.

■ Working in a system that often does not operate from a strengths perspective and does not allow clients much in the way of self-determination.

■ The work is stressful and can be emotionally draining. Self-care and having a balanced life is imperative.

Compensation and Employment Outlook

Because CPS workers are employed by local or state governments, they tend to earn higher starting salaries than many other social workers (though this certainly varies by region) and typically receive good benefits. Social workers who have a master's degree usually start at a higher level on the pay scale. Because child abuse and neglect will unfortunately continue to be a problem in this country, there will always be a demand for social workers to work in child protection. As shown in Table 4.1, there are a wide range of salaries depending on the state or region of the country in which a social worker resides, years of previous experience, and type of degree (undergraduate or graduate degree). Moving into a supervisory or program administrator role means a nice raise in your salary (see Connecticut below)!

Self-Assessment Checklist: Is this Job for Me?

☐ Do you have a passion for protecting children of all ages from diverse backgrounds and making sure they are safe?

☐ Are you able to work with parents from diverse backgrounds who have abused, neglected, or exploited their children?

☐ Do you enjoy having a job where your work day is often unpredictable and crisis-driven?

☐ Would you enjoy having a job where an important aspect of your work is to participate in court hearings within the family court system?

Table 4.1

SALARY RANGES FOR CPS CASEWORKERS IN SELECTED STATES, 2007

STATE	QUALIFICATIONS	SALARY RANGE FOR CPS CASEWORKERS (2007)
Texas	Bachelor's degree in social work or human services preferred	$2,636.70 to $3,491 per month
Oregon	BSW or human services degree, or bachelor's degree and 1 year of related experience	$2,903 to $4,229 per month
Illinois	BSW or related human service field and 4 years of related experience, or MSW or related human service field and 2 years of related experience	$3,645 to $5,437 per month
Connecticut	Only hire those with social work degrees: 1. Social Work Trainee (2-year training period)—need BSW or related field 2. Social Worker—must complete 2 years of training and pass exam 3. Social Work Supervisor—needs MSW 4. Program Supervisor	1. $43,075 to $47,450 per year 2. $56,209 to $71,539 per year 3. $61,858 to $78,410 per year 4. $68,565 to $87,947 per year

Sources: www.dfps.state.tx.us/ComeWorkForUs/fad.asp#
www.oregon.gov/DHS/jobs/salary.shtml
www.state.il.us/DCFS/library/com_communications_employment05.shtml
www.ct.gov/dcf/cwp/view.asp?a=2553&q=314424&dcfNav=

☐ Would you enjoy the challenge of working with involuntary clients who are not happy to have you in their lives?

☐ Would you be able to see and hear details of how a child has been abused and/or neglected including physical abuse, sexual abuse, emotional abuse, and various forms of child neglect and exploitation?

☐ Would you be comfortable having a job with unpredictable work hours?

☐ Would you be comfortable visiting with clients in their homes (e.g., parents, relatives, foster parents)?

☐ Do you have an assertive personality, and are you comfortable dealing with conflict?

☐ Would you be comfortable working for a government agency that is somewhat bureaucratic and has many rules, regulations, policies, and procedures to follow?

If you answered "yes" to seven or more of the above questions, then working in child protection might be for you!

RECOMMENDED READINGS/WEB SITES TO LEARN MORE

Child Welfare League of America: www.cwla.org

Court Appointed Special Advocates (CASA): www.nationalcasa.org

Crosson-Tower, C. (2003). *From the eye of the storm: The experiences of a child welfare worker*. Boston: Allyn & Bacon.

Crosson-Tower, C. (2007). *Exploring child welfare: A practice perspective*. Boston: Allyn & Bacon. Great chapter on child protection!

Prevent Child Abuse America: www.preventchildabuse.org

"The Case of Marie and her Sons" (July 23, 2006). New York Times Magazine. A moving profile of a Connecticut CPS caseworker.

Most states have a Web site for their department of children and families. For example, in Texas, visit: www.dfps.state.tx.us Just Google "Department of Children and Families" or "Children Protective Services" along with the state where you reside.

Child Protection Caseworker Exercise

Test your knowledge

1. CPS investigates the following allegations within families:
   a. Physical abuse
   b. Medical or physical neglect
   c. Sexual abuse or exploitation
   d. Abandonment
   e. Emotional or psychological abuse
   f. Inadequate parental supervision of a child
   g. All of the above
2. True or False
   Child *abuse* cases are more prevalent than child *neglect* cases.
3. Which of the following famous writers was an early advocate for children's rights and child protection?
   a. Jane Austen
   b. Charles Dickens
   c. Herman Melville
   d. Ernest Hemingway

4. True or False

   The Society for the Prevention of Cruelty of Animals (SPCA) was founded before the Society for the Prevention of Cruelty to Children (SPCC).

5. When CPS removes a child from their parent(s) or caregiver(s), the case gets heard in a _____ court.

   a. Criminal

   b. Civil or Juvenile

6. Which of the following is an example of a permanency plan for a child who has been removed from his or her home?

   a. Return home to parents/caregiver

   b. Permanent placement with a relative

   c. Adoption

   d. All of the above

7. True or False

   CPS agencies are typically funded by a combination of monies from the state and federal government.

8. When a child is being abused by a caregiver or family member, _____ investigates, but if a child is abused by a stranger, or someone who is not a family member, the _____ investigate.

   a. Police

   b. Child Protective Services

9. In any given year, there are usually approximately _____ children in the custody of CPS in the United States.

   a. 25,000

   b. 100,000

   c. 500,000

   d. million

10. True or False

    There is an abundance of foster and adoptive homes available for children in the child welfare system.

Answers: 1. g; 2. false; 3. b; 4. true; 5. b; 6. d; 7. true; 8. b, a; 9. c; 10. false.

ADOPTION SOCIAL WORKER

Many social workers who are interested in child welfare find themselves working in the fascinating field of adoption. This is a more positive side of child welfare because you get to witness the joyful experience of a child being placed into a new "forever" family. The job of the adoption social worker is to prepare the biological parents, the child, and the adoptive parents for the adoption. As you can imagine, it is a very exciting and emotional time for the child who needs a "forever home" and the families who want a child to love and parent. Many families who decide to adopt a child have not been able to conceive a child on their own.

It is important to know that adoption has changed in recent years. Due to the increased acceptance of abortion and birth control, as well as the trend toward teen mothers keeping their babies, there are fewer healthy infants available for adoption. Children available for adoption today are more likely to be older, nonwhite, and have special needs (medical or emotional problems). Social workers need to be skilled and creative to find the right homes for these children because many adoptive parents are seeking healthy infants.

Another major change is the increasing number of "open adoptions," adoptions that allow some continued contact between the biological parents, the child, and the adoptive parents. Sometimes, letters and pictures are exchanged, while in other cases, children may have periodic visits with their biological parents. Social workers assist parties in coming to an agreement that is in the best interests of all who are involved in the adoption triad.

New federal laws have been passed in recent years that emphasize the idea that children in foster care have the right to be in a permanent home as soon as possible. There is a strong emphasis on finding adoptive homes for these children, as soon as possible, so they do not grow up in the foster care system. Finally, it is important to know that adoption is a lifelong process, and the social worker's job often does not end when the child is placed in their new adoptive home. Many families will continue to need support and postadoption services to help with adjustment and ongoing issues.

Once families decide they want to adopt a child, they have a number of options: Do they want an international adoption? Do they prefer adopting through the child welfare system in the United States? Do they feel more comfortable going through a private adoption agency? Thus, you will find adoption social workers in each of these settings (e.g., state child welfare agency or private agencies that specialize in domestic or international adoptions). A growing number of "kinship adoptions" are also taking place (e.g., family member, typically a grandparent or aunt, adopts a child related to them because the biological parent is unable to parent the child, in many cases due to substance abuse problems). These families also need help and support, and there are a growing number of programs to meet this need. The following tasks are routinely performed by adoption social workers:

1. **Preparing children for adoption.** Before older children can be placed for adoption, they must be adequately prepared. In some cases, they may need counseling. Sometimes social workers help the child prepare a "Life Book," which helps them document their life before the adoption and to process why they could not continue to live with their birth parents. If children are not sufficiently prepared, there is a risk that the adoption process will be disrupted and the child will not be able to stay in the adoptive home.

2. **Counseling the birthparents.** As you can imagine, the decision to place a child for adoption is not easy. The parent(s) will need counseling and support to grieve the loss of the child and to help guide them through the adoption process. Some parents give their child up voluntarily, whereas those involved in the child welfare system sometimes have their parental rights terminated by the court against their will.

3. **Recruiting prospective adoptive parents.** It is unfortunate that there are not enough adoptive homes for all of the children who are available for adoption in this country. Recruitment is especially important for special needs children. Social workers may use a variety of strategies, such as community presentations, public service announcements on radio and television, and the Internet, to find homes for these children.

4. **Training and approving prospective adoptive parents.** Many adoption agencies require parents to complete training (typically 10 to 12 weeks) to learn the adoption process, all of the requirements, and also to prepare them for the challenges and benefits of adopting a child. An important part of this process is conducting a very thorough home study to assess the suitability of the parents to adopt a child. Parents will be assessed on their motivation for adopting a child, the stability of their relationship (if married), their physical and emotional health, and their financial stability. The agency will also perform a criminal background and child abuse check. Some social workers perform home studies on a contract basis with a state or private agency.

5. **Matching children and parents.** This is an art as much as it is a science. It takes experience and good assessment skills to match a child with the right family. Social workers must know the child and the prospective adoptive parents very well in order to make a good match. In some cases, the birthmother is allowed to select, or at least have input into selecting, the adoptive parents.

6. **Supporting families after the adoption placement.** Many agencies recognize that adoption is a lifelong process and that families may need short- or long-term services, such as counseling, support groups, in-home support by caseworkers, and referrals to other community resources, as needed.

7. **The legal work required to finalize an adoption.** Social workers need to become well versed on the legal process for finalizing an adoption. Adoption social workers will spend some of their time doing legal paperwork and appearing in court.

8. **Helping adoptees and birthparents with the search.** When a child or a birthparent decides they would like to search and meet each other, they will often need to seek the help of a social worker to guide them through this process so that it can be as successful as possible. This is an emotional journey for everyone involved!

Core Competencies and Skills

- Ability to do thorough assessments of children and families (home studies and matching children with adoptive parents).
- Strong counseling skills and understanding of the grieving process (birthparents who are losing a child or adoptive parents who were not able to conceive a child).
- Thorough understanding of the adoption process and how it affects each member of the adoption triad (e.g., child, biological parents, adoptive parents).
- Strong presentation and training skills (e.g., community presentations, training of adoptive parents).
- Understand the importance of cultural identity (this is especially important in transracial adoptions).
- Ability to mediate between biological parents and adoptive parents.
- Media and marketing skills (recruiting adoptive families).
- Good legal skills and knowledge of the laws surrounding domestic and intercountry adoption.

Educational and Licensing Requirements

You may be able to get a job as an adoption social worker with a BSW, but many employers prefer those with a master's degree and previous experience in child welfare. Agencies may also require a social work license, depending on the state where you reside.

Best Aspects of this Job

- Playing a role in creating a new family can be very rewarding!
- Finding a wonderful forever family for children, some of whom may have experienced abuse and/or neglect or a turbulent or uncertain beginning in life.
- Helping biological parents make peace with the decision that it would be in their child's best interest to be placed for adoption.
- Placing a child into an adoptive home, and helping adoptive parents realize their dream of having a child.
- Facilitating a successful open adoption so that a child can stay connected with their biological family and community of origin.
- Helping adoptive parents understand the importance of keeping a child connected to their culture or country of origin, especially when there are cultural differences between the child and the adoptive parents.
- Facilitating a successful reunion between an adopted child and a biological parent when the child reaches adulthood.
- Working in a field that is extremely fascinating and complex—the emotional rewards are great!
- Finding a loving home for an older child or a child with special needs is awesome!

Challenging Aspects of this Job

- Dealing with the stereotypes and myths surrounding adoption.
- It can be tough to balance the needs of the adoptive triad.
- Adoption often has happy endings, and yet it also involves grief and loss. Many families, children, and professionals have a hard time dealing with this concept.
- As with all social work, it is not an exact science and can be a roller coaster of emotions as you work with adoptive parents, children, and birthparents.

- Adoptive parents who are anxiously awaiting an addition to their family are looking for a sense of fulfillment; they want to "get from" the child and to feel the return love of a child. This doesn't always happen, especially not immediately.
- Working with children who have a difficult time attaching to their new family.
- Helping adoptive parents deal with not having the perfect, idealized child they have always dreamed of having.
- Convincing families that adoption is a lifelong process and will present new challenges at different life stages.
- Seeing some children wait for long periods of time for their "forever home," and others who will not be placed due to having significant physical, behavioral, or emotional needs.
- Working with children who have experienced abuse, neglect, and termination of parental rights can be challenging to deal with emotionally.
- When an adoption disrupts or does not work out, putting the pieces back together is very difficult. (The child and the adoptive parents are hurt and grieving. The child has experienced a rejection.)

Social Worker Spotlight: Agnes Zarcaro, LCSW
Spaulding for Children, Houston, Texas

I received my MSW in 1971 from the University of Houston. Today, I am a licensed clinical social worker (LCSW). I have worked in the field of adoption for 36 years.

My present position is manager of the South Texas Adoption and Family Support Programs of Spaulding for Children; these programs are located in Corpus Christi, McAllen, and Laredo, Texas. The Adoption Program centers on the adoption of older children who are in the Texas state foster care system—those who have had parental rights terminated and are awaiting a permanent adoptive home. The Family Support Program offers an array of services to the families as they await an adoptive placement. Once the adoptive placement occurs, the families and children are offered services through the finalization of the adoption and the post-legal adoption period. These programs include marriage communication; family, parent, and children's support groups; family retreats; and therapy.

The field of adoption has changed dramatically since I began, in November 1971, as a birthparent counselor, assisting "unwed mothers" (as they were called at that time) with making a decision about their "unplanned" pregnancy. Most birthmothers, at this time, did choose adoption for their babies. In the late 70s and 80s, birthmothers began parenting their children more and more, so the "homes for unwed mothers" began to change and began offering many more services to teens who decided to parent their children. In the 90s, infant adoptions were few and far between. International adoptions increased in numbers as U.S. families continued to want infants and found adopting domestically to be too expensive and complicated. The majority of children available today in the United States are older children or children with various special needs.

Within the field of adoption, there are many different areas where a social worker might concentrate. One can work with all triad members, or only one member of the triad. One can work in the preadoption, placement, or postadoption phase. One can work solely as a recruiter of adoptive families, or one can work in the clinical arena assisting families and children as they move through the phases and issues of the adoption. One can work in the legal system as a liaison with the courts on terminations and adoptions. Another area is postadoption, including the search and reunions of adoptees and birthparents. One can work for the state CPS agency or a private adoption agency that specializes in either domestic or international adoptions. Research is always an option as well. Our program is funded through two large federal grants, and we are obliged to have a research component which will help to advance the field as well as help in the evaluation and efficacy of the work.

The best part of working in adoption is that it is such a diverse field and it is very challenging. Families are made! Children will have a family in which they belong. When a teen who has been in the foster care system since age 2 is adopted at age 15, this is such a wonderful thing to happen for that child.

Compensation and Employment Outlook

Social workers who work in adoption are typically employed by either the state CPS agency or a private, nonprofit organization. For information on salaries for CPS caseworkers, please refer to the beginning of this chapter. Salaries for social workers working in a private adoption agency will vary greatly from agency to agency and by state. Due to the knowledge and skills required for this job, many social workers apply and get hired after gaining experience in other jobs within the child welfare system (e.g., CPS). In the state child welfare agency, jobs in the adoption unit are competitive and are reserved for experienced child welfare caseworkers. Seasoned caseworkers can enjoy a career transition to this division, which comes with the reward of finding children their "forever home."

Self-Assessment Checklist: Is This Job for Me?

- ☐ Do you have a passion for finding homes for children available for adoption?
- ☐ Can you work with and support birthparents who are placing their child for adoption?
- ☐ Do you believe there is a home for every child if you can just find it?
- ☐ Would you enjoy working with children, some of whom have experienced child abuse and have abandonment issues?
- ☐ Can you work with and support adoptive parents who are desperate for a child and have a history of infertility?
- ☐ Would you be comfortable making home visits?
- ☐ Are you comfortable asking people very sensitive questions to determine their suitability to be adoptive parents?
- ☐ Are you able to balance the needs of the child, the biological parents, and the adoptive parents?
- ☐ Would you enjoy the challenge of working with adoptive families after the child has been placed in order to support that placement?
- ☐ Would you be able to hear details of how a child has been abused and/or neglected including physical abuse, sexual abuse, emotional abuse, and various forms of child neglect and exploitation?

If you answered "yes" to seven or more of the above questions, then working in the field of adoption might be for you!

RECOMMENDED READINGS/WEB SITES TO LEARN MORE

AdoptUSKids: www.adoptuskids.org
Center for Adoption Support and Education (CASE): www.adoptionsupport.org

Child Welfare Information Gateway: www.childwelfare.gov

Crosson-Tower, C. (2003). *From the eye of the storm: The experiences of a child welfare worker*. Boston: Allyn & Bacon.

Crosson-Tower, C. (2007). *Exploring child welfare: A practice perspective*. Boston: Allyn & Bacon. Excellent chapter on adoption!

Crumbley, J. (1999). *Transracial adoption and foster care: Practice issues for professionals*. Washington, DC: CWLA Press.

The Evan B. Donaldson Adoption Institute: www.adoptioninstitute.org

Fahlberg, V. (1996). *A child's journey through placement*. Indianapolis: Perspective Press.

Jewett, C. (1978). *Adopting the older child*. Boston: The Harvard Common Press.

Jewett, C. (1994). *Helping children cope with separation and loss*. Boston: The Harvard Common Press.

The Joint Council on International Children's Services: www.jcics.org

Keck, G., & Kupecky, R. (2002). *Parenting the hurt child: Helping adoptive families heal and grow*. Colorado Springs, CO: Pinon Press

Levine, P., & Kline, M. (2006). *Trauma through a child's eyes: Awakening the ordinary miracle of healing*. Berkley, CA: North Atlantic Books.

National Adoption Day: www.nationaladoptionday.org

National Resource Center for Special Needs Adoption: www.spaulding.org

North American Council on Adoptable Children: www.nacac.org

FOSTER CARE SOCIAL WORKER

Though many child welfare social workers have a passion for adoption, others love the thrill of foster care. Because this field of practice has a lot of overlap with adoption, we advise you to read the previous section. Here, we will highlight some of the distinct aspects of working in foster care as a social worker. In the "old days," foster care and adoption were two very separate entities, and foster parents were not encouraged to adopt children in their care. This has definitely changed! According to the Child Welfare League of America, there are approximately 513,000 children in foster care, and 60% of children adopted from the child welfare system are adopted by their foster parents ("Quick Facts," n.d.).

However, at least initially, foster care is somewhat of a different experience from adoption because it is meant to be a temporary placement for the child while efforts are made to reunify the child with his/her parents. Foster parents must learn to deal with feelings of grief and disappointment when a child leaves their home to be reunified with their parents or is placed permanently with a relative, or when the child is exhibiting dangerous behaviors and needs to be placed in a more structured environment, such as a residential treatment center.

Unfortunately, many foster parents are often perceived in a negative light due to the small number of high profile media cases where foster parents have been found to be abusive to children in their care. However, most foster parents are generous, caring people who are willing to take children into their home who have suffered serious abuse and/or neglect at the hands of their caregivers. Foster parents come from all walks of life. They are childless young couples hoping to adopt, single parents, gay couples, older couples who have already raised their children, and families who already have biological children but want to add to their family.

Social workers who wish to work in foster care are typically employed by private foster care agencies that contract with the state to provide this service. The following tasks are very commonly carried out by foster care case managers:

- Recruiting members of the community to be foster parents—this is crucial since there is a severe shortage of foster parents in most states.
- Training and certifying individuals to be foster parents. Foster care agencies require prospective foster parents to complete a training (typically 10 to 12 weeks) to learn about the process, all of the requirements, and to prepare them for parenting abused children who often have a range of emotional problems and challenging behaviors. An important part of this process is conducting a very thorough home study to assess the suitability of these parents to foster a child. The agency will also perform background checks on all adults in the home.
- Supporting the foster parents after the child has been placed. The child typically has their own caseworker, so the social worker's job is to offer the foster parents guidance and support and ensure that they have the resources they need (e.g., counseling, clothing vouchers, adequate financial compensation).
- Advocating for the foster parents on your caseload and ensuring that they are treated as a respected member of the team by the state child welfare agency and judicial system.
- Making frequent home visits and monitoring the placement to evaluate whether the child is safe and is receiving good care. Ensuring that the foster parents are continuing to meet licensing requirements (e.g., ongoing foster parent training, fire inspection, CPR certification).

- Helping the family through the legal process of adopting the child if he/she becomes available for adoption, or providing emotional support if the child later leaves the home.

Core Competencies and Skills

Many of the same competencies and skills that are required for adoption social workers are needed for foster care social workers as well (see previous section). In addition, foster care social workers must have the ability to work with troubled or special needs children. Foster care social workers, in some cases, need to have the ability to support the child and foster families if and when the child leaves the foster home.

Best Aspects of This Job

- Seeing children who are dealing with the trauma of being removed from their home being placed in a safe, loving foster home—one that you were responsible for recruiting and training.
- The joy of finding the perfect foster home for a large sibling group so the children do not have to be separated.
- Witnessing the happy ending of a foster home placement that turns into a permanent adoption for a child in need of a "forever home."
- Working with amazingly giving foster parents who take "special needs" children into their home, some with serious physical and mental disabilities.
- Seeing children thrive in a foster home, with love and structure, and heal from the abuse and/or neglect they suffered.

Challenging Aspects of this Job

- Dealing with the shortage of foster homes in most communities can be very frustrating.
- Witnessing the devastation of foster parents who lose a child they have become extremely attached to. Helping foster parents accept the decision when it is in a child's best interest to go back home.
- Working with a foster family when a child has to leave the foster home due to escalating problems, or when a child is unable to attach to their new caregivers.

- Dealing with a child abuse allegation in a foster home.
- Balancing the needs of the child, the foster parents, and the biological parents.

RECOMMENDED READINGS/WEB SITES TO LEARN MORE

Casey Family Programs: www.casey.org

Crosson-Tower, C. (2007). *Exploring child welfare: A practice perspective.* Boston: Allyn & Bacon. Great chapter on foster care!

Fisher, A., & Rivas, M. (2001). *Finding fish: A memoir.* New York: HarperCollins.

National Foster Care Coalition: www.nationalfostercare.org

National Foster Parent Association: www.nfpainc.org

Pew Commission on Children in Foster Care: www.pewfostercare.org

Foster Care and Adoption Exercise

Case study

You are a caseworker in the adoption unit at the child welfare agency in your state, and your supervisor has just assigned a new case to you. Her name is Sarah, she is 10 years old, of Hispanic origin (she speaks Spanish and English), and she is available for adoption. You begin reading her file and see right away that this will not be an easy case. Sarah was sexually abused by her step-father for a number of years before she was removed from her home. As a result, she does not trust men. She has had a difficult time talking about this in therapy, as she is embarrassed and ashamed. She is still very angry and hurt that her mother did not protect her from this abuse.

Her adjustment to foster care has not been an easy one. She has been in a foster home for 2 years and has been able to maintain a stable placement, but her foster parents report that she will not let them get close to her. She has not been able to talk with them much about her life prior to foster care. On the positive side, she does well in school, gets along well with other children, and makes good grades. She is on the soccer team at school and plays the piano. She loves animals and would like to be a veterinarian one day. So far, she has expressed that she does not want to be adopted, even though her parents' rights have been terminated. She harbors fantasies of being reunited with her mother someday.

Questions

1. What thoughts and feelings do you have as you read this case scenario?
2. What do you think Sarah's chances are of being placed into an adoptive home?
3. How would you build a relationship with Sarah? Plan your first meeting with her.
4. How would you work with Sarah to help her be more open to the idea of being adopted?
5. Do you think Sarah is ready for adoption yet? If not, what kinds of services does she need to help her move forward?
6. What kind of family would be ideal for Sarah? List a few family characteristics that you feel would be important.
7. Do you think her current foster home might be an option for her? Why or why not?
8. Does Sarah have the right to decide whether she will be adopted?

REFERENCES

Child Welfare League of America. *Quick facts about foster care*. Retrieved June 18, 2008, from http://www.cwla.org/programs/fostercare/factsheet.htm

U.S. Department of Labor, Bureau of Labor Statistics. *Social workers*. Retrieved June 13, 2008, from http://www.bls.gov/oco/pdf/ocos060.pdf

5

School-Based and School-Linked Services

The United States has a long history of providing health and social services for children in school settings (Tyack, 1992). Social workers are often the link between the school and the family. School-based and school-linked health and social services utilize a systems approach that emphasizes the interconnection of health, welfare, and education and the need for immediate and comprehensive services and collaborative problem-solving methods. The evolution of school-based and school-linked services has not only been influenced by the political climate and economic condition of the time, but also the citizens' sense of responsibility and obligation to provide a wholesome environment to all children everyday, to act in their best interest, and to assist in their developmental adjustments in school settings (Kronick, 2000).

School-based and school-linked services are designed to be immediate and comprehensive in nature. These services include individual, group, and family counseling and therapy; adolescent group works; tutoring; recreation; National Head Start Association; and so forth. Many schools also offer free or reduced breakfast and lunch programs to deal with hunger. Likewise, other schools have programs that focus on college preparation for high school students.

Many of these services are provided by a team of individuals, which may include a school social worker, school counselor, school psychologist, after school program counselor, day care and school readiness program worker, or adult literacy program worker. All of these individuals may have varying degrees, licenses, and work experiences that they bring to their respective jobs. For this reason, it is important for school social workers to be comfortable operating in a collaborative environment.

School-based and school-linked services may be provided by social workers in community organizations, as well. Examples of community organizations in which social workers are employed and that commonly provide services in school settings include Americorps, Big Brothers Big Sisters, Boys & Girls Clubs of America, Communities in Schools, Teach For America, and so forth.

Although each state differs in their definitions and requirements of workers providing school-based and school-linked services, the following are commonly cited job descriptions as well as educational and licensing requirements for those with social work education, training, and work experience.

SCHOOL SOCIAL WORKER

As members of a specialized area of practice within the profession of social work, school social workers bring unique knowledge and skills to the school system and the educational team. They are committed to enhancing the educational experience of students, their families, and their community by providing social, emotional, behavioral, and adaptive functioning supports. They serve as the bridge between families and schools, on behalf of students.

In any given day, school social workers provide assessment for students with problems such as abuse, neglect, self-injury, substance abuse, and other issues. They plan and implement developmentally appropriate prevention programs, including educational groups on healthy self-image, prevention of adolescent pregnancy, substance abuse, violence, and other deviant behaviors. When necessary, these social workers also provide interventions, such as individual and group counseling for students and family counseling. They are key players in crisis intervention plans, both proactively creating them and offering support in the event of an incident (e.g., 911, school shootings).

Essentially, school social workers provide services to students in special education and work with at-risk adolescents, particularly in relation to school dropout prevention, violence prevention, depression, body image, teenage pregnancy, substance abuse, truancy, and other misconduct. They are valuable resources for students and teachers in terms of dealing with problem behaviors of students (School Social Work Association of America, 2005).

Social Worker Spotlight: Magda Flores, MSSW
School Social Worker, Communities in Schools, Austin, Texas

I received my MSW at the University of Texas at Austin. After years of working in child welfare (residential treatment and Children's Protective Services), I found myself wanting to do something dealing more with prevention. My job search led to me to school social work through a nonprofit agency called Communities In Schools (CIS), where I have worked for over 10 years now at both the elementary and junior high school level. What initially drew me to school social work was the agency's mission, which basically states that we help children prepare for a successful life by helping them stay in school. The longer I worked at CIS, the more I realized just how many things get in the way of a child's academic success, and how many social problems could be alleviated when children are able to complete their education and acquire viable job skills.

In my work as a school social worker, I am able to address a wide variety of issues and my client is always there, meaning I don't have to concern myself with missed appointments or an inability to pay. School social work often includes individual and group counseling, which covers topics such as domestic violence, substance abuse, self-esteem, social skills, self-harm, divorce, grief issues, empowerment, and a variety of other issues that may present themselves. Because of the flexibility and independent nature of my work, I am able to address these topics in whatever manner is most effective. I can utilize the school district's ROPES course, or I can do art activities, or I can do traditional talk therapy. In true social work fashion, my work also involves linking children and families with community resources, advocacy (within the complex and sometimes intimidating educational system), and assistance with basic needs. Recognizing that so many children lack exposure to many experiences, I am able to take students on field trips to universities, cultural events, overnight camping trips, and other activities. Furthermore, my job often includes planning and implementation of school-wide family events, sponsorship of school activities (e.g., chess club), and tutoring.

Topics and events often change from year to year, just as the student population changes. Part of a school social worker's job is to work in conjunction with school personnel and administration to provide the most pertinent and effective programming in order to adapt to the changing needs of students. Because the work is so flexible and dynamic, and because I can truly see and feel the positive impact that my work has on children's lives, I go to work each day with a smile on my face, anticipating what the day's challenges (and rewards) will bring.

AFTER SCHOOL PROGRAM COUNSELOR

After school program counselors may be members of a school's educational team or a community organization that provide services, such as after school tutoring; study hall; music, dance, and art groups; and recreational programs, to students in need of additional support. These counselors are committed to providing support for a student's academic progress, including tutoring on specific subjects and a study hall to complete homework. They are committed to strengthening the student, family, community, and school relationship. They are vital to keeping students supervised, occupied, and engaged in positive activities which help keep them out of trouble.

DAY CARE AND SCHOOL READINESS PROGRAM WORKER

Day care and school readiness program workers provide child development, mental health supervision and management, and head-start services to children up to age 12. They plan and implement daily programs and services that help children develop educationally and personally. For instance, development of self-esteem, imagination, speech, physical skills, health, and nutrition are daily tasks of these workers. They provide parent conferences, home visits, socialization groups, psychosocial and developmental assessments, crisis intervention, and community collaborations to improve children's educational experience. It is the oath of these day care and school readiness program workers to maintain a professional image and treat all children with dignity and respect (National Association for the Education of Young Children, 2007).

ADULT LITERACY PROGRAM WORKER

Adult literacy program workers provide literacy, remedial, and self-enrichment education to out-of-school youths and adults. They work with individuals from a variety of cultures, languages, education levels, and economic backgrounds to meet their needs in reading, writing, and speaking English; basic mathematics; and other subjects. These workers help youths and adults who did not make it through the mainstream educational system develop the knowledge and skills necessary to participate in their communities, hold a job, complete the General Educational Development exam, or pursue higher education. With the changing demography of the United States, it is common place for these workers to assist immigrants whose native language is not English (U.S. Department of Labor, Bureau of Labor Statistics, Occupational Outlook Handbook, 2007).

SPECIAL EDUCATION SOCIAL SERVICE WORKER

In the school system and organizations that provide services to the school, certain social workers specialize in offering services to children and youth in special education. These workers are involved in the creation and implementation of the Individualized Educational Program (IEP), for each student who utilizes the school's special education services. They conduct assessments of the student's physical and mental disabilities and family situations, which help in creating the IEP. As part of a team that acts in the best interest of the student, a special education social service provider facilitates the involvement of the family, community, and other organizations in the development of a sound educational program for the student. Several of the specific services provided to the student and family include individual and family counseling, social skills classes, tutoring, parenting classes, and other services to help students and families cope with the disability. In addition to providing micro-level services, these social workers are also involved in policy development and advocacy for students with disabilities.

As shown by the descriptions above, there are many career opportunities for social work in school settings. As providers of school-based and school-linked services, these social workers promote educational and personal development and growth of all students in their families and communities.

SOCIAL WORKER ON A COLLEGE CAMPUS

When we think about school social work, we usually think about social work in a public school. However, another exciting career option for social workers includes working for a university. Some social workers work in the university counseling center, where they provide therapeutic services to college students who are experiencing a variety of problems, both personal and academic. Problems might include anything from dealing with a sexual assault to depression, to coping with the stress of working and going to school full time. These positions require an earned master's degree in social work (MSW) as well as licensure.

Social workers are also hired to work in various university programs, sometimes referred to as student services. They might be in charge of educational programming on issues such as date rape, violent dating relationships, and substance abuse. They might also run support groups on campus for gay/lesbian college students or other groups of students in need of this type of service. Some of these positions are more specialized and are termed *wellness coordinators* or *sexual assault advocates*. More and more universities are recognizing the value of having social workers and other mental health professionals on campus to help support students and address the wide array of problems and needs they often experience in today's college environment.

Core Competencies and Skills

- Passion for working with students, including those at risk and in special education.
- Comfortable working in a bureaucratic yet fast-paced environment and maintaining. cooperative relationships with multiple parties, including students, families, community, politicians, etc.
- Comfortable working with a diverse population of students, particularly in urban schools.

- Excellent knowledge of child and adult growth, development, and behavior characteristics.
- Excellent knowledge of methods for supervising, managing, motivating, and remediation of students.
- Excellent verbal and written communication skills for meetings, documentation, court reports, etc.
- Strong educational and career counseling, crisis management, and problem-solving skills.
- High degree of cultural sensitivity toward bicultural students, their families, and community; ability to work respectfully with children, families, and communities regardless of age, gender, sexual orientation, race/ethnicity, national origin, immigration status, disabilities, and socioeconomic status.
- Ability to work with bilingual students and their families (e.g., provide access to information in the appropriate language as well as provide translators).
- Excellent assessment and decision-making skills.
- Excellent skills in prevention and intervention, particularly related to school dropout, teenage pregnancy, substance abuse, truancy, gangs, and youth violence (e.g., parent conference, home visit, socialization group, psychosocial and developmental assessment, crisis intervention, community collaborations).
- Self-care as school settings are demanding and multifaceted.

Educational and Licensing Requirements

School social workers can be employed in school settings with a bachelor's, master's, or PhD degree in social work, depending on the policies of the particular school system. In the United States and its territories, many MSW education programs have concentrations or specializations in school social work that prepare students specifically for this career. Licensure in school social work requires an individual to meet both the Standards for School Services Professionals and the Standards for School Social Work Professionals (School Social Work Association of America, 2005).

Qualifications of after school program counselors vary tremendously by state and program. However, the emphasis of these counselors are on knowledge, skills, and experiences such as the ability to work with children, communicate effectively, time management and organization, analytical abilities, sound judgement, and being a good role model. Although there is no specific licensure for after school program counselors, licensing is required at the agency/organizational level according to specific fields (e.g., child day care licensing, social work).

The educational requirements for day care and school readiness program workers range from high school diploma, knowledge of child development, and on-the-job training to courses in education, nutrition, psychology, and speech or an associate's degree in early childhood education. For workers interested in administrative positions, a bachelor's degree and sometimes a state teacher certificate/license or master's degree is required.

Educational and licensing qualifications for adult literacy program workers vary by state and program. For example, most states require at least a bachelor's degree and preferably a master's degree. Others require the state teacher certificate/license and a certificate in English as a second language or adult education (U.S. Department of Education, Office of Vocational and Adult Education, 2007).

As discussed thus far, school-based and school-linked service providers have a very delicate and precious population for whom they are responsible, including children and disenfranchised adults who were unable to successfully progress through a traditional educational system. Because of the length of time children spend in school as well as the intensity of the demand and responsibility for the care of children and disenfranchised adults, a high degree of knowledge, skills, and training are required to successfully and effectively meet their needs. Consequently, workers with a social work degree or related field are needed in school settings.

Best Aspects of this Job

- Working with students, their families and communities.
- Contributing to the lives of adults who are more than likely vulnerable to social problems due to limited education or under education.
- Expanding knowledge about diverse cultures including those of immigrants and developing cultural competency skills.
- Expanding knowledge about languages and skills to mobilize resources to ameliorate the negative impacts of language barriers.
- Expanding knowledge about risk and protective factors (e.g., personal, family, peer, school, community-based) that contribute to or hinder the educational achievements and aspirations of students.

- Opportunity to work with schools, families, and communities to mobilize resources that will help students, both children and disenfranchised adults, with their families and community.
- Opportunity to be a part of an educational team with teachers, counselors, coaches, etc. for the best interest of the student.
- Being important in the lives of the students with which one has been entrusted.
- Being a significant influence on students, both children and disenfranchised adults.
- Being a witness to achievements such as change to appropriate behavior, increased classroom performance, self-enrichment, and graduation.
- Working with motivated, self-directed, and confident adults who are seeking self-enrichment opportunities.
- Every single day in the school system is unique and exciting!

Challenging Aspects of this Job

- Possible difficulty in engaging parents as team members.
- Occasionally, difficulty in working with school professionals who do not have social work education or experience.
- Sometimes a school social worker's workday expands beyond the school to the home.
- Witnessing academic failure and unwillingness to try again.
- Knowledge of problems in the home that negatively impact innocent students.
- Knowing that sometimes the problems stem from the traditional educational system (e.g., inaccessibility to needed resources and information).
- The heavy burden of being responsible for appropriate assessments and making decisions that affect children and disenfranchised adults.
- Sometimes working with at-risk students who are unwilling to collaborate on a solution.
- Sometimes a schools social worker's safety is at stake.
- Because demands are extremely high in school settings, caring for oneself and having a balanced life can be difficult.
- Standing, walking, carrying materials, and talking all day can sometimes take a toll, physically.

- Having a successful program eliminated from the school because funding is not available.

Compensation and Employment Outlook

School-based and school-linked service providers are employed by both public and private entities, thus compensation varies by setting, program, state, and region. Those working for a school system or government typically receive good salaries and benefits. School social workers and school counselors with master's degrees usually start at a higher level on the pay scale. For instance, in 2004, school social workers median annual income was $34,820 and ranging from $23,000 to $57,000. The median annual income for social workers in elementary and secondary schools was $44,300 (U.S. Department of Labor, Bureau of Labor Statistics, Occupational Outlook Handbook, 2007).

With the increased demand for school counselors and the expansion in their responsibilities, earnings may change dramatically. In 2004, the median annual earning was $45,570, with a range of $26,260 to $72,390. Because school counselors have summer breaks, summer work in the school or other settings may also provide additional income. The following are 2004 figures (Table 5.1) for some of the largest employers of educational, vocational, and school counselors (U.S. Department of Labor, Bureau of Labor Statistics, Occupational Outlook Handbook, 2007).

Depending on the program, geographical location, and qualifications of the individual, after school program counselors may be paid hourly wages ranging from as little as $7 to $25 or higher. Some of these counselors are hired by the school, whereas others are hired by agencies and organizations in the community who are stakeholders with students in the school.

Day care and school readiness program workers tend to be low-paid compared to other school-based and school-linked positions. Depending on geographical location, program, and qualifications of the individual,

Table 5.1

Elementary and secondary schools	$51,160
Junior colleges	$45,730
Colleges, universities, and professional schools	$39,110
Individual and family services	$30,240
Vocational rehabilitation services	$27,800

day care and school readiness program workers may earn about $15,000 annually in Virginia to about $25,000 annually in Hawaii in 2006 (PayScale Inc., 2007).

Among adult literacy program workers, in 2000, the median hourly earning was $16 and ranging from $9 to $28. Part-time adult literacy workers are paid hourly or per class and receive no benefits, whereas full-time teachers are paid a salary and receive good benefits if they work for a school system or government (Bureau of Labor Statistics, U.S. Department of Labor, Occupational Outlook Handbook, 2007). As indicated earlier, there is a wide range of salaries for school-based and school-linked service providers depending on the position, employer, program, state or region, years of previous experience, and type of degree (e.g., undergraduate or graduate degree).

In terms of outlook, employment of school social workers is not only expected to grow, but will also be competitive due to increases in student enrollments, diversity in the schools, and the increase in academic, personal, social, and mental health needs of both students in the general school population and special education. Nonetheless, the greatest determining factor in this growth within the schools remains to be funding available from the federal, state, and local governments (U.S. Department of Labor, Bureau of Labor Statistics, Occupational Outlook Handbook, 2007).

The increase in student enrollments in colleges and other postsecondary school settings will positively impact growth in the job outlook for school counselors. Likewise, the increase in K-12 enrollments, the expansion of the responsibilities of school counselors, and the increased demand for schools, particularly elementary schools, to employ counselors adds to the positive outlook on jobs for school counselors. Although budget instability dampens the forecast for school counselors, federal grants and subsidies may help ameliorate the situation, particularly in rural and inner-city schools (U.S. Department of Labor, Bureau of Labor Statistics, Occupational Outlook Handbook, 2007).

After school programs have been a resource for working parents for decades. The employment outlook for after school program counselors may be positively impacted by the increase in school enrollments, student needs for social and behavioral prevention and intervention, and the demand for after school programs by women and men with children who are working outside of the home.

The job outlook for day care and school readiness program workers is very good through 2014 due to high turnover rates and increases in the number of children needing day care because mothers are entering or returning to the labor force (National Association for the Education of Young Children, 2007). In terms of adult literacy program workers, opportunities are expected to be very good through 2010, especially for teachers of English as a second language due to large increases in immigrant populations and self-enrichment courses because of the current trend of embracing lifelong learning. The large number of people retiring and the constant high demands for teachers will also create jobs. Like other employment opportunities, the demand for literacy education fluctuates with the economy (U.S. Department of Education, Office of Vocational and Adult Education, 2007).

Self-Assessment Checklist: Is this Job for Me?

☐ Do you have a passion for working with children from diverse backgrounds and ensuring their educational, personal, social, and mental health needs are met?

☐ Do you think that you are able to work with parents from diverse backgrounds, both culturally and linguistically, and their communities?

☐ Do you enjoy having a job where your workday is spent working with multiple systems, including students, teachers, families, communities, and courts, to mobilize resources for the best interest of the child?

☐ Would you enjoy having a job where you are able to contribute to the betterment of the lives of disenfranchised adults who otherwise did not have the opportunity to succeed in a traditional educational system?

☐ Would you enjoy the challenge of working with a range of individuals from at-risk children to motivated adults?

☐ Would you enjoy advocating for access to resources and information for children, their families, and communities?

☐ Would you be comfortable visiting with children in their homes (e.g., parents, relatives, foster parents)?

☐ Do you have an assertive personality and are comfortable dealing with conflict?

☐ Would you be comfortable working for an agency that is somewhat bureaucratic and has many rules, regulations, policies, and procedures to follow?

If you answered "yes" to seven or more of the above questions, then working at a school setting might be the place for you!

RECOMMENDED READINGS/WEB SITES TO LEARN MORE

Dupper, D. (2002). *School social work: Skills and interventions for effective practice.* Somerset, NJ: Wiley Higher Education Publication.

Education Encyclopedia: http://education.stateuniversity.com/pages/2000/FullService-Schools.html

National Association for the Education of Young Children: www.naeyc.org

School Social Work Association of America: www.sswaa.org

School Social Work Exercise

Birat Rahim is a 6-year-old boy who is in the first grade. His parents emigrated from Pakistan when he was 3, and the family speaks both Urdu and English at home. Birat's teacher has noticed that for the past 2 weeks since report cards went home for the second quarter, he has been very withdrawn in class. Birat has not been playing with his usual friends, and he also has not been touching his school lunch. At least three times a week, Birat asks to visit the school nurse at the clinic, telling the nurse he has a stomach ache. The teacher contacts the school social worker for assistance.

Questions

1. As the school social worker for this referral, what is the first step you would take in assessing this child?
2. What could be the possible areas of concern causing such a change in Birat's behavior?
3. Before you work with this family, what kinds of things would be important to learn about the family's native culture and language?

REFERENCES

Kronick, R. F. (2000). *Human services and the full service school.* Springfield, IL: Charles C. Thomas.

National Association for the Education of Young Children. (2007). *Promoting excellence in early childhood education.* [Online]. Retrieved December 1, 2007, from http://www.naeyc.org/about/

PayScale, Inc. Salary Survey Report for Industry: Child Care/Day Care (2000–2007). Retrieved April 19, 2008, from http://www.payscale.com/

School Social Work Association of America. (2005). About School Social Work Association of American. [Online]. Retrieved April 19, 2008, from http://www.sswaa.org/

Tyack, D. (1992). *Health and social services in public schools: Historical perspectives.* Future of Children 2, 19–31.

U.S. Department of Education, Office of Vocational and Adult Education. (2007). *Strategic Plan for Fiscal Years 2007–12.* [Online]. Retrieved December 1, 2007, from http://www.ed.gov/about/reports/strat/index.html?src=ln

U.S. Department of Labor, Bureau of Labor Statistics. (2007). *Occupational outlook handbook, (2006–2007 ed.).* [Online]. Retrieved December 1, 2007, from http://www.bls.gov/oco

6 Social Work with Older Adults

Though many social workers choose to work with children, others enjoy working with individuals at the other end of the age spectrum. In the coming years, there will be an increasing demand for social workers who work with older adults. The proportion of Americans aged 65 and older is rapidly growing and has been termed the "graying of America." The U.S. Census Bureau estimates that by 2020, one in five Americans will be classified as an older adult! This has created a number of important challenges and opportunities for the social work profession as we strive to ensure that the needs of older Americans are met.

Most of us can identify with this because we have parents and grand-parents, and we want them to be able to live independently for as long as they can and to have a high-quality life. We look to federal government programs, such as Medicare, Social Security, and subsidized housing, to help ensure that older adults have access to medical care and enough money to meet their basic needs when they retire. Other services, such as Meals on Wheels and community senior centers, are important programs for older adults at the local level.

Social workers who work with older adults are concerned with a variety of issues and problems, including elder abuse, Alzheimer's disease and dementia, assisting grandparents who are raising grandchildren, age discrimination, and end-of-life care. Older adults with physical or mental impairments, or who are suffering from a chronic disease, may need assistance at home or in a long-term care residence. Many older adults suffer from depression or substance abuse, and they need the care of a mental health professional.

Working with older adults requires a high degree of knowledge and skills and can be a very rewarding career. This chapter profiles a number of important work settings for social workers who want to work with older adults.

Gerontology, the study of the biological, psychological, and social aspects of aging, is a relatively new field in social work; it became an established field of social work practice in the 1980s. According to Segal, Gerdes, and Steiner (2004), "The goal of gerontological social workers is to promote and advance older clients' social, emotional, and physical well being so that they can live more independent and satisfying lives" (p. 173).

ADULT PROTECTIVE SERVICES CASEWORKER

Most people are familiar with Children's Protective Services (CPS) and the role that this agency plays in their state. However, many are less familiar with the concept of elder abuse and do not realize that many states employ APS caseworkers who investigate allegations that an older adult, or disabled adult, is being abused or neglected by a family member or caregiver. According to the National Center on Elder Abuse (2008), the best available estimates suggest that between 1 and 2 million Americans aged 65 or older have been subject to some form of elder abuse, and the majority of abusers are family members, typically an adult child or a spouse.

Elder abuse may take the following forms: physical abuse, sexual abuse, emotional abuse, neglect, exploitation, and abandonment. APS workers perform many of the same tasks as CPS workers: they investigate reports of abuse and neglect, interview the victim and the alleged perpetrator(s), work within the court system, arrange needed services for the family, and sometimes arrange an alternate placement for the victim to keep them safe. (**Note**: Please read the description of the CPS caseworker in chapter 4, as the skills and competencies needed for APS casework are very similar to the casework performed by CPS caseworkers.)

However, there are also a few differences between CPS and APS work. The major difference is that the APS victim is an adult, not a child, so they have a choice in whether they want to receive help and assistance from APS. This is very different from the CPS system where the laws mandate that caseworkers protect the child, and sometimes remove them from their home, even when this is against the child's wishes. Anecdotally, many APS caseworkers report that their jobs are less stressful than that of CPS caseworkers and that the caseloads are more manageable. In some states, APS caseworkers also investigate allegations of abuse and neglect occurring in nursing homes and other residential care facilities.

Social Worker Spotlight: Lori Delagrammatikas, MSW/PhD Candidate and Program Coordinator, MASTER, Academy for Professional Excellence, San Diego State University School of Social Work

I didn't get involved with social work until I was in my 40s. My first social work job was determining the amount of home care needed by impoverished, disabled seniors through California's In-Home Supportive Services program. I loved the job because I was able to provide the kind of help that truly makes a difference in clients' lives. I met some fascinating individuals, like the wheelchair bound woman who, despite insufferable pain, went to a nursing home every morning to read to the blind, or the elderly Dutch woman who had hidden Jewish families during World War II and now hid food throughout her home.

My next job was as a program specialist for APS. Although this was an administrative job, without direct client contact, I liked the wide variety of duties and experiences. APS social workers investigate abuse of elders living in the community (as opposed to abuse of elders living in nursing homes). The types of abuse range from financial scams to physical/sexual abuse and include self-neglect situations. My job included working with both social workers and management to develop policies and procedures about how workers conducted investigations, delivered services, and managed cases. I met with other community agencies (e.g., law enforcement and mental health) to determine how our agencies could work together. My duties included developing materials to teach the public about elder abuse and reviewing new legislation to determine how it would affect practice. In the process, I became very passionate about elder abuse. I eventually got involved at the state level by volunteering to sit on a statewide APS committee. I helped write the California elder abuse regulations and I chaired the committee when it published a study of all the elder abuse reports received in California on a specific day.

During the time I worked in APS, I came to realize that we know very little about the dynamics of elder abuse, the size of the problem, and the best ways to intervene. The baby boomers are aging and we are facing a tidal wave of abuse. We need to be ready! So, I recently retired from my government job to return to school and earn my PhD in social research. I am also working part time developing an APS Training Academy, in association with the National APS Association, to provide standardized training to new APS social workers.

I invite new social workers to consider a career in APS. The field is growing. It's never boring. And, there are very few jobs as rewarding!

SOCIAL WORK IN ADULT DAY CENTERS

Adult day centers are daytime programs that serve older adults who are living at home. By providing older adults with a supervised place to stay during the day, they offer respite for caregivers, particularly caregivers who are caring for someone with Alzheimer's or other cognitive impairments. This is an extremely valued service for caregivers who need a break from the daily grind of caring for someone who needs full-time care. This gives caregivers the opportunity to run errands or just have some time for themselves. However, adult day centers also provide a valuable service to the older adults and help to meet their health and mental health needs, as well as reduce their social isolation.

Adult day centers usually provide a range of services, including educational, recreational, and self-help groups. Some might also have a health or wellness component. They often serve meals and offer transportation to and from the center.

There are a number of roles for individuals who have received a bachelor's in social work (BSW) or a master's in social work (MSW) to play in adult day centers. They can act in an administrative capacity and may have the title of director or program manager in one of these programs. In this role, the social worker would be charged with developing programs, working with the community, and managing the funds of the organization. Social workers can also act in the role of care coordinator or case manager. In this role, they will assess the client's needs to determine eligibility and appropriateness of services and provide information and referrals, thereby linking them to other programs in the community.

RESIDENTIAL CARE CASE MANAGER

There are a number of residential settings for older adults, depending on the level of care and support required. Adults who are healthy and are able to live independently may choose to live in a retirement community for seniors. Those who need more care may reside in a skilled nursing or assisted living facility. Those with the highest level of care may need to reside in a long-term care rehabilitation facility or nursing home. Social workers can be found working in these various residential settings for older adults. Social workers often perform a case management role to ensure that clients receive services appropriate to their needs, and they work with family members by providing support and information. Psychosocial supportive and educational counseling is often a component of working with adults to help them plan for and cope with life changes.

CAREERS IN PSYCHOGERIATRICS

Some social workers work with older adults who are suffering from depression or other emotional or psychiatric conditions. According to the Centers for Disease Control and Prevention (2007):

- Almost 20% of Americans age 55 and older experience specific mental disorders that are not part of "normal" aging, including depression, anxiety disorders, and dementia (including Alzheimer's disease).
- Between 8% and 20% of older adults in the community, and up to 37% in primary care settings, suffer from depressive symptoms.

■ Among Americans 65 years and older, approximately 6% to 10% have dementia, and two-thirds of people with dementia have Alzheimer's disease.

Recent research, on the other hand, has focused on "healthy aging" and on activities older adults can do to preserve and maintain their mental and emotional health.

This is a burgeoning field and a good fit for those interested in the behavioral and biological aspects of geriatric mental health. Some social work clinicians in private practice specialize in bereavement and loss. There are a growing number of hospitals around the country that have specialized psychiatric programs for older adults. For more information on social work in the field of mental health, please refer to chapter 8.

SOCIAL WORK IN HOSPITALS AND OTHER HEALTH CARE SETTINGS

Older adults suffer from a wide range of illnesses, for which they need medical, social, and emotional support. According to the Centers for Disease Control and Prevention (2007), 88% of those older than 65 years of age have at least one chronic health condition (e.g., heart disease, cancer, stroke, diabetes).

Gerontological social workers in this setting provide a range of services, including psychosocial assessments, family support services, home health care, hospice, discharge planning, and counseling and support. For more information on social work in the medical field, please refer to chapter 7. Here, we will focus on two popular settings when working with older adults in a medical setting: hospice and home health care.

Social Worker Spotlight: Sheryl Bruno, MSW
Social Work Supervisor, Providence ElderPlace, Portland, Oregon

My family always "told" me that I'd be a nurse. However, in college, I realized that I hated bodily fluids, science, and math, so I switched to other aspects of the human spirit and mind. In 1984, I graduated from the University of Hawaii, having received a bachelor's degree in human development. For the most part, I decided to pursue my MSW for two reasons: I wasn't quite ready to leave college, and I wasn't sure what reaction I would get from potential employers to a degree called "human development." So, by December 1986, I graduated and considered myself ready. For what, I had no idea.

I've always had a strong affinity for older adults, and I was continually exposed to this population with my work in acute care settings as a discharge planner for numerous hospitals in Hawaii and Washington (Seattle and Bellevue). My work took on a different focus while at Harborview Medical Center, however, when I worked as a case manager for the AIDS clinic, then later as a therapist for women and children who were sexually abused. Throughout these experiences, I continued to have a "calling" to go back to geriatrics. With my relocation to Portland, Oregon, I was hired as a social work case manager for Providence ElderPlace, and I have been here for the past 12 plus years. My professional growth continued with Providence, from being a direct line staff member to that of supervisor and manager.

Providence ElderPlace is a comprehensive care program that offers a range of services to older adults and their families—medical and mental health services, housing assistance, social services, recreational therapy, end-of-life care, care coordination, and more—all in one program! To learn more about this model of care, please visit: www.providence.org/oregon/Programs_and_Services/ElderPlace/default.htm

Social workers at Providence ElderPlace provide: case management; relocation planning of patients to appropriate housing settings such as adult foster homes, residential care facilities, and assisted living facilities; financial planning; family conferencing; strong interdisciplinary team work; home visits; detailed psychosocial assessments; crisis management; discharge planning; and mental health counseling.

The running theme for my professional career is the desire to help those who are vulnerable and in extreme need. This theme worked well at all of my jobs, but particularly with my job within the Providence Health System, given their strong mission and their values of justice, stewardship, compassion, respect, and excellence. Perhaps, this explains why I have been with Providence Health

System for over 12 years and have no intentions of leaving soon. I've also stayed in social work due to the fact that the field allows one to explore many areas in helping others such as a direct case manager, therapist, and most recently in my professional career as a supervisor and manager. Although stressful as most jobs in the health care field can be, I continue to see the value of the social work role everyday by virtue of the commitment of my staff and the people we serve everyday.

HOSPICE SOCIAL WORKER

Generally speaking, hospice agencies provide services for people with terminal illnesses who are expected to die within 6 months, either in the patient's home or in an inpatient hospice facility. Due to the growing number of older Americans, usage of hospice services is rising and will continue to do so. According to the National Hospice and Palliative Care Organization (2007), an estimated 1.3 million patients received services from hospice in 2006, a 162% increase in 10 years.

The role of the hospice social worker includes helping the dying patient and their loved ones prepare for the end of their life, assisting the patient and the family with bereavement, providing relief from pain (e.g., palliative and supportive care), improving the patient's quality of life, assisting with difficult decision making, and mediating between the patient and the medical professionals involved in the patient's care. Because the focus of this work is on death and dying, there is often a spiritual or religious component to this work as well. Hospice social workers work with a team of professionals, including hospice nurses, physicians, and chaplains.

Social Worker Spotlight: Mary Jane O'Rourke, MSW
Hospice and Palliative Care of Washington County, Hillsboro, Oregon

I have an MSW from Eastern Washington University. As a medical social worker at Hospice and Palliative Care of Washington County (HWC) in Hillsboro, Oregon, I assume a variety of social work roles. For the past 2.5 years, I have provided direct social work services to hospice patients and families as part of HWC's in-home hospice, which is designed to meet terminally ill patients and families physical, social, psychological, and spiritual needs. I serve as a resource coordinator, counselor, and educator for patients and families. When a patient's physician refers him or her to hospice, an MSW and RN meet with the patient and family to educate them about hospice, assess individual needs, and gather the various resources needed for particular patients.

Hospice is a concept of care designed to provide support and care for patients with incurable diseases, so they may maintain quality of life and comfort as they journey through the dying process. Hospice social workers are required to have a BSW, yet at HWC, an MSW is preferred.

Working with people at the end of their lives is a privilege and an honor. The end of life can be a vulnerable yet meaningful time for hospice patients and families. The gift lies in the invitation to enter one's home and life at such a vulnerable time. Respecting each person for whom they are, how they have lived their life, and how they ultimately want to leave this world is the main task of a hospice social worker. I am constantly learning valuable lessons about the human spirit and the beauty of life and death.

HOME HEALTH SOCIAL WORKER

Private home health agencies have proliferated in recent years, as the number of adults who need care but want to remain in their home continues to grow. This service will continue to be in demand in the coming years. Social workers employed in home health agencies primarily play a case-management role. They refer families to needed services and programs; "trouble-shoot" problematic situations between the care giver and the care receiver; arrange alternative care options; facilitate communication between family members, medical professionals, and service providers; and counsel families dealing with illness and end-of-life issues.

GERIATRIC CASE MANAGER

This is a growing field of social work practice that will continue to expand in the coming years as more and more families need assistance from a professional in managing the needs of their loved ones. Any family member who has been faced with the daunting decision to move an older family member to a care facility knows how overwhelming it can be. In a very short period of time, the family must sort through where their parent should live, whether they will be eligible, how to pay for it, and cut through the red tape of Medicare and Medicaid. And on top of all of this, they want to ensure that their loved one will be in a place where they will be safe and cared for.

Geriatric case managers may work in a private, for-profit agency or have their own private practices. Social workers in this role commonly perform the following tasks: conduct care planning assessment and link the client with appropriate resources and providers; assist with arranging in home services or moving an older adult to a retirement community, assisted living facility, or nursing home; provide counseling and support, including crisis counseling; assist with medical, legal, and financial issues; provide case management and facilitate communication between family members, medical professionals, and service providers; monitor service delivery to ensure that the patient is receiving high quality care that is timely; and provide advocacy when necessary. This job has the potential to be quite lucrative because many case managers are in business for themselves and the number of families in need of this type of service will continue to grow.

Social Worker Spotlight: Simon Paquette, LCSW, RC Medical Social Worker, Independent Case Management, Camas, Washington

In 1992, I received my MSW from Springfield College in Springfield, Massachusetts. I had many years of experience as a practicing social worker before going back to graduate school at age 40. In graduate training, I became sensitized to the issues and family dynamics when a family member is dying from an illness, as part of my hospice career path. I found myself gaining tremendous experience in the medical management of terminal illness and supportive interventions to family members. I gained knowledge about poor medical practice, social work interventions, and evidence-proven pathways. I remained in this field for 9 years. I began a transition process of immersing myself back into mental health, chronic disease management, pain management practice reform, regulating long-term care, nursing home social service, and home health, ultimately dissatisfied with the choices. I found my knowledge of medical management being useful but not contributing to improving the lives of others.

The role I evolved into was independent case management of the total care of persons with guardians, conservators, and trust officers. I found an outlet for my skills in situations where a client requires comprehensive care solutions. I took on several difficult cases with clients involving families at odds with the legal system, each other, and the guardianship community. I became valued for my skills and knowledge base by those who were contracting with me. My clients achieved more independence, quality of life, and consistent care. I also found the recognition of other medical disciplines because I could deal with the total care need. I had found a niche, and more importantly excitement, in finding solutions resulting in the kind of care outcomes I had been frustrated in achieving in the past. This time, however, I was able to continue to facilitate and coordinate care over time, resulting in increased quality of life, reduction of medical needs, and stable health/mental health disease process. The many years of work experience involving mental/medical health, disease process management, funding streams, legal, ethical, and values issues had all come together for me. I have more value as a professional in contributing to the well being of others and personal satisfaction with the outcomes of my work.

I have experienced successful outcomes with clients that had required immense resources being reduced to routine care management. A lifetime of gained experience has translated into the most satisfaction I could have ever imagined in the practice of social work. I am independent, valued, and growing as a professional in the later stages of my career. I had gained the knowledge base to understand funding, care management systems, medical culture, and the politics involved from macro to the micro levels. I have discovered a new career area for myself and colleagues that is quite remarkable in providing all the supports, tools, and team work to fulfill all aspects of social work practice. The impact of aging in our society has yet to be fully understood. The challenges it poses are ideal for the advanced social work practitioner.

CAREERS IN RESEARCH AND POLICY

There are some social workers who choose to work in research and/or policy. Social workers work as lobbyists or in advocacy organizations, such as the American Association of Retired Persons (AARP), to try to pass legislation that improves conditions for older adults. Areas of focus might include making improvements to the Medicare and Social Security programs, making prescription drugs more affordable, providing financial and other benefits to grandparents who are raising grandchildren, and affordable housing for seniors. Social workers also work as researchers in the field of aging/gerontology. They typically work for universities, the government, or a nonprofit research organization.

CAREERS WITH THE GOVERNMENT

There are social workers all across the country who begin working for the government (city, county, state, or federal) after having some direct experience in gerontology. Many states and localities have an Office or Department of Aging. For those interested in working at the federal level, there is the Administration on Aging under the auspices of the Department of Health and Human Services. Most of these jobs include working in policy or program planning. They may also involve applying for a grant to start a new outreach program, or other needed program, for older adults in your community. The upside of working in a high-level government job is that it includes good benefits, regular working hours, and often higher salaries because you are recognized as an expert in your field.

Core Competencies and Skills

- Knowledge of the aging process, chronic illnesses and mental impairments of the aging, and commonly used medications and medical interventions.
- Knowledge of the stressors that can occur as one adjusts to older adulthood such as retirement, widowhood, physical decline, loss of loved ones, and approaching end of life.
- Strong advocacy and mediation skills are needed to ensure that older adults are receiving the professional care and services to which they are entitled.
- Awareness of cultural and religious/spiritual differences when it comes to attitudes and beliefs on aging and death and dying.

- Effective working with large systems of care, such as the medical and mental health systems.
- Knowledge of and sensitivity to the dynamics and risk factors related to elder abuse and neglect.
- Strong knowledge of the latest research on loss, bereavement, and death and dying.
- Strong assessment and counseling skills with a life-course perspective.
- Knowledge of the major government programs, laws, regulations, and public policies that pertain to older adults such as Medicare, Social Security, Social Security Supplemental Income (SSI), guardianship, living wills, power of attorney, and end-of-life care.

Educational and Licensing Requirements

It is a good idea to attend workshops in your community that pertain to social work with older adults, many of which will emphasize end-of-life care, mental health, or medical issues. There are BSW-level positions available in gerontology if you are interested in working in residential settings, such as independent and assisted living centers, rehabilitation centers, community senior centers, or APS.

Many social work jobs that involve working with older adults require a master's degree and specialized training, particularly if you are interested in working in the fields of health care, mental health, or hospice. Some jobs may also require licensure. There are a number of ways to get experience and specialized training if you are interested in working in this field. It would be advisable to choose field internships in this area when you are completing your undergraduate or MSW. Additionally, there are some MSW programs that offer concentrations in gerontology or certificate programs that allow for advanced training in the field. You may also look for social work programs that offer elective courses on aging, grief, or death and dying. The Council on Social Work Education's (CSWE) Gero-Ed Center Web site maintains a list of accredited programs that feature gerontology (http://depts.washington.edu/geroctr/Resources4/sub4_4_5GeroSWPrograms.html).

Best Aspects of this Job

- Working in a multidisciplinary setting with other professionals (e.g., physicians, nurses, dietitians, occupational and physical therapists, mental health, professionals, chaplains) makes for an interesting and diverse work environment.

- Working with older adults enables you to work with individuals from diverse backgrounds who have lived varied and interesting lives.
- Many social workers who work with patients who are dying feel it is an honor to be able to provide comfort to patients and their families in their final days.
- Hearing the stories of older adults as they share their wisdom and life experiences with you is a privilege.
- Working with persons as they grow older helps you keep your own priorities in perspective.
- Protecting older adults from abuse and neglect and helping them achieve a high-quality life can be very rewarding.

Challenging Aspects of this Job

- Seeing patients who are dying or in pain takes an emotional toll; self-care is very important.
- It is difficult to watch an older adult giving up their independence and to see their quality of life decline when support and resources are not available.
- Assisting families with making end-of-life decisions for their loved one (e.g., when to remove the feeding tube) can be challenging.
- Setting clear boundaries with patients and families.
- Understanding and working with your own grief can be challenging.
- Dealing with societal views around issues of grief, death, and aging can be frustrating.
- Must be flexible and willing to change course when patients and families are in crisis.

Compensation and Employment Outlook

According to the U.S. Department of Labor (2008), "The rapidly growing elderly population and the aging baby boom generation will create greater demand for health and social services, resulting in particularly rapid job growth among gerontology social workers" ("Social Workers," p. 3). Thus, social workers interested in working with older adults will be in great demand in the coming years due to these changing demographics.

Salaries for APS caseworkers are comparable to the salaries of CPS caseworkers in each respective state. Salaries for those jobs requiring an MSW (e.g., hospice, mental health settings, medical settings) will be significantly higher than those jobs requiring a BSW (e.g., community senior centers or residential settings, such as nursing homes and assisted living facilities). Administrative and supervisory positions in agencies and organizations serving older adults will also pay higher salaries.

Self-Assessment Checklist: Is This Job for Me?

- ☐ Do you have a healthy respect and admiration for older adults and the rich life experience they bring to the table?
- ☐ Would you enjoy working with and supporting the family members of older adults?
- ☐ Would you find it interesting and exciting to work with an interdisciplinary team of medical and mental health professionals?
- ☐ Are you comfortable seeing adults who are ill and working with issues of death and dying?
- ☐ Do you enjoy the company and companionship of older adults?
- ☐ Would you be able to see and hear details of how an older adult has been abused and/or neglected by one of their family members or in a residential facility?
- ☐ Are you creative in terms of planning social and recreational activities for older adults?
- ☐ Are you able to keep you own values and beliefs (e.g., religious or spiritual in nature) related to death and dying to yourself and not push them onto the patients you will be working with?
- ☐ Are you good at taking care of yourself in order to deal with the emotional toll of working with issues of death and dying?
- ☐ Would you be comfortable working in a host setting with other professionals who were educated differently and may have different views and values than those of social workers?

If you answered "yes" to seven or more of the above questions, then working with older adults might be for you!

RECOMMENDED READINGS/WEB SITES TO LEARN MORE

General Information on Aging

Administration on Aging, U.S. Department of Health and Human Services: www.aoa.dhhs.gov/

American Association of Retired Persons (AARP): www.aarp.org

American Society on Aging: www.asaging.org/about.cfm

Council on Social Work Education Gero-Ed Center: http://depts.washington.edu/geroctr/

Grobman, L. M., & Bourassa, D. B. (2007). *Days in the lives of gerontological social workers: 44 professionals tell stories from real life social work practice with older adults.* Harrisburg, PA: White Hat Communications.

National Association of Professional Geriatric Care Managers: www.caremanager.org/index.cfm

Elder Abuse

Clearinghouse on Abuse and Neglect of the Elderly: http://db.rdms.udel.edu:8080/CANE/index.jsp

Mellor, J., & Brownell, P. (2006). *Elder abuse and mistreatment: Policy, practice, and research.* Philadelphia: Haworth Press.

National Center on Elder Abuse: http://www.ncea.aoa.gov/NCEAroot/Main_Site/Library/CANE/CANE.aspx

National Committee for the Prevention of Elder Abuse: http://www.preventelderabuse.org/

Woolf, L. Elder abuse and neglect. Retrieved August 7, 2008, from http://www.webster.edu/~woolflm/abuse.html

Visit the Web site below to watch a Web video of a real APS case in Texas: http://www.dfps.state.tx.us/Adult_Protection/video/default.asp

Hospice/Death and Dying

Albom, M. *Tuesdays with Morrie.* New York: Doubleday. (A beautiful true story of a man suffering from Lou Gehrig's disease who lived and died with great dignity.)

Kubler-Ross, E. (1989). *On Death and Dying.* London: Routledge.

National Hospice and Palliative Care Organization: www.nhpco.org

Alzheimer's Disease

Alzheimer's Association: www.alz.org/

Social Work with Older Adults Exercise

Case Study

You are an APS caseworker and have been given the following case to investigate: Mr. Harris is 77 years old and lives with his 52-year-old son. The caller reports that the son hits his father and constantly calls him names and threatens to throw him out of the house when he has had too much to drink. The caller has seen bruises on the face and arms of the victim on numerous occasions. The caller also alleges that the son is taking his father's social security money each month. He uses the money to finance his hunting trips with friends and to purchase alcohol and other expensive gifts for himself. His father often goes without needed medication for his high blood pressure and diabetes. The caller is very worried about the victim and feels he needs to be living in a safer environment, where he is cared for and loved. The caller believes that Mr. Harris is scared of his son and would like to be living elsewhere but feels he has nowhere else to go.

Questions

1. What are your thoughts and feelings as you read this case?
2. If you were the APS caseworkers assigned to investigate this case, what would your next steps be?
3. Who would you talk to and what questions would you ask?
4. What would you do if Mr. Harris denies the allegations even though other close family members report that he is being abused?
5. What if Mr. Harris confirms the allegations but refuses your help and services and says he is fine to deal with this on his own? What would you do then?
6. How would you deal with the son if he is hostile and angry and denying that he does anything to harm his father?
7. If these allegations are true, what kinds of services could be provided to help this family?

REFERENCES

Centers for Disease Control and Prevention. (2007). Health information for older adults. Retrieved June 17, 2008, from http://www.cdc.gov/Aging/info.htm#3

National Center on Elder Abuse. Elder Abuse Prevalence and Incidence, Fact Sheet. Retrieved August 12, 2008, from http://www.ncea.aoa.gov/NCEAroot/Main_Site/pdf/publication/FinalStatistics050331.pdf

National Hospice and Palliative Care Organization. (2007). *NHPCO Facts and Figures: Hospice Care in America.* Retrieved June 17, 2008, from http://www.nhpco.org/files/public/Statistics_Research/NHPCO_facts-and-figures_Nov2007.pdf

Segal, E. A., Gerdes, K. E., & Steiner, S. (2004). *Social work: An introduction to the profession.* Belmont, CA: Brooks/Cole.

U.S. Department of Labor, Bureau of Labor Statistics. (2008). *Social Workers.* Retrieved June 13, 2008, from http://www.bls.gov/oco/ocos060.htm

7   Social Work in Health Care

Kissing the boo-boo doesn't help the pain. . . .
It helps the loneliness. —*Rachel Naomi Remen (1996)*

When we examine the mission of social work, a case may be made that all social work involves the practice of healing. This is no more evident than the diverse roles of social workers in the field of medicine.

The health care delivery system in America is complex and varied. At the turn of the 20th century, the focus on medical care began to shift from individual patient disease and pathology to a broader understanding of public or community health, with an emphasis on prevention. This was most notable during the devastating flu epidemic of 1918 that killed thousands of people in America and abroad. The first Public Health recommendation in the wake of this human disaster resulted in a public education campaign to promote the value of frequent hand washing as the primary prevention measure in combating the transmission of deadly communicable diseases. Social workers had a major role in this campaign since they were known as "community workers" in densely populated urban centers, which appeared to be the focus of several communicable diseases. The Public Health system is where the role of the medical social worker was born (Fort Cowles, 2003).

Health care in the United States has certainly undergone many trans-formations over the past 100 years, and with it, the role of social work.

There are currently more than 47 million people in the United States who do not have health insurance coverage (U.S. Census Bureau, 2007). Unequal access to comprehensive care is a major barrier in the treatment and prevention of illness in populations of people who are the most vulnerable: children, women, ethnic minorities, persons living in poverty, and older Americans. Grave disparities in receiving medical care persist due to chronic poverty and/or belonging to a particular minority or ethnic group.

The rapid development and growing availability of medical technology have created more options for care and improved quality of life. However, this growth has also contributed to exorbitant costs in providing health care and introducing social, legal, and ethical dilemmas for individuals, families, communities, and health care providers. A major role for social workers in health care is to help people navigate the system and manage the psychosocial stressors of entering the system and making health care decisions (Darnell, 2007).

> Social workers look at the person-in-environment, including all of the factors that influence the total health care experience. Social workers practice at the macro and micro level of health care and thus have the ability to influence policy change and development at local, state, and federal levels and within systems of care. (National Association of Social Workers, 2005, p. 8).

Social workers are found in many areas of the health care system and help to ensure that as patients move throughout the system they receive the appropriate level of care they need. Social workers practice in the public health system, acute and chronic inpatient hospitals, rehabilitation and residential care settings, home health agencies, hospice centers, doctor's offices, outpatient clinics, and ambulatory care centers. They provide an array of services including health education, psychosocial support through counseling and group work, crisis intervention, and case management. The common thread throughout the various social work settings and functions in health care is the value and importance of the role of patient advocacy. (For a discussion of social work in nursing homes, hospice, and other settings where care is provided for the elderly, please see chapter 6.)

In today's world, health care social workers are increasingly relied upon to respond to regional, national, and global critical incidents, providing intervention for traumatic events and disasters.

SOCIAL WORK IN HOSPITALS

Social workers who work in hospital settings help patients and their families cope with a new diagnosis, injury, or chronic illness by providing direct services to meet their needs in assisting them to return to independent functioning within the community. Medical social workers provide psychosocial support to people, families, or vulnerable populations so they can better cope with their diagnosis and treatment.

As part of a multidisciplinary team, medical social workers have many functions. Social workers provide a valuable resource to doctors and nurses by providing them with critical information for the treatment and recovery process of patients by obtaining in-depth social histories and assessments. The following scenario provides an example of a medical social worker in action:

Mr. Fuller was admitted to the hospital for severe and chronic back pain. His doctor decided to hospitalize him because Mr. Fuller required increasingly higher dosages of pain medication, which prevented the patient from returning to work, and he still was not feeling any better. A social worker was given the referral for an assessment of Mr. Fuller, and through the course of their conversation, the social worker learned that Mr. Fuller's only son died 6 months earlier. It was shortly after his son's death that Mr. Fuller's back pain severely increased. The social worker understood that the mental health condition of depression often intensifies the physical experience of pain for persons with a pre-existing condition. She provided the doctor with her information and assessment of Mr. Fuller's present condition. The doctor was unaware of the extreme grief the patient was experiencing, and she promptly contacted her colleague, a psychiatrist, to evaluate Mr. Fuller for depression. The psychiatrist met with Mr. Fuller, and subsequently prescribed an antidepressant. Mr. Fuller was discharged to home, and the social worker followed up with him a week later by telephone. She learned that Mr. Fuller was sleeping better and felt less pain. The social worker suggested attending a bereavement group close to where he lived, and Mr. Fuller agreed to participate. During a 6 week follow-up phone call, Mr. Fuller reported that he was using less pain medication and was able to return to his job.

Other functions medical social workers may provide include:

- Facilitating psychosocial support groups for persons newly diagnosed with a condition or recovering from treatment.
- Finding help for caregivers.

- Educating patients and families by helping them understand the treatment plan and adhere to the doctors' recommendations.
- Promoting wellness by helping people change unhealthy behaviors.
- Helping people access insurance and financial benefits and understand their rights as patients.
- Communicating with their doctors and medical team.
- Screening and assessment for neglect and abuse, psychosocial high-risk factors, and other needs.

Many medical social workers are able to specialize in an area of medicine by population (e.g., pediatrics or gerontology), or by specific illnesses or conditions, (e.g., renal disease, diabetes, cancer, obstetrics and gynecology, HIV/AIDS, pain management).

Social Worker Spotlight: Maya Doyle, LCSW
Senior Social Worker/Camp Coordinator, Division of
Pediatric Nephrology/Children's Hospital at Montefiore

I was diagnosed with insulin-dependent diabetes at the age of 8, and I struggled with the disease throughout my adolescence. Few people understood how difficult it was for me to be "in control," to be adherent with a medical regimen, and to reconcile my body and self-image. It was hard for me to take care of myself, but I was determined to live independently.

I spent one summer answering phones at a drug and alcohol treatment program, and I met a compassionate and competent group of social workers, people who "spoke my language"—of empathy, advocacy, and problem solving. I decided to pursue a masters in social work and entered the program at NYU. My goal was to work with young people coping with chronic and life-threatening illness.

My second-year internship was in the adolescent health program at a city hospital, and afterwards, I was hired to cover the inpatient pediatric medical unit. There, I encountered trauma, child abuse, devastating diagnoses, and chronically ill children brought from other countries on visitor visas by parents desperate to get them medical care. I had to learn to think on my feet, to multitask, to document painstakingly, and to keep resources at my fingertips.

Six years later, I became the social worker for the Ira Greifer Children's Kidney Program at Montefiore Medical Center, in Bronx, New York. It was, literally, my dream job. I worked with children and teens along the continuum of their illness, from diagnosis with chronic illness, through dialysis, transplant, and sometimes back again. Wherever they were in the medical center—outpatient clinic, dialysis unit, inpatient admission, transplant evaluation, posttransplant care—I followed them and provided clinical social work services, discharge planning, and all things in between. Our multidisciplinary team was filled with strong personalities who supported and challenged each other continually. Ethical issues, such as the health care and end-of-life decision-making of our adolescents or assessing our patients' readiness for transplant and allocating a precious donor organ, were ever-present.

In addition to my traditional social work role, I also became one of the coordinators of the Ruth Gottscho Dialysis and Children's Kidney Program at Frost Valley YMCA. Starting in 1975, it was the first place in the world to allow children on dialysis to attend a mainstream summer camp program. My role has come to include outreach to pediatric nephrology centers throughout the Northeast, as well as marketing, staffing, vendor relations, and fundraising. More fun is helping families prepare for sending their child to camp, often their first time away from home, and then seeing the kids "just being kids,", far away from the hospital setting. A chance for greater independence, self-care, and self-confidence, a chance to make friends—I know personally the value of such things.

In 2007, I took an extended maternity leave after my own high-risk pregnancy. I am coordinating our camp program and (slowly) pursuing a doctorate in clinical social work, while watching the development of my own son. An eye-opening experience after years of counseling parents! My advice to those considering social work as a profession? There are so many options within the field—the role, the population, the setting—in which to apply our unique bio-psycho-social perspective. Choose the thing you feel passionate about, and let it lead you.

For more information of the kidney camp program at Frost Valley, please visit: http://www.frostvalley.org and enter the search term "kidney."

EMERGENCY ROOM SOCIAL WORKER

This is a specialized area of medical social work that requires skills in crisis intervention, critical incident debriefing (CID), helping people cope with acute trauma and loss, preparation for public health emergencies, and providing victim assistance. Emergency room (ER) social workers work in an extremely fast-paced environment, and usually do not have a 9-to-5 schedule. They often work different shifts in the same manner that doctors and nurses do.

ER social workers are essential in a "liaison" role to the medical team and patient's families, when patients need to be transferred for further treatment in an appropriate intensive care unit (ICU) within the hospital or another facility (e.g., large community hospital with a burn unit).

In many instances, ER social workers provide to patients, victims, families, and communities, "psychological first-aid" (PFA). Emergency room social workers are on the forefront of helping people cope with and recover from crisis and trauma, from the children injured in a school bus accident, to helping a "lost" loved one with Alzheimer's disease. The ability to translate critical information, navigate complex service delivery systems, and advocate for the best interests of patients and families are the primary functions of social work practice in the ER.

DIRECTOR OF SOCIAL WORK

Because of their expertise, it is not surprising to find medical social workers employed as part of the administrative team in health care delivery systems. As directors of social work departments, case management, or quality assurance departments, social workers in these managerial roles play a vital part in the day-to-day functioning of providing care to patients and families, in addition to providing professional support to social work staff, other health care employees, and the community.

Social work managers are responsible for the supervision, professional development, and continuing education of social service staff in order to maintain the highest standards in service delivery as required by accreditation standards of hospitals and clinics, in addition to the National Association of Social Worker's Code of Ethics. Improving patient care, in the context of managing available financial resources, is part of the daily routine for social work administrators.

Social workers in this role examine and address issues such as:

- The types of patients staying too long in the hospital because they are homeless or there is no one to take care of them if they are discharged.
- The increased number of ER referrals for persons with mental health issues because of too few treatment providers in the community.
- The large number of uninsured women who are being discharged too quickly after delivering a baby, only to return with complications and be readmitted.

Social work directors are often part of multidisciplinary bioethics review teams and quality improvement committees in hospital settings. Social work directors are members of these teams and committees because of their professional knowledge of human behavior and the social environment, as well as the leadership and facilitation skills they bring to the problem-solving process.

PUBLIC HEALTH SOCIAL WORKER

Social workers in the field of public health utilize their skills with the broad focus of community health. They work primarily in organizations focused on prevention and risk reduction, such as Planned Parenthood, infant and toddler early intervention programs, Head Start programs for pre-kindergarten children, child and infant mortality teams with the Centers for Disease Control (CDC) and state health departments, and HIV prevention programs with nonprofit human service agencies.

Public health social workers are found in government regional emergency response centers to help educate the community regarding emergency preparedness in times of disasters and epidemics, where everyone in a specified geographic area would be affected by an outbreak of pandemic flu, tuberculosis, or salmonella, or what to do in case of a biohazard threat (e.g., a toxic chemical spill). They will often be trainers of volunteers in the public health system, for example the Medical Reserve Corps, and help train others to provide psychological first aid (PFA) in the event of a community emergency or disaster.

Family violence prevention, healthy eating and weight loss, smoking cessation, and substance abuse awareness programs are other public health issues that concern these medical social workers. Public health social workers may even be employed at your workplace through an employee assistance program.

Public health social workers who work for the federal CDC or state health departments may have specialized knowledge and skills in epidemiology, which is the study of the origin and spread of disease. Some social workers supplement their bachelor's degree in social work (BSW) or master's degree in social work (MSW) coursework with additional courses in epidemiology, attend a dual degree program in social work and public health, or pursue a doctorate in epidemiology or a related field after completing their MSW.

Social Worker Spotlight: Erica Solway, MSW, MPH Doctoral Student in Sociology, University of California, San Francisco

Upon graduation from college, I decided to continue my education and enter a dual master's degree program in social work (MSW) and public health (MPH). Although still a student, I was relatively certain, given my previous volunteer, work, and research experiences with older adults that I wanted to work in the area of aging. Before deciding on the program, I spoke with many people regarding a career in aging, and I was advised that social work and public health training would provide a strong foundation for understanding the experiences of older adults. It was also suggested that there is a considerable need to study social policy and aging—in particular aging services. This was extremely valuable advice. While pursuing advanced education in social work and public health, I had the opportunity to work with the local long-term care ombudsman program, to plan a conference on the health of older women of color, and to work on several research projects that focused on both the health and mental health of older adults and family caregivers. All these opportunities were enlightening and allowed me to contribute in meaningful and diverse ways to improving the lives of older adults.

I am now in a doctoral program in medical sociology. While I am currently focused on a new discipline, it serves to enhance and enrich the many skills and interests I developed as a social work and public health student. Since the beginning of the doctoral program,

I have worked with Students for Social Security (SSS) and Concerned Scientists in Aging (CSA), two nonprofit, nonpartisan organizations that work to raise awareness about the important role of social insurance as a foundation of economic and health security through public education. I have worked on organizing campus events; developed the Web site (www.studentsforsocialsecurity.org) and newsletter; created a documentary film on the importance of Social Security; and am now in the process of editing a book on social insurance with some of my SSS/CSA colleagues Leah Rogne, Carroll Estes, Brian Grossman, and Brooke Hollister tentatively titled, *Social Insurance, Social Justice, and Social Change.* Furthermore, I am focusing my dissertation research on activities and efforts to help lower the rates of smoking among people with mental illness through a social movement perspective. I became interested in this area of research after I was offered an opportunity to work with an initiative to try and address this important issue thanks to my background in social work and public health. Although I have not worked as a clinical social worker like many of my colleagues in this field, my social work background has opened many doors and has led to enormously fulfilling opportunities in research, advocacy, and social policy in the areas of aging, social insurance, mental health, and smoking cessation.

REHABILITATION SOCIAL WORKER

Rehabilitation social workers are medical social workers who specialize in rehabilitation medicine and are employed in many of the settings noted above, in addition to places such as Veterans Affairs (VA) hospitals and clinics.

Rehabilitation social workers provide counseling and psychosocial support as well as direct services to individuals in their process of recovery from various illnesses, accidents, and traumas that resulted in a disabling condition. Persons injured by a medical condition, such as a traumatic brain injury or stroke, as well as those who have survived a car accident or fire or are coping with the disabling effects of a progressive disease, will most certainly encounter a social worker on their road to recovery.

Social workers in this field may also be employed as *disability experts* who are trained to assist persons in obtaining financial benefits once they have become disabled.

Rehabilitation social workers are in great demand, particularly those who work with American veterans. According to the Defense and Veterans Brain Injury Center, which provides many kinds of rehabilitation for those in active military service and veterans, traumatic brain injury was present in at least 14% to 20% of those surviving combat casualties in previous military engagements. Preliminary information from the current conflict in the Middle East suggests that this number is now much higher. (For more information about working with the military, see chapter 8).

HEALTH CARE POLICY SPECIALIST

Health is a matter of both economics and social well-being. Social workers in this area of health care are knowledgeable about the larger health care system and have an in-depth understanding of the social, political, and economic factors impacting health. They examine financial expenditures, political reforms, service delivery systems, insurance programs, and community behaviors that either promote health or contribute to illness. Policy social workers in health care are committed to advocating through the political process for policies that will reduce disparities in access to care and improve the quality of life for all.

Social workers in this area are employed with organizations such as the national American Cancer Society, American Heart Association, the March of Dimes, and Easter Seals. Social workers in health care policy also work in regional organizations for HIV awareness and prevention, family violence prevention, and local agencies focused on insuring the medically underserved and low income population, as well as providing accessible transportation for persons with disabilities.

Core Competencies and Skills

- Strong assessment and interviewing skills.
- Knowledge of physical health and medicine.
- Care coordination and case management skills.
- Crisis intervention skills.
- CID skills.
- Cultural competency with diverse populations.
- Ability to utilize spirituality in social work practice.
- Engage in advocacy efforts.
- Knowledge of bioethics.

- Group work skills.
- Planning, administration, program development, and evaluation skills.
- Strong counseling skills.
- Knowledge of economics and finance.
- Knowledge of benefit programs, such as Medicare and Medicaid.

Educational and Licensing Requirements

A BSW is required to be employed in nursing homes and public health clinics where the social worker's primary responsibilities are in case management. Most other areas of medical social work require a master's level degree. There is a growing requirement of having specialty certifications, such as a case management credential, or additional licensing.

Many social work programs offer course work and field experience in all aspects of health care. Great educational opportunities exist to do both micro and macro social work practice in health related field placements.

Best Aspects of this Job

- Working in a fast-paced environment.
- The ability to multitask and have concrete results.
- Opportunities to address inequality in access to care and treatment on an individual and "big picture" level.
- Working with interdisciplinary teams, doctors, and nurses.
- Education opportunities with ongoing training and specialization.
- The ability to listen to personal narratives of patients.
- Networking with many community agencies and organizations
- Promoting wellness, resiliency, and recovery as a "first responder."
- Helping to prevent illness and loss of functioning.
- Resolving ethical dilemmas and mediating conflict.

Challenging Aspects of this Job

- The need to maintain personal health and wellness in the face of great demands may be difficult to do.
- Limited economic means for indigent groups often make it hard to locate resources and services.
- Availability to work various shifts or be "on call" may not be good if you like predictability and a set work routine.

- Helping people cope with loss and bereavement on an ongoing basis may be emotionally draining for you if you do not have a balance of activities.
- Working with patients who are very ill and/or in pain may depress you.
- Involvement with chronic and long-term care may provoke heightened anxiety or depression for yourself, especially if you have a family member or friend who is in a similar circumstance.
- Change efforts in policy work often takes years to achieve.

Compensation and Employment Outlook

In general, employment for social workers is expected to grow much faster than the average rate of growth for all occupations through 2016. Increases for medical and public health social workers alone are anticipated to be 24%. Because hospitals continue to limit the number of days a person stays in the hospital for treatment, the demand for social workers will slow down in hospitals. However, with quicker returns of patients to their home and the growing aging population, social work employment is expanding in the area of home health services. In 2006, the median salary for medical and public health social workers was approximately $44,000 (Bureau of Labor, Occupational Handbook, Social Workers).

Self-Assessment Checklist: Is this Job Right for Me?

- ☐ Are you able to work in an emergency room or medical environment where you cannot control who or what you will see?
- ☐ If you have had a family member or friend in the hospital, were you able to visit with them despite the physical environment or their medical condition?
- ☐ Do you like to multitask?
- ☐ Are you flexible when your day does not go as planned?
- ☐ Can you communicate well when you speak and write?
- ☐ Are you able to "think on your feet"?
- ☐ Is it possible for you to care about persons from different cultural and religious backgrounds and advocate for their needs?
- ☐ Would visiting patients in their home interest you?
- ☐ Do you like looking for community resources and working with health care professionals from diverse disciplines?

☐ Would you be able to work during a religious or cultural holiday that you typically observe?

If you answered "Yes" to seven or more of the above questions, you may want to do some more research on social work in health care!

RECOMMENDED READINGS/WEB SITES TO LEARN MORE

Association of Oncology Social Workers: www.aosw.org

American Public Health Association: Social Work specialty group: www.apha.org

Cowles, L. F. (2003). *Social work in the health field* (2nd ed.). New York: Haworth Social Work Practice Press.

Garret, L. (2000). *Betrayal of trust: The collapse of global public health.* New York: Hyperion Publishers.

Meenaghan, T. (2001). Exploring possible relations among social sciences, social work, and health interventions. *Social Work in Health Care, 3* (1), 43–50.

Mizrahi, T. & Berger, C. S. (2001). Effect of a changing health care environment on social work leaders: Obstacles and opportunities in hospital social work. *Social Work, 46,* 170–182.

Moore, M. (Director). (2007). Sicko[Motion Picture]. United States: Dog Eat Dog (health care documentary film directed by Michael Moore): www.michaelmoore.com

National Association of Social Workers-Health Specialty Practice Section: www. socialworkers.org

National Institutes on Health: www.nih.gov

National Library of Medicine: www.nlm.gov

Society for Social Work Leadership in Health Care: www.sswlhc.org

SOCIAL WORK IN HEALTH CARE EXERCISE

See if you can locate a hospital, veteran's hospital, or rehabilitation facility in the community in which you live. Call and ask for the director of social work or social services, and request an appointment to meet with them or some one on their staff so you can tour the facility and ask questions about the profession.

Another way for you to find out more about social work in health care is to volunteer in a medical setting and begin working with patients and their families. You may want to volunteer as a "reader" to kids receiving treatment for cancer or for persons who have limited sight or are blind. Gaining experience through volunteer work can help you decide what you would enjoy doing most and help you plan your educational goals.

REFERENCES

Darnell, J. S. (2007). Patient navigation: A call to action. *Social Work, 52*(1), 81–84.

Defense and Veterans Brain Injury Center [online]. Retrieved June 19, 2008, from http://www.dvbic.org/cms.php?p=FAQ

Fort Cowles, L. A. (2003). *Social work in the health field: A care perspective* (2nd ed.). Binghamton, NY: Haworth Press.

National Association of Social Workers. (2005). *Standards for social work practice in Health care settings.* Washington, DC: Author.

Remen, R. N. (1996). *Kitchen table wisdom* (p. 60). New York: The Berkley Publishing Group.

U.S. Census Bureau. (2007). *Income, poverty and health insurance coverage in the United States: 2006.* [Online]. Retrieved on 13 August 2008, from www.census.gov/prod/2007pubs/p.60-233.pdf

8   Social Work in Mental Health and Addiction

Social work practice in mental health has certainly come a long way, especially over the past 50 years. It was not too long ago when someone who was diagnosed with a mental illness was institutionalized for an indeterminate period of time, whether they consented or not to their confinement. The history of mental illness is the history of "insanity." Centuries ago, anyone who did not conform to societal norms was viewed as insane. Individuals deemed "insane" were often incarcerated in prisons and left to languish until their death. During the mid 1750s, physicians in England began to lobby Parliament to build hospitals to cure the condition of "lunacy." Asylums were built in the early 1800s across England, Ireland, Canada, and America to more humanely house and treat persons with "insanity," apart from the penal system. Often, those who had developmental disabilities or "mental retardation" could not be distinguished from other "lunatics" and they, too, were committed to asylums (Torrey & Miller, 2001).

In 1835, American social activist Dorothea Dix made a trip to England to recover from a long-term illness caused by tuberculosis. While in England, she became acquainted with the readings of a French physician, Dr. Philippe Pinel, and a British doctor, William Turke, who worked on behalf of prison reform and humane treatment for the mentally ill in the

1700s. In 1837, Dorothea Dix returned to the United States committed to improving the conditions for those affected by mental illness in the United States. With the help of Horace Mann, educator; Charles Sumner, the abolitionist; and Samuel Gridley Howe, head of the famous Perkins Institute for the Blind, Dix lobbied to secure legislation in Massachusetts to fund appropriate care for mental illness conditions. Worcester State Hospital became the first publicly funded hospital for treating mental illness in this country (Bookrags.com, 2008).

Mental illnesses were not very well understood for the next 175 years, until a research revolution took place in the 1990s, which the National Institute of Mental Health refers to as "the decade of the brain." It was during this time that medical science and technology was developed to literally look inside the brain and give us better information on how to treat mental disorders and addictions.

A recent World Health Organization report, *The Global Burden of Disease*, examines the impact of a wide range of diseases on the loss of years of healthy life. This extensive study found that four out of the top ten causes of disability in the world are mental illnesses: major depression, bipolar depression, schizophrenia, and obsessive-compulsive disorders. Across all age groups worldwide, depression will produce the second largest disease burden in the year 2020 (National Alliance on Mental Illness, 2008). In the United States, 50% of people between the ages of 15 and 54 reported experiencing at least one psychiatric disorder (National Association of Social Workers [NASW], 2008). Mental illness is costly to society, due to what it takes away in productivity to the economy and in people's lives.

The next leading high-cost problem in mental health treatment is the devastation caused by substance abuse and dependency. According to the 2006 National Survey on Drug Use and Health, an estimated 22.6 million people had substance abuse or dependency problems in the previous year. The survey showed that 2.5 million people received substance abuse treatment at specialty facilities in 2006.

The costs of substance abuse are enormous. In 1992, a study funded by the National Institute on Drug Abuse and the National Institute on Alcohol Abuse and Alcoholism found the total economic cost of alcohol and drug abuse to be $245.7 billion for that year. This estimate encompasses treatment and prevention costs, health care costs, costs related to lost earnings and reduced job productivity, an increase in related crime, and social welfare (National Institute on Drugs and Alcohol, 2008). As with other chronic diseases, many people afflicted with drug addiction require continuous mental health care and support to remain drug free and regain control of their lives.

It should be noted that mental disorders and substance abuse issues are often linked, so many clients that are seen by social workers will have co-occurring disorders and will need treatment for both (or several) mental health issues simultaneously.

Thanks to improvements in psychopharmacology and psychotherapeutic treatments, individuals with mental disorders and addictions can recover and reclaim their lives. This is largely due to access to newer kinds of medications that have fewer side effects and proven treatment models of care that can reduce hospital stays, incarceration, and homelessness.

Social workers are the largest professional group of trained mental health providers in the United States today. In our profession, all social workers can provide counseling and psychosocial support to clients, and in any number of settings, social workers may encounter clients with substance abuse and/or mental disorders. However, clinical social workers specialize in the treatment of psychiatric and substance abuse disorders. "Clinical social work has a primary focus on the mental, emotional, and behavioral well-being of individuals, couples, families, and groups. It centers on a holistic approach to psychotherapy and the client's relationship to his or her environment" (NASW, 2005).

Many social workers practice in the area of prevention and policy, with respect to mental health or behavioral health issues. Prevention programs, for example, help people maintain their emotional and psychological health under crisis conditions. Policy practice focuses on areas of need, such as increased federal funding in research on mental illness and universal access to mental health treatment. Whatever direction you take in mental health and substance abuse, social workers are highly skilled and needed professionals.

CLINICAL SOCIAL WORKER

Clinical social work is defined as "the application of social work theory and methods to the treatment and prevention of psychological dysfunction, disability, or impairment, including emotional and mental disorders." The terms *social casework* or *psychiatric social work* are used interchangeably with clinical social work (Barker, 2003, p. 76).

Clinical social workers are found across wide and varied practice settings such as nonprofit family counseling centers, public community mental health centers, psychiatric hospitals and medical facilities, day treatment and residential settings, and private independent or group mental health counseling practices. Clinical social workers are employed to help individuals, families, couples, and small groups identify the issues they are facing and to provide specific strategies to improve their unique situation. In this way, clinical social workers help enhance and maintain the coping skills of the consumers they serve within the context of the person's environment to achieve a better balance in living when confronted by life's challenges.

One type of treatment does not work with all people needing help, so clinical social workers must be knowledgeable and skilled in many different therapeutic techniques (e.g., cognitive-behavioral therapy, solution-focused interventions, narrative therapy, play therapy). In addition to the therapies mentioned, there is growing interest to work with expressive therapies that incorporate art, music, drama, and journal writing into the therapeutic process (see chapter 18 for more about integrating the arts into social work).

Clinical social workers may also specialize with particular populations (e.g., children, teens, families, older adults) and within specific mental health areas (e.g., schizophrenia, addictions, anxiety and depression, sleep disorders, sexual orientation and gender identity).

Social Worker Spotlight: Sue Matorin, MS, ACSW Treatment Coordinator, Affective Disorder Team, Payne Whitney Clinic, New York Presbyterian Hospital; Faculty Member, Department of Psychiatry, Weill College of Medicine at Cornell; and Adjunct Associate Professor, Columbia School of Social Work

In a long, rich career in health/mental health I have worn many hats—clinician, program developer, social work department director in an academic medical center, and adjunct professor. I serve on boards, have published works in the area of stigma and mental illness, and have proudly received some honors, but at the center of my career have always been my remarkable clients. I am relieved that I have the skill to help those damaged by serious psychiatric and medical illnesses reclaim their lives. I am still haunted by my first fieldwork cases in an urban welfare center—what did a naïve young Massachusetts-born student have to offer to these lives of desperation?

Fast forward—I now save lives, often suicidal ones. At the Payne Whitney Clinic, I work with adults with depression and bipolar disorder after they have been hospitalized, some also struggling with serious medical illnesses and/or economic problems. In my private practice at Cornell, my clients often function well in their work lives but have a myriad of marital and family problems usually fueled by the psychiatric illness of one family member. I lend out my classical music CDs to clinic clients for stress reduction. I discuss movies, favorite television shows, make-up, diet, and exercise endlessly—anything is grist for the therapy. My best conversations about race are with my minority clients.

Check out my video on the National Association of Social Workers Web site "On Any given Day"—my 88-year-old mother disliked how I looked, but my clients loved it, and I was thrilled for the opportunity to describe what I do. (Available at: http://www.socialworkers.org/pressroom/events/anyGivenDay1007/default.asp)

SOCIAL WORK WITH GROUPS

Social work with groups is an important skill used frequently by social workers. Knowledge and skill in social work practice with groups require specialized education and the ability to understand when group work is the preferred intervention while working with individuals, families, small groups, organizations, and communities.

Many social workers spend much of their day creating, planning, facilitating, and evaluating groups for many different treatment purposes in a variety of practice settings. The most important function of group work is to help each member become part of a collective of mutual aid and support where individuals learn from and help each other to be more independent in how they cope with change or adversity.

The role of the social worker as a *facilitator* of the group process requires a high level of training and expertise. In 1998, the Association for the Advancement of Social Work with Groups (AASWG) published the first edition of the *Standards for Social Work Practice with Groups*. The standards outline the values, knowledge, and skills required for professional social work practice with groups, and reflect core principles from the NASW Code of Ethics. They are applicable to a wide range of different types of groups, which include treatment groups, support groups, psycho-educational groups, task-centered groups, and community action groups.

Professionally led groups are often found in school settings with children and parents, mental health treatment programs, homeless shelters, drug and alcohol awareness programs, family violence prevention programs, victim services, and health care facilities. Group interventions range from learning new social skills, changing unwanted or unhealthy behaviors, learning trust, gaining insight into personal problems, to experiencing mutual support and understanding, achieving stated goals and objectives, or organizing for action.

Social Worker Spotlight: Mary Kiernan-Stern, MSW, LCSW Northern Virginia Cancer Center, Alexandria, Virginia

After a number of years working in administration and medical social work in hospitals, I began to work at an outpatient cancer treatment center. My role at the cancer center was to assess patients for various needs and to identify risk factors that may have prevented them from completing their treatment. Cancer care is often very costly, and the treatment can be physically challenging to endure at times. For many, treatment may be ongoing with no definite end in sight, so part of my intervention with people was to help them learn to cope with a catastrophic diagnosis, as if it were a long-term chronic illness. To do this would require collective and consistent support.

Extensive research from the 1980s and 1990s, most notably in the work of Dr. David Spiegel, reported that the life expectancy for cancer survivors was longer for those who participated in a therapeutic support group. There was also research indicating that patients who were in a support group coped better with their treatment and more often completed the course of treatment prescribed. One of my first tasks at the center was to create and facilitate a general support group for any patient in the hospital community with a diagnosis of cancer. This group would meet every other week at the cancer center.

Over time as our group met, certain members made various requests. A couple of members wanted to have an additional forum to discuss particular books they found helpful for coping with their cancer experience. Other members of the general group requested a support group with a spiritual focus. With assistance and guidance from the members, I developed a Cancer Recovery Book Group and a nondenominational Pastoral Care Support Group.

The hospital chaplain agreed to facilitate the Pastoral Care group on the same day of the week during the weeks in between my facilitation of the general support group. In this way, I was able to have a support group every week at the cancer center for those patients who needed an extra level of psychosocial and spiritual care. The nondenominational support group was a model soon adopted by other area hospitals providing cancer care.

At the same time, I was able to give great thought to the creation of a book group using bibliotherapy as an expressive arts intervention for the framework of this particular group. I was concerned about having the hospital as the only focal point of psychosocial support. Patients with long-term illnesses and treatments spend many hours and days at hospitals and this can be psychologically draining. I wanted to be able to help "patients" return to being part of the wider community.

So, I approached the community relations director at a local Borders bookstore, and asked if I could use their space to hold a monthly Cancer Survivors Book Group. Not only did they allow us to have space, but they added us to their book group calendar, gave us 10% discounts on book titles used for the group, and provided us with free coffee. Shortly after we started our book group, a Borders employee was diagnosed with cancer, and she was given time off from her work schedule to come join us for group. I am proud to say that this group went on for 7 years at Borders, and I was able to replicate a similar group at a Barnes and Noble in Washington, DC.

Many people who came to group and shared with us information they received from a doctor that their life expectancy was limited to months, were participants in these groups for years and continued to be cancer survivors. This is why, as a clinical social worker, I love group work—because of the collective dynamic in the power to heal mind, body, and spirit.

SOCIAL WORK AND SUBSTANCE ABUSE INTERVENTION

Substance abuse intervention is a specialty area in the field of social work, yet it is a specialization in which you may find social workers in almost every practice arena. Substance use disorders (SUDs) know no boundaries. They affect the lives of individuals, families, and every community.

Social workers in this field are employed in hospitals, mental health centers, homeless shelters, local government agencies for drug and alcohol services, drug and alcohol treatment centers, court systems and probation offices, schools, and workplaces. As the largest provider of mental health services in the United States, social workers routinely confront problems associated with addictions in their work. "There are many pathways to treatment for people with SUDs; however, the wide range of settings in which social workers practice allows the profession to address the needs of the whole person as he or she seeks to recover from a SUD" (NASW, 2005, p. 6).

One such pathway is in the field of alcohol, tobacco, and other drugs (ATOD), where treatment interventions are crisis oriented or short term, (e.g., smoking cessation program). When working with people with serious drug addictions (e.g., methamphetamines, prescription drugs, cocaine, heroin), newer research has provided evidence that these addictions are chronic and require much longer term and intensive treatment options for recovery. Social workers are professionally trained to integrate emerging research and translate that knowledge into essential interventions for persons with substance abuse disorders.

Social Worker Spotlight: Robert Klekar, LCSW, LCDC
Social Work and Substance Abuse*

I received my bachelor's in social work from Southwest Texas State University (now Texas State University) in San Marcos, Texas, and my MSW from Our Lady of the Lake University in San Antonio, Texas. At the beginning of my university years, I studied art. After about 2 years, I became depressed and sought out counseling. Finding this experience helpful, I opted to change majors and wanted to do something where I could help others (not to suggest art doesn't impact others in a healing way) on a one-on-one basis. At the time, the only thing I knew about social work was from a leaflet advertising the George Brown School of Social Work stapled to a bulletin board in the Liberal Arts Building. My reaction was, *"What in the world is social work?"* I found an answer to that question after I combed through the university catalogue and read the various degree outlines. Upon reading about social work, I discovered it resonated with me for two reasons; it involved helping others and social action. At the time, I fancied myself a quixotic, social revolutionary, so the latter had great importance. Eighteen years have elapsed since I completed my MSW. During that time, I have worked a couple of administrative roles but mainly in the area of direct clinical practice. While I wouldn't describe what I do as radical or revolutionary at a macro level, it does involve helping others. Most of my work has been in the areas of mental health and substance abuse treatment for adolescents and adults. For the past 13 years, my primary focus has been providing substance abuse services to male offenders within a prison setting.

For a social worker considering a career in criminal justice, there may be many questions and concerns. When others talk to me about working in a prison setting, I'm often asked, *"Is it dangerous in there?"* My answer, *"Possibly."* Moving past razor wire each working day is a reminder that I've entered a zone that's potentially hazardous, where some of the inmate histories include the commission of violent crimes. So, it is important to be vigilant and mindful, always keeping personal safety at the forefront of your mind. But, the work itself is not all that different from what I've done in other settings. As I see it, risk has always been a part of the change process, regardless of the setting, especially when we work with people who are distressed, in some cases desperate, agitated, or struggling from the change process. It is my belief the education and training of social worker students, with its dual emphasis on person and environment, is ideal preparation for social work within drug treatment and prison settings. Sure, the work is challenging, but aside from a paycheck, there are limitless other incentives. To name a few, helping clients make subtle, and in some cases, dramatic changes in their lives; shaping service delivery; receiving professional training and continuing education; and personal growth.

When people find out that I work in a drug abuse treatment program or prison, the next question I typically encounter is, *"What exactly do you do?"* In general, I retort, *"Ask and answer a lot of questions."* For those inclined to hear me out, I'm likely to give a longer, well-rounded answer. That is, I provide group psychotherapy to clients most of the time. Ironically, I was initially interested in helping people at a one to one level, but now I prefer the dynamism of group settings.

During these sessions, clients talk about their drug abuse histories and actions they are taking towards living a drug and crime free life. Of course, there are other duties such as providing drug education classes, performing assessments, treatment planning, individual counseling, copious amounts of documentation, and discharge planning. In some cases, crisis intervention. I also have had the opportunity to receive training and participate on a hostage negotiation team and a crisis support team, both geared towards managing critical incidents that may arise within a prison setting.

Finally, there are those who ask, *"Do you like what you do?"* I answer with a resounding, *"Absolutely!"* Sure, there are periods of professional burn-out but I have means to cope with those times. The most interesting and sustaining part of my job are the daily conversations I have with clients. This is where the 'ask and answer' part of my job comes into play. For me, the heart and soul of the change process lies with a social worker's ability to establish rapport with a client and work collaboratively towards problem resolution. This is an exciting, engaging, and often unpredictable endeavor. Someone, and it might be me, is going to change due to this process. While there have been considerable efforts to introduce evidence-based approaches into social work practice, the actual process of direct social work practice reminds me more of the creative arts. Clients have a way of influencing me to tailor interventions to fit their story, rather than the other way around. It never ceases to amaze me that clients, even those with severe deficits, have the means to generate solutions to their problems once they are engaged in a conversation about change. While these solutions do not solve all the distal factors that come about, (e.g., a drug dependency), they are a step towards enhancing client autonomy. After all, two of my favorite axioms from social work practice are 'start where the client is at' and 'honor the client's right to self-determination'.

---

*Opinions expressed in this article are those of the author and do not necessarily represent the opinions of the Federal Bureau of Prisons or the Department of Justice.

Social Worker Spotlight: Shana Seidenberg, MSW, LSW MISA (Mental Illness Substance Abuse) Coordinator, Kauai Community Mental Health Center

After attending Mount Holyoke College in South Hadley, Massachusetts, I had the awesome opportunity to participate in a community service organization called City Year in Boston. My participation in City Year further confirmed my interest in social work as I mentored youth in the public school system. I received my masters in social work from Simmons College in 2005. Shortly after graduation, I went to Kauai for a vacation. Now I call Kauai home, and I work for the Kauai Community Mental Health Center (CMHC) as their Mental Illness Substance Abuse Coordinator. Community mental health centers provide services that help people with severe and persistent mental illness, live out in the community rather than in institutions; being a part of the team at Kauai's CMHC is an exciting and challenging career.

My role is to provide consultation and training to case managers for their clients with co-occurring disorders (also referred to as a dual diagnosis). My favorite part of my job is facilitating groups for clients with co-occurring issues. The group emphasizes psycho-education, relapse prevention skills, and peer support for clients recovering from mental illness and a substance abuse disorder. The clients have taught me much of what I know, and I am very grateful to everyone I have worked with. Education can teach you a lot, but the experiences of working with people are sometimes more revealing. I really enjoy listening to people's stories and learning about the local culture.

My favorite part of being a social worker is empowering people to make positive choices. People with mental health issues and addiction issues face many difficult choices every day. I am thrilled to be a part of a support network for people in recovery. Social workers need to promote education and awareness of co-occurring issues and battle the ongoing stigma facing this group of people.

EMPLOYEE ASSISTANCE WORKER

The field of employee assistance practice developed with the social work profession during the 1970s in response to employers' and workers' growing social, financial, and emotional needs at the workplace. Today, many large employers, such as Verizon, Apple, and the National Brick-layer's Union, as well as moderate-sized organizations, such as utility companies or county governments, offer workers the benefits of employee assistance programs (EAPs). Any size business or agency may create an EAP inside their own organization, or they might contract with another outside organization to provide EAP services to their employees. Research has shown that paying and providing such services to workers is a win-win situation for employers in reduced time off from work and improved morale and productivity. The benefits to workers include less lost wages and improved health and mental health. For every dollar invested in an EAP benefit, the financial return is large.

Social workers in EAPs assist both employers and workers with various workplace issues. They provide services in behavioral health and wellness, crisis intervention, work-life issues, career transitions, and information and referrals for a great many resources. Employee assistance social workers are trained in critical incident and stress debriefing (CISD) interventions in response to a workplace trauma and often provide psycho-educational workshops and trainings focused on prevention and wellness, in addition to specialty services in substance abuse.

MILITARY SOCIAL WORKER

Military social workers support members of the Armed Services and their families, both at home and in overseas assignments. They usually provide services ranging from individual counseling and rehabilitation, the development of summer programs for children and teens of military personnel, to victim advocacy, drug and alcohol counseling, family violence prevention programs, and marriage and family counseling. The Veterans Administration Social Work Web site includes a list that shows the varied range of services provided by military social workers:

- Health care for homeless veterans.
- Physical and rehabilitation services.
- Substance abuse.
- Geriatric and extended care.
- Spinal cord injury.
- Posttraumatic stress disorder.
- Community re-entry for incarcerated veterans.

- Women's health.
- Community support/mental health intensive case management.
- Community residential care.

In addition to the VA, military social workers may be directly employed by a branch of the military (e.g., the Army Medical Command), or they may work as independent contractors with a firm hired by the military.

The trauma of participating in or witnessing combat has led to high levels of mental health issues among the military. Various studies show that incidence of posttraumatic stress disorder (PTSD), depression, suicide, and substance abuse are all high in this population, hence the need for social workers who are educated and trained to treat these conditions.

Another primary focus of military social work is on the family and the multitude of stressors they confront, particularly those related to displacement and relocation. This role has been growing in importance since the 1990 U.S. Gulf War, and the need for military social workers has dramatically increased since 9/11 and the subsequent involvement of U.S. troops in Iraq.

Core Competencies and Skills

- Be able to interpret social, personal, medical and mental health information.
- Evaluate and treat mental health conditions.
- Establish rapport with clients over the short term or long term.
- Facilitate psychological, emotional, and behavioral change.
- Identify appropriate resources.
- Advocate for client services.
- Collaborate effectively with multidisciplinary professionals.
- Evaluate the outcomes of treatment services.
- Demonstrate in-depth knowledge about multidimensional problems and services.
- Be knowledgeable about psychiatric illnesses, developmental disabilities, and the addiction and recovery processes.

Educational and Licensing Requirements

An accredited master's degree in social work (MSW) is required for all of the above jobs. The areas of mental health and addictions is typically regulated by the state, and social workers are required to obtain a clinical license (see chapter 3) to practice in the state where they are employed. There is a growing trend in state regulations, and with employers of social workers in the addiction and EAP fields, to require additional certifications beyond that of a clinical license. There are national and state organizations that provide certifications in these specialty areas, and some of your graduate level social work courses and previous employment experiences may be credited toward certification.

Best Aspects of this Job

- Crisis-oriented.
- Offering hope and healing in the recovery process.
- Specialization of skills.
- In-depth knowledge base of expertise.
- Ability to work with clients for a long period of time.
- Access to highly specialized trainings.
- Work with professionals from many different areas.
- Helping to change lives.
- Membership opportunities with peers in the same specialty.
- Opportunities for solo or group private practice in counseling services.
- Career development opportunities toward consultant/trainer and self-employment.

Challenging Aspects of this Job

- Emotionally difficult to watch a person relapse or come out of remission.
- The road to recovery is very long for some clients.
- Coordination of care can be tedious given all of the professionals and services involved.
- Time and money is needed to meet licensing and certification requirements.
- Coping with suicide or violence may be emotionally and physically taxing.
- Being "on call" and available for emergencies may make life planning difficult for yourself.
- Traveling to remote locations may be stressful.

Compensation and Employment Outlook

Employment projections from the Bureau of Labor indicate there is rapid growth in the need for social workers in the area of mental health and substance abuse. In particular, social workers in substance abuse will continue to be in high demand since substance abusers are increasingly being diverted to treatment programs rather than prison (U.S. Bureau of Labor Statistics, 2007). Because of the level of knowledge and training required, including licensure and certification, social workers with these credentials earn substantially better salaries. In 2006, the top 10% of social workers in this field earned more than $57,630.

Self-Assessment Checklist: Is this Job for Me?

- ☐ Can you work independently and defend your viewpoint when working with psychiatrists, nurses, and other well-trained professionals?
- ☐ Would you be able to compassionately work with a population that is difficult and alienating to others?
- ☐ Are you able to "reserve judgment" with people who are substance abusers?
- ☐ Do you like working primarily with families?
- ☐ Are you willing to spend the time to obtain a license and a credential?
- ☐ Can you handle crisis and emergency situations?
- ☐ Do you like working with people over a long period of time in an institutional setting?
- ☐ Would you be able to manage your own emotions in helping others to cope with death and bereavement?
- ☐ Are you comfortable providing intensive services to people in their homes and communities?
- ☐ Do you see yourself as an "expert" in an area as your career develops?

If you answered "Yes" to seven or more of the above questions, then being a social worker in this field may offer opportunities for you to be in a rewarding career.

RECOMMENDED READINGS/WEB SITES TO LEARN MORE

American Psychiatric Association: www.psych.org
Association for the Advancement of Social Work with Groups: www.aaswg.org

Clinical Social Work Association: www.cswf.org

Family Secrets: Inside Addictions (2007 documentary DVD from ABC News Primetime): available at www.Amazon.com or www.netflix.com

Kaysen, S. (1994). *Girl, interrupted.* New York: Vintage.

Mental Health America: www.mha.org

National Alliance on Mental Illness: www.nami.org

National Association of Social Workers: www.socialworkers.org

National Institute of Drugs and Alcohol: www.nida.gov

National Institute of Mental Health: www.nimh.gov

Out of the Shadows (film showing the impact of mental illness and recovery for the person and family): www.outoftheshadows.com

Sheff, D. (2008). *Beautiful boy: A father's journey through his son's meth addiction.* Boston: Houghton-Mifflin Co.

Treatment Advocacy Center: www.psychlaws.org

Veterans Administration Social Work: http://socialwork.va.gov

Mental Health and Addiction Exercise

Case Scenario

Mrs. Reynolds is a 46-year-old married mom of a 15-year-old daughter. She is currently receiving medical treatment for breast cancer at a local community hospital. In visiting her doctor, she learned that her prognosis for a full recovery is good and that she will be finished with her treatments soon. Mrs. Reynolds cries when she hears this news, and proceeds to tell the doctor she has thought of killing herself recently, since the stress of coping with years of her husband's excessive drinking has now become unbearable. The doctor spends more time in talking with Mrs. Reynolds and obtains her consent to make a referral to a mental health social worker.

Questions

1. As the clinical social worker for Mrs. Reynolds, what would be your first step in helping her?
2. What diagnosis would you give to Mrs. Reynolds?
3. What type of treatment intervention would you discuss with this client?
4. Do you know the community resources available to help in her situation?
5. Would you involve the other members of her family in the treatment process?
6. How would you follow up with Mrs. Reynolds once she leaves your office that day?

REFERENCES

Barker, R. (2003). *The social work dictionary (5th ed.)*. Washington, DC: NASW Press.

Bookrags.com (2008). *Biography: Dorothea Dix*. [Online]. Retrieved on April 21, 2008, from http://bookrags.com/biography/dorothea-lynde-dix-woh

National Alliance on Mental Illness. (2008). *Federal funding of mental health research*. [Online]. Retrieved April 07, 2008, from http://nami.org/PrinterTemplate.cfm?Section=Issue_

National Association of Social Workers. (2005). *NASW standards for clinical social work in social work practice*. Washington, DC: Author.

National Association of Social Workers. (2005). *NASW standards for social work practice with clients with substance abuse disorders*. Washington, DC: Author.

National Institute on Drugs and Alcohol. (2008). *NIDA InfoFacts: Costs to society*. [Online] Retrieved April 8, 2008, from http://www.nida.nih.gov/InfoFacts/costs.html

Substance Abuse and Mental Health Services Administration. (2007). *New National Survey Reveals Drug Use Down Among Adolescents in U.S.-Successes in Substance Abuse Recovery*. [Online]. Retrieved June 18, 2008, from http://www.samhsa.gov/newsroom/advisories/0709043102.aspx

Torrey, F. E., & Miller, J. (2001). *The invisible plague: The rise of mental illness from 1750 to the present*. New Brunswick, NJ: Rutgers University Press.

U.S. Bureau of Labor Statistics. (2007). *Occupational outlook handbook, (2006–2007 ed.)*. [Online]. Retrieved December 1, 2007, from http://www.bls.gov/oco

U.S. Department of Veterans Affairs. (2007). *Social Work Jobs*. [Online]. Retrieved June 18, 2008, from http://www.socialwork.va.gov/jobs.asp

9 Careers in Crisis Intervention

When you watch a television show like *ER*, news footage of a hurricane or other natural disaster, or a depiction of a violent crime or murder, does your adrenalin start pumping as you visualize yourself intervening to help others in these situations? If so, crisis intervention may be the career path for you! This is an important and valuable skill, as crisis situations require social workers and other helping professionals who can remain calm and composed under pressure in order to aid others in a time of great need. Social workers are often called to help in a variety of crisis situations such as terrorist attacks (e.g., Oklahoma City bombing in 1995; September 11th bombing of the World Trade Center in 2001), natural disasters (e.g., Hurricane Katrina in 2005), and random acts of violence (e.g., school shootings in high schools and college campuses, rapes, assaults, murders, muggings, gang violence).

Social workers can be found working and volunteering in various government and nonprofit organizations, such as the Red Cross, Salvation Army, Federal Emergency Management Agency (FEMA), and victim's services programs, which are typically found within police departments. Social workers who work internationally may assist people in the throes of war, displacement, and genocide. They provide a range of services such as immediate help with food, shelter, and clothing; relocation; information and referral; critical incident debriefing immediately after the

121

trauma exposure; short-term crisis counseling; and ongoing treatment for posttraumatic stress disorder (PTSD). Please see chapter 8 for more information on working with individuals and groups in a therapeutic context.

However, it is important to understand that crisis intervention is provided in almost every social work setting. No matter where you work, you may come into contact with individuals who find themselves in a crisis situation (e.g., a client who is suicidal, a family who has just lost their housing, a child who has just lost a parent). It is important that all social workers are skilled in the art of crisis intervention.

For some individuals in crisis, their normal coping mechanisms do not work, and they experience a range of emotions such as helplessness, confusion, anxiety, depression, and anger. Crisis intervention work typically involves providing short-term treatment to help people return to their precrisis level of functioning. Individuals suffering from PTSD emotionally re-live the event and may experience nightmares and intrusive thoughts and are observed to be in a highly agitated state. Without treatment, these symptoms may last for a long time after the original trauma.

That being said, there are some fields of social work practice where working with individuals and families in crisis is a primary focus of the job:

- Child Protective Services caseworkers (chapter 4).
- Homeless outreach caseworkers (chapter 13).
- Emergency room social workers (chapter 7)
- Working with suicidal patients or the severely mentally ill (chapter 8).
- Victim's Services (assisting victims of crime and their families) (chapter 10).
- International social work (chapter 12).

The careers that are profiled in other chapters of this book will not be described again here. The focus of this chapter is to profile careers that employ social workers who are highly skilled in crisis intervention: the fields of disaster and emergency management, family violence, and sexual assault. Careers in policy as related to these areas will also be discussed.

CAREERS IN DISASTER AND EMERGENCY MANAGEMENT

Webster's Dictionary defines disaster as "a sudden calamitous event bringing great damage, loss, or destruction." According to the National

Association of Social Workers, social workers are "uniquely suited to interpret the disaster context, to advocate for effective services, and to provide leadership in essential collaborations among institutions and organizations" (National Association of Social Workers, 2005). Since the beginning of the profession, social workers have responded to the call to offer disaster assistance. Because many social workers are trained in crisis intervention, they are uniquely positioned to aid people in need after an emergency or natural disaster. Even though social workers are concerned about the impact of disasters in general, they are particularly concerned about the impact to vulnerable populations such as children, people with disabilities, poor people, and older adults. During Hurricane Katrina, for example, we watched in horror while many poor people and residents of hospitals and nursing homes were unable to flee.

One technique that is commonly used by social workers after a disaster is called critical incident stress debriefing (CISD). Responses to trauma can include shock, confusion, depression, anxiety, nightmares or other sleep disturbances, survivor's guilt, and even suicidal ideation. Debriefing allows those involved with the incident to process the event and reflect on its impact. It also allows individuals to vent their emotions and express their thoughts associated with the crisis event. Debriefing is typically provided during the first 24 to 72 hours after the initial impact of the critical event. CISD is provided to individuals to help mitigate the development of posttraumatic stress.

Even though disaster relief work is not a common career for most social workers, social workers are needed as volunteers in this realm, so we thought it was important to mention. A small number of social workers work for organizations such as the Red Cross, Salvation Army, or FEMA and do this kind of work full-time, but most social workers volunteer their time with these various agencies to help out in a time of crisis.

Social Worker Spotlight: Brian Rivers, BSW, LSW
Case Manager/Volunteer Coordinator, East Biloxi
Coordination, Relief, and Redevelopment, Biloxi,
Mississippi

I am a 26-year-old graduate and licensed social worker (LSW) from the University of Southern Mississippi School of Social Work. My current occupational field is disaster relief, recovery, and redevelopment. The field is just as stated: first comes the disaster, then the initial relief and recovery (also referred to as the crisis intervention stage), and then the redevelopment stage (assisting the community in re-establishing connections and resources). This is a field, I admit, I never imagined I would be interested in.

I am employed with East Biloxi Coordination, Relief and Redevelopment Agency in Biloxi, Mississippi. I also lead the committee for the Finish the Job Fund, which I spearheaded prior to the second anniversary of Katrina. My social work education gave me the foresight to see that a crisis was in the making and that the shift of funding and attention would no longer remain with us in Mississippi. At the time of initiating this fund, many organizations had limited or no correspondence with others who were serving the same arena.

With national attention and funds being diverted to current disasters nationwide, the responsibility has fallen on grassroots organizations and social welfare groups to answer the call of replacing the diminished resources. Today, Mississippi has 65,000 homeless families statewide, and current statistics show that one-third of this population has an "unmet need" related to Hurricane Katrina. Unmet needs vary from a client that has yet to get themselves in the position to provide food for themselves and their family to a client who resided in an heir property that needs legal assistance, before any other form of assistance can be pursued. Throw into the equation a 40% illiteracy rate for the state, and you can begin to grasp the situation here in Mississippi.

The most important aspect of my work is advocacy. The hurricane ravaged people from all economic backgrounds, yet the recovery tools were not available to those who could not afford insurance or to those with no funds to go through a court proceeding to have a deed transferred. I consider myself to be in the "trenches," because my position is the first point of contact for clients seeking assistance. This, in itself, adds excitement to the job. The average workday does not exist. I may be fielding client intakes all day on a Monday; Tuesday may require an appearance in court or at a city council meeting; Wednesday may require leading a group of volunteers doing manual labor; Thursday may involve presenting at a conference; and Friday might be spent doing crisis intervention or gathering statistics. The following week may consist of none of the above tasks! Grant writing is a daily task that is required, especially to be a successful helping professional in the community in this line of work. As you can see, the skill set for a social worker in this field must be pretty broad.

The question most asked of me is "Why do you do what you do?" My answer is simple. I see jobs in two ways, you can work FOR someone or you can work WITH someone. This is how I see my role as a social worker, working WITH a client to meet 1 goal or 100 goals. In my current job, working in disaster recovery, I find more personal satisfaction than I ever imagined.

FAMILY VIOLENCE COUNSELOR

All men, women, and children should have the right to be free from violence and to be safe in their own home. Unfortunately, domestic violence (DV) is a major social problem in this country that affects millions of families each year. According to the National Coalition Against Domestic Violence, one in four women will experience DV in her lifetime. (A small but significant number of men are also victims of DV.) DV can be defined as a pattern of abusive behavior that is used by one intimate partner to gain or maintain power and control over another intimate partner; this can include physical abuse, sexual abuse, economic abuse, emotional, and psychological abuse.

The most common setting for social workers who work in the field of DV is in the battered women's shelter. Temporary/emergency assistance shelters for women and children can be found in communities around the country, though many would argue that there are not enough of them. Women in urban areas may be turned away or put on a waiting list due to lack of space in these shelters. Rural areas may not have any services at all.

Other social workers may work with perpetrators of violence, to help them understand the root causes of their behavior and hopefully learn alternatives to violent behaviors. This work may take the form of group counseling, which is often known as batterer intervention programs.

SEXUAL ASSAULT COUNSELOR

Sexual assault is nonconsensual sexual contact. Women, men, and children can all be victims of sexual assault, though according to experts in the field, the vast majority of victims are female and the vast majority of perpetrators are male. The perpetrator may be a stranger, an acquaintance, or a relative. It may take years for a victim to recover from the psychological effects caused by the sexual assault. Because DV and sexual assault are linked to the oppression of women and children in this country and around the world, this is a social justice issue that has particular relevance for the social work profession.

Services for victims of sexual assault are typically provided by a community rape crisis center. In some communities, the women's shelter and the local rape crisis center are housed in the same agency. The following services are commonly offered by social workers doing rape crisis or domestic violence work:

1. **Prevention and community education.** Social workers focus on preventing violence and promoting safe and healthy relationships through community education and school-based programs. Educating the community about DV and sexual assault and giving a voice to survivors who need help and understanding is vital. This can be accomplished through community fairs, media campaigns, community presentations, professional trainings, school-based programs to reach young people, distributing brochures and other informational materials, and public awareness events.

2. **Crisis intervention.** This is perhaps the defining feature of the battered women's shelter and rape crisis center. Most offer a 24-hour hotline and an emergency shelter for women and their children who need a safe place to stay and have nowhere else to go. Over the phone, hotline counselors listen, counsel, provide information and referral, and do safety planning to help a woman come up with a safe plan for leaving her intimate partner. The shelter is a temporary solution until a more permanent living situation can be secured. A range of services are offered to women served by a rape crisis center or staying in an emergency shelter:

   ■ Individual and group counseling; many shelters have special groups and activities just for the children in the shelter.
   ■ On-call work in health care settings, where social workers will meet sexual assault victims at the emergency room to offer information and support while they undergo a rape exam.
   ■ Case management services where clients are connected to needed resources in the community.

- Legal advocacy, which includes help obtaining protective restraining orders, prosecuting offenders, and getting clients connected to attorneys and organizations that offer legal advice.
- Helping clients prepare for, and navigate through, the legal system (if they choose to pursue legal measures) and deal with the psychological impacts of testifying, cross-examination, and other court procedures.
- Life-skills training for victims of DV so they will be prepared to live and work on their own.
- Many shelters offer transitional housing (typically in an apartment complex) for women and children to live after they leave the shelter, but before they are ready to live on their own in the community.

3. **Collaboration.** Meeting the needs of DV and sexual assault survivors often requires collaboration with other community organizations, such as the police department along with their victim's services program, Children's Protective Services (because children are often at risk when a woman is being abused), the District Attorney or County Attorney's office, hospitals, housing programs, and programs offering mental health services.

POLICY ADVOCATE

Social workers interested in family violence and sexual assault can work at the micro or macro level. As discussed in the previous section, many social workers choose to work directly with victims or perpetrators of abusive relationships or sexual violence. It can be very gratifying to provide a range of therapeutic interventions that help these clients leave an abusive situation and heal from years of violence.

Other social workers passionate about decreasing DV and sexual assault work to create social change by educating people about family violence or working in the political arena to pass laws helpful to those who are victims of these crimes. This involves lobbying legislators at the local, state, and national levels to get laws passed that help victims of DV and sexual assault, and to advocate for increased funding for family violence shelters and rape crisis centers. Many states have advocacy organizations that focus their efforts at the state level. There are also a number of prominent organizations, such as the National Coalition Against Domestic Violence and the National Network to End Domestic Violence, which are national in scope.

Social Worker Spotlight: Cindy Southworth, MSW
National Network to End Domestic Violence, Washington, DC

I am the Founder and Director of the Safety Net Project at the National Network to End Domestic Violence (NNEDV), based in Washington, DC. I have been working to end violence against women since before I received my BS in Human Development and Family Studies in 1993. As an undergraduate student, I volunteered at a local domestic violence shelter and rape crisis center in State College, PA. After volunteering, I moved into a part-time position educating children and parents about child sexual abuse, and then I moved onto a full-time job coordinating a transitional housing program. I answered hotline calls, met with survivors every week, trained and supervised volunteers and interns, accompanied victims to court hearings, and saw first-hand the resilience of women who survived horrific abuse. I was, and remain, in awe of their strength.

After several amazing and rewarding years of working with survivors, I decided to get my masters degree in social work (MSW) in order to give me more tools to change a system that I saw not working as well as it could. After receiving my MSW, I worked in Maine, organizing local domestic violence awareness month activities and improving the law enforcement system's response to domestic violence. I also chaired the state domestic violence coalition's legislative committee.

In 1998, a colleague encouraged me to apply for a national manager position leading an internet project focusing on violence against women. This technology-focused position led to work supporting another technology project: working with the courts to implement a state-wide restraining order database. Through both of these systems advocacy positions, I realized that front-line victim advocates and the sexual and domestic violence survivors who turn to them did not fully understand the ways in that technology could benefit victims and be misused by abusers.

In 2000, two colleagues of mine at the Pennsylvania Coalition Against Domestic Violence and I developed a curriculum on technology, privacy, and victim safety and presented it at a national conference. I quickly realized there was an urgent need for more information to help survivors understand how to strategically use technology to increase their safety. In 2001, I began looking for an organization to house the project that I was creating, and in 2002, I officially launched Safety Net Project at NNEDV, with seed money from the AOL Time Warner Foundation.

As the Director of the Safety Net Project, I and my team of three trainers present workshops on technology and stalking, databases and confidentiality, and other technology topics to victim advocates, law enforcement, attorneys, judges, and government officials at state and national conferences. I work with government agencies such as the U.S. Department of Justice, U.S. Department of Health and Human Services, and the Federal Trade Commission, to ensure that victims' stories are heard and that technology-related policies do not inadvertently put survivors in more danger. I also provide hands-on assistance when local advocates are trying to help a victim of technology stalking and connect service providers to tech-savvy law enforcement allies, I have developed through my work. Recently, I have been working with companies such as AOL and Google on increasing victim privacy and safety. From testifying before the U.S. Senate on victims and stolen phone records, to answering a call from a survivor who read a handout we created on SpyWare use by abusers, every day I feel like I make a difference.

One of the most rewarding parts of this work is knowing how many people are impacted and occasionally making a connection with someone whose life has been touched by this issue. Since studies show that one in three women will be assaulted by an intimate partner in her life time, there are survivors everywhere. Sometimes during training, survivors share their own experience while others quietly and intently catch my eye and say "you do really important work."

Core Competencies and Skills

- Excellent counseling skills (individual and group).
- Strong crisis intervention skills.
- Understanding of DV and sexual assault as larger issues that are linked to the status and oppression of women in society.
- Sensitive to the shame that victims often experience and the lengths they will sometimes go to, to keep the violence and abuse a secret.

- Knowledge of the legal system and laws governing DV and rape (e.g., protective orders).
- Ability to assess risk to children and women.
- Knowledge of battered women's syndrome and the dynamics of domestic violence.
- Strong advocacy skills.
- Ability to collaborate with others systems in the community to meet the needs of your clients (particularly the legal and court systems).

Educational and Licensing Requirements

You will find social workers with bachelor's degrees and master's degrees working in emergency women shelters and rape crisis centers. Some social work students will complete their field work in these organizations while completing their undergraduate degree and then obtain a job there after graduation. This is a wonderful learning experience for a new social worker. In most of these settings you will be provided with in-depth training on the causes and dynamics of sexual violence and intimate partner abuse and many hours of supervised training. Certain jobs at the shelter, such as therapist or administrative positions, may require a master's degree and a specified number of years of previous experience.

Best Aspects of this Job

- Working with a diverse group of individuals and organizations to increase people's awareness and knowledge of DV and sexual assault.
- Having the opportunity to be a supportive presence in a victim's life; to be someone who believes the victim and understands.
- Having a supportive work environment and working with colleagues who understand the emotional ups and downs of the job.
- Seeing victims of DV heal from the abuse they have suffered and take steps toward living a life free from abuse.
- Having the opportunity to educate the community and to work on the prevention of problems dealing with DV.
- Helping women and children who find themselves in a serious crisis, and providing immediate help and a safe place to live.
- Having the opportunity to prevent DV and sexual violence by educating the public about healthy relationships and the effects of violence on men, women and children.

Challenging Aspects of this Job

- When the system cannot prevent serious or deadly harm to victims.
- Seeing firsthand victims who suffer the effects (emotional and physical scars) of domestic violence and sexual violence.
- If you have a history of being a victim of abuse, it can be challenging to do this work unless you have worked through your emotional scars and healed.
- Working with people who blame the victim instead of the perpetrator (e.g., asking why the victims stay instead of why the perpetrator abuses his loved ones), and why we as a society tolerate this.
- Working with victims who are not yet ready to leave an abusive situation or when they are forced to return to an abuser due to financial reasons or lack of support.
- Balancing the needs to support and advocate for the victim with the need to make sure the children are safe and protected.
- Finding the line between educating and empowering a victim, and allowing her to make her own decisions about her life.

Compensation and Employment Outlook

Salaries for social workers working in domestic violence shelters and rape crisis center, most of which are nonprofit organizations, will vary greatly from agency to agency and by state. Salaries will be higher for those who are in supervisory or administrative positions.

Self-Assessment Checklist: Is this Job for Me?

- ☐ Do you enjoy doing work that is crisis-driven? Can you stay calm in a crisis?
- ☐ Do you have a strong empathy for people who have been traumatized by disaster or violence?
- ☐ Would you be able to see physical injuries and hear details of how someone has been sexually assaulted or abused (including physical abuse, sexual abuse, and emotional/psychological abuse)?
- ☐ Can you respect someone's self-determination or choice to stay with an abusive partner?
- ☐ Do you have a passion for helping people to live lives free from fear and abuse?

☐ Would you enjoy educating the public about DV and sexual violence and getting the community to get involved in solving this
problem?

☐ Are you a patient person? (because it may take a long time until a
victim is ready to leave an abusive situation)

☐ Would you be comfortable working in a shelter environment
where women and their children are living?

☐ Would you enjoy the legal work involved in this field?

☐ Do you have a strong empathy for people in abusive relationships
or who have experienced sexual violence?

☐ Would you enjoy the challenge of empowering victims of abuse
or assault?

If you answered "yes" to seven or more of the above questions, then
working in crisis intervention might be for you!

RECOMMENDED READINGS/WEB SITES TO LEARN MORE

Crisis Intervention

James, R. K., & Gilliland, B. E. (2007). *Crisis Intervention Strategies.* Florence, KY:
Brooks/Cole.

Kanel, K. (2006). *A guide to crisis intervention.* Florence, KY: Brooks/Cole.

The National Child Traumatic Stress Network: www.nctsnet.org/nccts/nav.do?pid=
hom_main

Psychological First Aid: Field Operations Guide: www.ncptsd.va.gov/ncmain/ncdocs/
manuals/nc_manual_psyfirstaid.html

Rosenfeld, L. B., Caye, J. S., Ayalon, O., & Lahad, M. (2004). *When their world falls
apart: Helping families and children manage the effect of disasters.* Washington, DC:
NASW Press.

Wise, J., & Bussey, M. (Eds.). *Transforming trauma: An empowerment perspective.* NY:
Columbia University Press.

Family and Sexual Violence Web Sites

Family Violence Prevention Fund: www.endabuse.org
National Center on Domestic and Sexual Violence: www.ncdsv.org
National Coalition Against Domestic Violence: www.ncadv.org
National Domestic Violence Hotline: www.ndvh.org
National Network to End Domestic Violence: www.nnedv.org
National Sexual Violence Resource Center: www.nsvrc.org
U.S. Department of Justice, Office on Violence Against Women: www.usdoj.gov/ovw

Domestic Violence

Barnett, O. W., Miller-Perrin, C., & Perrin, R. (2005). *Family violence across the life span: An introduction*. Thousand Oaks, CA: Sage Publications.

Davies, J., Lyon, E., & Monti-Catania, D. (1998). *Safety planning with battered women: Complex lives/difficult choices*. Thousand Oaks, CA: Sage Publications.

Jones, A. (2000). *Next time she'll be dead: Battering and how to stop it*. Boston: Beacon Press.

Nicarthy, G. (2004). *Getting free: You can end abuse and take back your life* (4th ed.). Seattle: Seal Press.

Renzetti, C. M., Edleson, J. L., & Bergen R. K. (Eds.). (2001). *Sourcebook on violence against women*. Thousand Oaks: Sage Publications.

Roberts, A. (2007). *Battered women and their families* (3rd ed.). New York: Springer Publishing Company.

Schecter, S. (1983). *Women and male violence: The visions and struggles of the battered women's movement*. Cambridge, MA: South End Press.

GLBT

Lundy, S., & Leventhal, B. (1999). *Same-sex domestic violence: Strategies for change*. Thousand Oaks, CA: Sage Publications.

Legal Issues

Lemon, N. (Ed.). (2001). *Domestic violence law: A comprehensive overview of cases and sources*. Eagan, MN: West Group Publishers.

Mental Health

Herman, J. (1997). *Trauma & recovery: The aftermath of violence – from domestic abuse to political terror*. New York: Basic Books.

Women of Color

Malley-Morrison, K., & Hines, D. A. (2004). *Family violence in a cultural perspective: Defining, understanding and combating abuse*. Thousand Oaks, CA: Sage Publications.

Sexual Violence

Buchwal, E., Fletcher, P., & Roth, M. *Transforming a rape culture* (2nd ed.). Minneapolis: Milkweed Editions.

Crisis Intervention Exercise

Case study

You got hired a few weeks ago as a social worker in the battered women's shelter in your area. You are really excited, because of all the jobs you applied for, this was your first choice. You are being trained by your new supervisor and are learning new things every day about women who are abused by their intimate partners. It is difficult to see these women with their physical and psychological wounds.

A new client has been referred to the shelter, and you are finding this to be a challenging case. Sylvia has recently lost custody of her three children (Sophia, Brittney, and Justin) to the state child welfare agency. According to CPS, Sylvia was being emotionally and physically abused by her husband, and he had complete control over his family. The children witnessed their father's violence against their mother on many occasions. However, the children were removed due to Sophia's allegations that she was being sexually abused by her father for the past 4 years. She told the CPS investigator that her mother knew this was happening and had even walked in on them on a couple of occasions. The other children report knowing that their sister was being sexually abused. They report living in terror with their father who was often drunk and who would have violent unpredictable outbursts. They are terrified of him.

Their father has been arrested and the case will be taken to the grand jury. The children have been placed in a foster home together while the caseworker investigates whether there are any relatives who might be able to care for them. Sylvia is extremely distressed that her children have been taken from her. The child welfare agency views her as a mother who did not protect her children from abuse that has been detrimental to their health and safety. Sylvia denies that she knew that her daughter Sophia was being sexually abused, and she downplays the abuse from her husband. In her view, they did not have a perfect marriage, but she believes that through counseling she and her husband can get back on track. She is extremely upset at CPS for removing her children and feels this is unfair and unjust. Your supervisor disagrees with CPS' characterization of Sylvia as a nonprotective mother. She sees Sylvia as a battered woman who needs help and support, not punishment. She attributes this to CPS' lack of sensitivity and understanding of women who are severely abused by their husband over a long period of time. What do you think?

Questions

1. What thoughts and feelings come up for you as you read this case scenario?
2. Do you sympathize with Sylvia or are you upset with her for not protecting her children?

3. Do you agree with CPS' decision that it was in the children's best interests to take them into custody? Do you think they could be safe with their mother, or do you agree that they need to be in foster care for the time being?
4. What kinds of services would you arrange for Sylvia? What are the short- and long-term goals for Sylvia?
5. What can be done to get social workers from these two agencies to work together so they are not working against each other?
6. Do you think there is any chance of reuniting this family?
7. What do you hope happens in this case?

REFERENCE

National Association of Social Workers. (2005). Social workers and disaster relief. Retrieved June 19, 2008, from http://www.socialworkers.org/ldf/legal_issue/200509.asp?back=yes

10 Careers in Criminal Justice and the Legal Arena

If you are passionate about working with offenders or victims of crime, or are intrigued by legal dramas such as *Law and Order*, then this may be a career option for you. In the early days of the social work profession, social workers provided services primarily in the jails and prisons. Today, social workers are employed throughout the criminal justice system and legal arena in settings including the courts, police departments, and community-based treatment programs.

The need for social workers throughout the criminal justice and legal systems is more pronounced today because of the rapid increase in the general incarcerated population, the rapid increase of incarcerated women and mothers, large increases of incarcerated individuals with undocumented immigrant status, and ongoing disproportionate increase among incarcerated people of color. Furthermore, the association between mental health issues, socioeconomic disparities, criminal activity, and the large percentage of substance abuse–related offenses among offenders is proof that there is an urgent need for social workers in the criminal justice system (Orzech, 2006). Intersected with the above issues are complex family and personal health problems that inflict those who come in contact with the criminal justice system.

Equipped with a dynamic theoretical orientation, professional education, and licensure, social workers in the criminal justice system are well positioned to focus on rehabilitation and prevention rather than punishment. Social workers work with individuals to ameliorate risk factors for involvement in the criminal justice system, while strengthening protective factors for living productive lives. With expertise in policy advocacy, protection of rights, and provision of clinical services, including family services, case management, and crisis intervention, they are able to provide quality services to individuals from diverse backgrounds. Quality social work services can not only positively impact treatment of offenders in terms of preventing recidivism, re-entry, and initial contact with the system, but also prevent victimization of individuals, families, and communities.

The following sections outline some commonly cited job descriptions and educational and licensing requirements for those with social work education, training, and work experience in the criminal justice system and the legal arena.

Social Worker Spotlight: Lyn K. Slater, MA, MSW, PhD
Interdisciplinary Center for Family and Child Advocacy,
Fordham University, New York

I have always been interested in the intersection between social work and the law. My first graduate degree was in criminal justice, and my first job was in a residential treatment center for delinquent girls. It was in my first job that I was introduced to the field of social work and began to be more interested in the clinical, rather than correctional, aspects of working with court-placed adolescents. I later became the director of a small residential treatment facility in New York City and decided to obtain an MSW.

Throughout my early career, I had frequent interaction with the legal system, both Family Court and Criminal Court. Because of my position as an administrator I became aware of the enormous influence federal laws and state statutes and regulations exerted on my social work practice. There were times that regulations were not in the best interest of my clients and I had to find unique and creative ways to persuade the judge to make exceptions. When those situations occurred, I worked very closely with the lawyers assigned to my client's cases, and this was when I realized the power and influence I could have as a social worker when I was teamed with a lawyer who shared my client's goals and my professional value of social justice.

For the last 12 years, I have worked side by side with lawyers working on behalf of children and families. First, I worked at Lawyers for Children, one of the first legal organizations in the country to assign interdisciplinary teams of attorneys and social workers to represent children in foster care. I not only worked on individual cases, but also population-based advocacy projects, such as researching and writing a handbook for children in foster care who had been sexually abused and developing testimony for use in class action lawsuits that addressed unsafe and discriminatory practices in the local child welfare system.

Currently, I teach at Fordham University and co-supervise, with a law professor, the Family Advocacy Clinic. Law and social work students are placed together as interdisciplinary teams and represent parents living in poverty who have children with special needs. The approach is a holistic one in that we may represent a family when they have a housing issue, a special education issue, or a child welfare concern. Evidence-based social work assessment is the cornerstone of our practice and when combined with the processes in the law that allow client's to have a voice and challenge decisions they do not agree with, participation in the clinic is an empowering experience not only for the client, but for the social work and law students as well. It has been an enormous privilege for me to learn how, by working with lawyers, to amplify my client's voice and have their story be told.

PROBATION OFFICER

Probation officers with social work backgrounds provide expert knowledge and skills that contribute to innovation in the criminal justice system. As part of a team working with offenders, probation officers are committed to enhancing the social functioning of individuals (both juveniles and adults) who are placed on probation rather than incarcerated in prison.

Probation officers provide supervision through personal contact with the offenders and their families, home visits, workplace visits, and electronic monitoring. They also work together with community entities, such as churches, residents, and neighborhood organizations, to monitor the progress of offenders. Services provided to offenders include individual, group, and family therapy; counseling; substance abuse rehabilitation; and job training. Probation officers primarily work with the courts, investigating offenders' backgrounds, providing presentence reports, recommending sentences, reviewing sentencing recommendations with offenders and their families, testifying in court, and providing ongoing reports on the offenders' rehabilitation and compliance efforts (American Probation and Parole Association, 2008).

PAROLE OFFICER

Parole officers provide many of the same services as probation officers; however, they monitor and supervise individuals who have been released from prison. Their goals include helping released individuals prevent recidivism, committing of new crimes, and re-entering the justice system.

CORRECTIONAL OR DETENTION OFFICER

Correctional or detention officers with educational and employment backgrounds in social work are in positions to positively impact the correctional systems. Their job is daunting as they are responsible for monitoring and supervising over a million offenders in the United States awaiting trial or who have been sentenced to serve time in a jail or prison. They ensure security and order and enforce adherence to rules and regulations within the correctional facility to prevent jail or prison riots, assaults, and escapes. They monitor daily activities and work assignments; enforce discipline; conduct regular inmate and cell searches for weapons, drugs, and other contrabands; facility searches; and inspect mail and visitors. The correctional or detention officers' daily report of activities keeps everyone in-check, and the officers enforce regulations primarily through their interpersonal communication skills and through the use of progressive sanctions (e.g., the removal of some privileges). Depending on the offenders' security classification within the institution, correctional officers may have to restrain inmates in handcuffs and leg irons to safely escort them to and from cells, to other areas, and to see authorized visitors. Officers also escort prisoners between the institution and courtrooms, medical facilities, and other destinations outside the institution (U.S. Department of Labor, 2007).

CORRECTIONAL TREATMENT SPECIALIST

Correctional treatment specialists provide expertise in case management, counseling, and creation of effective treatment plans for offenders upon release from the secured facility. They work in jails, prisons, and parole and probation agencies. In jails and prisons, correctional treatment specialists evaluate the progress of offenders using psychological tests, and they work with offenders, probation officers, and community agencies to develop parole and release plans, including educational and job training plans, life skills training on coping, anger management, substance abuse treatment, and sexual offender counseling either individually or in groups (U.S. Department of Labor, 2007).

JUVENILE JUSTICE COUNSELOR

Juvenile justice counselors work in the probation system and residential treatment programs, primarily providing individual or group counseling to juveniles as well as specialty programs, such as substance abuse and sex offender treatment. These counselors also provide counseling to at-risk youth, assisting youth with court appearances and advocating for appropriate services, aiding in educational placements, and linking youth to school officials. Likewise, they work in community corrections as counselors to juvenile offenders who may have served their sentences and have been released to a community-based program that provides less structure and supervision, and more autonomy to work towards adjusting to life back in society (Peat, 2004).

GANG PREVENTION COUNSELOR

Social workers who specialize in gang prevention customarily educate children and youth, families, schools, and communities about gangs, risk and protective factors for gang involvement, roles of each party in preventing gang involvement, and consequences of such involvement. Social workers who engage in gang prevention work bring extensive creativity; theoretical orientation; cutting-edge knowledge and research; and advanced skills in the assessment, prevention, and treatment of violent behavior. These social workers may also draw on their expertise in program development, community mobilization, and culturally competent practices with families in the quest to prevent gang involvement among children, youth, and adults.

FAMILY COURT SOCIAL WORKER

Family court social workers may serve as forensic social workers, mediators, and guardians working in drug courts, truancy courts, or mental health courts. Typically, they advocate on behalf of juveniles who must appear in court (although they may also represent adult offenders). These social workers attempt to provide social services in lieu of incarceration, if possible. They utilize their expertise in assessment and subsequently may recommend services such as counseling, specialized treatment, or residential care. Their recommendations must be approved by a judge and adhered to by the client (who in turn reports to a probation officer). However, if the client is found out of compliance with the recommendations, incarceration may result. The same services may also be available to adult offenders who may have the opportunity to engage in a diversion program in lieu of incarceration. (Refer to chapter 11 for further information on forensic social work.)

Social Worker Spotlight: Brandy Macaluso, BSW, CVP Coalition for Independent Living Options, West Palm Beach, Florida

After an internship for my BSW, I started work at a Center for Independent Living in Florida. The focus of my job was empowering and focusing on strengths as a way to promote independence for people with disabilities. The crime victim practitioner (specializing in people with disabilities) position opened up a few months into my employment as a life skills specialist. I was offered the job and excitedly accepted. I sat for my victim practitioner designation through the Office of the Attorney General, State of Florida.

The job itself exists to assist victims through the legal system that either acquired a disability through an act of violent crime or who were exploited and/or abused due to their disability. I was in charge of assisting in filing compensation claims through various programs within the state, providing counseling, facilitating peer support groups, advocating with various agencies and law enforcement to assist with the victim's needs, providing information and referral services to programs in the area, and providing court accompaniment to victims for restraining order and criminal case hearings.

Being a specialized victim advocate, I sit on various task forces, councils, and coalitions in Palm Beach County, to ensure that the specialized needs and accommodations are represented for people with disabilities. I also provide training on how other entities such as law enforcement, domestic violence shelters, and other victim service agencies can better assist victims with disabilities.

A crime victim practitioner's job can be outwardly challenging. Victim reprogramming for such things as guilt, helplessness, vulnerability, and extremely low self-esteem can be the most difficult, especially when compounded with a newly acquired or newly exploited disability. The most gripping is when the victim wants to return to the abuser. The biggest component to leave with them is knowledge. There is help if they need it, and I will be here if they need to talk or need information. However, being able to help that person begin a new life without the abuser is the most rewarding. I am able to share in their triumphs in court, their milestones in counseling, and their breakthroughs with empowerment. I turn into their biggest cheerleader.

It's those moments that I take home with me. I have learned so much while working at the center. I know I have changed the lives of victims with disabilities by helping them convert such a negative event into a positive new start. There is nothing more rewarding.

PRISON/JAIL SOCIAL WORKER

Social workers who work in prisons or jails generally provide individual and group counseling to inmates. In particular, these social workers provide specialized treatment to substance abusers and sex offenders. Their extensive social work knowledge and skills, particularly in assessments and group works, are beneficial to the inmate population. Although these social workers are integral to the prison/jail system, the high worker-to-inmate ratio often only results in more focused specialized treatments.

CAREERS IN VICTIM ASSISTANCE

Social workers who specialize in victim assistance typically provide services to police officers and assist in police-community activities. They provide crisis intervention to officers in relation to mental health, substance abuse, or domestic issues. They also assist officers in crime prevention activities, securing social services for issues of domestic violence, homelessness, school shootings, deaths, etc. These social workers utilize their expertise to deescalate conflict situations and facilitate the building of policy-community cooperation.

Likewise, these social workers are utilized by the police to provide services to victims of rape, assault, family violence, and other crimes. The services provided might include counseling for the victim and the victim's family, helping the victim understand their options in pressing criminal charges, and helping the victim through the legal process. These social workers also provide death notification to families when someone has been killed in a violent crime or traffic accident. (For more information on this type of work, see chapter 9.)

Social Worker Spotlight: Marilyn Peterson Armour, MSW, PhD Institute for Restorative Justice and Restorative Dialogue, Austin, Texas

I was a family therapist for over 30 years before being introduced to restorative justice. During that time, I often stood in awe as I witnessed the healing that family members experienced once they could be fully authentic and open to each other—a healing far more powerful and sustaining than anything I could give them as a therapist. The field of restorative justice is not only my home, but a home that feels familiar because it does the same thing that family therapy does. It attempts to heal the harms caused by crime by bringing together the victim and offender to engage in a dialogue about what happened, the impact of the crime on others, and what can be done to restore the brokenness that others feel.

I am fortunate to live in Austin, Texas, and work in the School of Social Work at The University of Texas at Austin. As a researcher, my primary interest is in evaluating the effectiveness of restorative justice programs in an attempt to mainstream restorative practices. I've worked on several innovative restorative justice programs in Texas. For example, Victim Offender Mediated Dialogue is offered by the Victim Services Division of the Texas Department of Criminal Justice. This program brings together victims and offenders of severely violent crime (e.g., homicide, rape) for a mediated dialogue after a 6-month preparation. Bridges to Life is another in-prison restorative justice program that brings together unrelated crime victims and offenders to meet in small groups over 12 weeks, for the purposes of reducing recidivism and advancing the healing of both victims and offenders. Both of these programs are ground-breaking and provide real avenues for victim and offender healing. My interest is in understanding the dynamics of these programs and how the interactions between key people provide experiences of healing and meaningful accountability. Indeed, I believe that if we can discover the mechanisms that make restorative justice work, then we can create interventions to break through denial while addressing the pain and destructive consequences from social injustices and interpersonal conflicts on all sides.

Part of my joy is being able to teach a course in restorative justice to social work and law students together. Their different perspectives enrich their responses to the material I teach and model the learning that comes from exploring each other's worlds. I use numerous panels of victims, offenders, and community members to teach the course. Many of the law students have never heard, firsthand, the experience of a crime victim who was mugged nor had a loved one murdered. Many of the social work students have never considered the perspective of anyone other than those who are socially disadvantaged. The course, therefore, stretches students' hearts and minds in unpredictable ways and exposes the assumptions we all make about each other. It also forces students out of their usual dichotomous thinking, because they have to hold onto many differing perspectives at the same time.

I'm proud to be part of a movement that holds such hope and promise and a movement which challenges the cynicism and despair that erodes our connections with each other. Although restorative justice is considered a multidisciplinary field, it is also values-based and, like social work, uses those values to guide practice. Moreover, many of the values overlap making social work a natural and future home for restorative justice.

CAREERS IN RESTORATIVE JUSTICE

One positive movement within the criminal justice system is the promotion of a restorative justice framework in which social workers are not only working with offenders but are also strong advocates for victims' rights and services, whether the victim is an individual, family, or community (Ivanhoff, Smyth, & Dulmus, 2007; Showalter & Hunsinger, 2007). Basically, restorative justice focuses on offender accountability through the provision of opportunities to offer recompense for the harm caused to the victim.

Restorative justice often features face-to-face meetings (mediated by social workers or other mental health professionals) between victims and offenders in which both sides have a chance to discuss the crime and its consequences. Successful restorative justice interventions may help victims feel a sense of empowerment and "closure," and for offenders to understand the full impact of their crime and offer restitution for their actions. Some studies have shown that these interventions may lead to lower recidivism rates among offenders.

Restorative justice has been used between individual offenders and victims, families, communities, and even representatives of warring nations. This framework not only advocates for change in the criminal justice system, but also resolution of various issues such as child abuse, school bullying, human rights violations, and international conflict (Strang & Braithwaite, 2002).

Core Competencies and Skills

- Embrace a more restorative justice approach to working with individuals, families, and communities.
- Promote policy change, particularly for access to and availability of resources for individuals reentering their communities, research on innovative approaches to issues, and best practices within the criminal justice system.
- Advocate for equality and safe and humane environments for at risk and incarcerated individuals, protection of the public and community, and provision of culturally relevant services to people of color and other vulnerable populations (e.g., transition planning, substance abuse treatment, mental health services).
- Advocate for policies to combat ethnic minority disproportionality and institutional racial discrimination in the justice system.

- Advocate for availability and accessibility of social work services, quality health care, and educational and vocational opportunities in the criminal justice system.
- Advocate for continuous special training for social workers in the justice system.
- Advocate for forensic social work practice standards to rehabilitation.
- Provide bilingual services in health, mental health, and rehabilitation.
- Take leadership in educating the justice system regarding cultural competency in services, equal treatment of people, and social work professional values and ethics.
- Advocate for more community-based options that allow offenders to remain within their communities, therefore, accessing their families, cultures, and relevant treatment.
- Utilize excellent assessment, decision-making, crisis intervention, case management, program development, mediation, and community organization skills.

Educational and Licensing Requirements

Educational and licensing qualifications for social workers in the criminal justice system vary by state, territory, and facilities. Depending on the state or territory within the United States, officers, specialists, and counselors can be employed in the criminal justice system with a bachelor's (BSW), master's (MSW), or PhD degree in social work. Likewise, those who hold the title of social worker can be employed with a BSW, MSW, or PhD in social work. Throughout the United States and its territories, many MSW education programs have concentrations or specializations in social work within corrections, which prepare students specifically for a career in the criminal justice system. Social workers who provide specialized services, such as substance abuse and sex offender treatment, may also complete certifications or special trainings. Licensure in social work requires an individual to meet the respective state's or territory's standards for licensing and 2-year supervised clinical experience for clinical social workers.

As discussed thus far, social workers in the criminal justice system provide critical services to vulnerable populations, consisting of both offenders and victims, on a variety of levels, including individuals, families, groups, and communities. Consequently, a high degree of knowledge, skills, and training is required to successfully and effectively meet their needs. Social workers are indeed needed in these settings.

Best Aspects of this Job

- Working with both offenders and victims in terms of advocating for self-determination and client-centered approaches to promoting social functioning.
- Working to demistify a system that has been viewed as intimidating, adversarial, punitive, and coercive.
- Providing both prevention and intervention as needed by individuals in the justice system.
- Working with individuals, families, and communities to mobilize resources and promote the social functioning of all parties involved.
- Contributing positively to the lives of offenders and victims.
- Expanding knowledge about diverse cultures and developing cultural competency skills.
- Opportunity to combat disproportionality of people of color in the system.
- Opportunity to advocate for equality, protection of rights, self-determination, and humane treatment.
- Numerous opportunities for policy advocacy on availability and accessibility of services to offenders and victims.
- Expanding knowledge about risk and protective factors (e.g., personal, family, peer, school, community-based) that contribute to the risk for involvement in the justice system.

Challenging Aspects of this Job

- Safety is sometimes an issue when working in the justice system.
- Working with victims and offenders can be stressful, hazardous, and overwhelming.
- Sometimes one's workday expands beyond the workplace.
- Sometimes it is difficult to build relationships with involuntary clients and ensure client self-determination.
- Working with offenders who do not respond to treatment (e.g., sex offenders) and working with offenders whose actions may be personally objectionable.

- Witnessing offender difficulty in rehabilitation and recovery.
- Knowing that policies and racial profiling are possible risk factors for disproportionality in the system.
- The heavy burden of being responsible for appropriate assessments and making decisions that affect children, youth, families, and communities.
- Because demands are extremely high in criminal justice systems, caring for oneself and having a balanced life can be difficult.
- Having a successful program eliminated from the criminal justice system because funding is not available.
- Working with professionals who do not have social work backgrounds.

Compensation and Employment Outlook

Social workers in the criminal justice system are employed by both public and private agencies, thus compensation varies by setting, program, facility, state, and region. For instance, the emphasis on rehabilitation and probation resulted in an excellent employment forecast for probation officers through 2014. In 2004, the median annual income for probation officers was approximately $39,000. Overall, the employment forecast for social workers in the criminal justice system is excellent, with correctional officers growing faster than the average for all occupations due to population growth and increase in incarceration. In 2006, median annual income for correctional officers was about $36,000 (U.S. Department of Labor, Occupational Outlook Handbook, 2006). Depending on the setting, counselors and specialists may be paid hourly wages ranging from $7 to $25. In relation to those who hold the title of social worker, in 2006, median annual earnings of child and family social workers was about $38,000, mental health and substance abuse social workers was approximately $36,000, and all other social workers had a medium annual earning of about $44,000 (U.S. Department of Labor, Occupational Outlook Handbook, 2006).

Self-Assessment Checklist: Is this Job for Me?

- ☐ Do you have a passion for working with individuals involved in the justice system, and making sure their educational, personal, social, and mental health needs are met?

☐ Do you think that you are able to work with people from diverse backgrounds, both culturally and linguistically, and their communities?

☐ Are you passionate about policy advocacy on behalf of offenders and victims?

☐ Do you enjoy having a job where your work day is spent working with multiple systems, including individuals, families, schools, communities, and courts, to mobilize resources for the best interest of the individual offender or victim?

☐ Would you enjoy the challenge of working with a range of individuals from at-risk children to motivated adults?

☐ Would you enjoy advocating for access to resources and information for those incarcerated, their families, and communities?

☐ Would you be comfortable working under stressful and hazardous conditions?

☐ Do you have an assertive personality and are comfortable dealing with conflict?

☐ Would you be comfortable working for an agency that is bureaucratic and has many rules, regulations, policies, and procedures to follow?

☐ Are you committed to restorative justice for victims and offenders?

If you answered "yes" to seven or more of the above questions, then working in a criminal justice setting might be the place for you!

RECOMMENDED READINGS/WEB SITES TO LEARN MORE

American Correctional Association: www.aca.org

American Jail Association: www.corrections.com/aja

Bing, L. (1992). *Do or Die*. New York, NY: Harper Perennial.

Briar-Lawson, K., Lawson, H., & Sallee, A. (Eds.). *New century practice with vulnerable families*. Dubuque, IA: Eddie Bowers Publishing, Inc.

Federal Bureau of Prisons: www.bop.gov

Center for Court Innovation: http://changingthecourt.blogspot.com/2007/04/social-workers-and-criminal-justice.html

National Center for Victims of Crime: www.ncvc.org

Restorative Justice Online: www.restorativejustice.org/

U.S. Department of Labor, Bureau of Statistics, Internet: http://www.bls.gov/oes/current/oes211029.htm#nat

Van Wormer, K., & Bartollas, C. (2007). *Women and the criminal justice system* (2nd ed.). Boston, MA: Allyn & Bacon.

Criminal Justice Exercise

While television shows regarding legal issues are plentiful, many court hearings in local communities are actually open to the public. Research the court services available in your neighborhood, and investigate which sessions are open to the public to attend. You may also want to contact your local Legal Aid Society and ask to visit their offices. Learn the difference between criminal and civil courts. You can make an appointment to "interview" a legal aid attorney and talk to them about the types of clients they serve and the issues they address.

Go to the FBI Web site (**www.fbi.gov**) and research the crime statistics nationally and for your state. There is a lot of information you can review, and you may be surprised to learn what has been happening in your own community.

REFERENCES

American Probation and Parole Association. (2008). About APPA. [Online]. Retrieved April 17, 2008, from http://www.appa-net.org/about/

Ivanhoff, A., Smyth, N., & Dulmus, C. (2007). Preparing social workers for practice in correctional institutions. In A. R. Roberts & D. W. Springer (Eds.), *Social work in juvenile and criminal justice settings*, 7(1), 341–350. Springfield, IL: Charles C Thomas.

Orzech, D. (2006). Criminal justice social work: New models, new opportunities. *Social Work Today*, 6(6), 34.

Peat, B. (2004). *From College to Career, A Guide for Criminal Justice Majors*. Boston, MA: Pearson Education.

Showalter, D., & Hunsinger, D. (2007). Social work within a maximum security setting. In A. R. Roberts & D. W. Springer (Eds.), *Social work in juvenile and criminal justice settings* 366–375. Springfield, IL: Charles C Thomas.

Strang, H., & Braithwaite, J. (Eds.) (2002). *Restorative justice and family violence*. Melbourne, Australia: Cambridge University Press.

U.S. Department of Labor, Bureau of Labor Statistics. (2007). *Occupational Outlook Handbook*. [Online]. Retrieved April 17, 2008, from http://www.bls.gov/OCO/

11 Careers in Forensic Social Work

You may be familiar with the term *forensic* if you are an avid fan of the television series *CSI* (Criminal Services Investigation), or if you were a member of your high school or college debate team. *Forensic* comes from the latin word "forensis" meaning "before the forum" or the court. You are probably not old enough to remember ancient Rome; however, during that time a person charged with a criminal offense would be given the opportunity to present their case in full view of the public. The person accused of the crime, as well as their accuser, would be given an opportunity to make a speech offering their side of the story. The person who made the most compelling and skillful argument would essentially "win" their case.

Forensics (or forensic science) is the application of several sciences, including social sciences, used to answer questions of interest to the legal system. *Forensic social work* refers to the practice of social work that focuses on the law, legal issues, and litigation in both criminal and civil legal systems (Barker, 2003, p. 166).

As you may have noticed from chapter 10, social work and the law have always been related to one another. In fact, the historical connection between the two professions goes back to the late 1800s and the Settlement House movement, with the eventual creation of the first juvenile court.

In today's world, *forensic social work* is a term used more frequently in the profession, and the roles played by social workers in this area are quite diverse, with more roles emerging. Forensic social workers are employed as mediators, victim advocates, family court evaluators, mental health evaluators, expert witnesses, mitigation specialists, and risk assessors.

Forensic social work is a specialized focus of practice that bridges both civil and criminal justice systems. It is the assessment and evaluation expertise of the social worker, as an unbiased party in the legal system, that forms the foundation for this type of social work practice. Many social workers, based on their knowledge, skills, and professional experiences, have been qualified by both civil and criminal courts to be an *expert* in their field. This means they can appear in court and testify in various situations.

Typically, social workers have appeared in court as expert witnesses in the area of adoption, termination of parental rights, child abuse and neglect, substance abuse and various addictions, emotional distress or trauma, and mental illness. Such testimony may be given in person or in a written document, and the testimony is based on the social worker's professional experience and the currently accepted theories of human behavior and social environment in the field (Tyuse & Linhorst, 2005).

CUSTODY EVALUATOR

Sometimes, when families break up, in the wake of a difficult divorce or after the death of a sole parent, the court has to determine who is the best custodian of the minor child (or children). In these cases, social workers may be called upon by a judge in a Domestic Relations Court to prepare an evaluation of the minor child. The purpose of the evaluation is to determine who should have custody of the child. This legal decision is based on the concept of what is considered to be "in the best interest of the child," and the decision may include factors such as the child's level of attachment with each potential custodian, the financial means of each potential custodian, and the child's social and educational needs.

To make this evaluation, the social worker may interview the child (or children), parent(s), and other family members. After evaluating all the available materials, the social worker prepares a written assessment of what he or she thinks is in the best interests of the child. The social worker may also have to testify in court. The social worker's testimony as an "expert witness" assists the judge in making the legal decision regarding who will have the physical and legal responsibility for the child or children under review.

MENTAL HEALTH EVALUATOR

In some criminal or civil cases, individuals brought before the court may be suffering from mental illness or developmental disabilities, which impact their ability to participate in, and understand, the court proceedings. In other words, their level of competency to make appropriate decisions may come under question. Criminal and civil courts require a specific evaluation to determine whether or not an individual is competent. Social workers are frequently called upon by courts for competency evaluations, where the social worker helps the courts with these types of decisions. These evaluations often involve interviews with the individual and other family members, mental health assessments, medical and developmental histories, and other materials.

MITIGATION SPECIALIST

A mitigation specialist is a social worker who attempts to present evidence that will justify a more lenient sentence for a person convicted of a crime. The intention is not to excuse the crime, but to provide the judge and jury with a better understanding of why the person committed the act. Mental and physical health issues, substance abuse, family history of abuse and neglect, and community or cultural values all may be presented as mitigating factors.

Mitigation specialist is an emerging area of recognition for social work practice; however, the scope of this practice rests on the foundation of basic social work skills—engagement, interviewing, and assessment.

Perhaps the most crucial cases in which mitigation testimony may have an impact are those involving the death penalty. The death penalty currently exists in 38 states. Each state allows for the provision of mitigating factors to be presented to the court on behalf of the defendant. Lawyers working for the defense have been using social workers more often in preparing for the penalty phases of capital punishment trials. Social workers are skilled in interviewing clients and other relevant parties, conducting mental health assessments, presenting the client as a human being in written social histories, and managing conflict between the victim's family and family members of the defendant (National Association of Social Workers [NASW], 2003).

Social Work Spotlight: Alison Cusick, MSW Candidate George Mason University, Intern, Office of the Public Defender, Montgomery County, Maryland

I recently completed my field practicum as a graduate social work intern at the Office of the Public Defender (OPD) in Montgomery County, MD. I did this internship as my first year field practicum requirement in my MSW program at the George Mason University in Arlington, Virginia. At OPD, I was part of the Neighborhood Defense project, a team that consists of three social workers, a civil attorney, an education attorney, several law clerks, and three graduate social work interns. Since my supervisor, Melissa, oversaw all of the social workers in the state of Maryland, she was only in our office once a week for supervision. Therefore, I spent a lot of time working directly with the social workers in the office, to discuss cases and seek advice on clients, school, and my own career.

When I began my internship at OPD, I had no idea what to expect. I double majored in criminal justice and psychology, so I was familiar with the criminal justice system and the role that mental health professionals play in the system. In my first week at OPD, Melissa organized an orientation for all social work interns across the state. We spent a day in Baltimore discussing what our role would be with clients, how the social worker code of ethics applied to our work, and what ethical situations we may encounter working with this particular client base. We also discussed how attorney-client privilege may cause ethical conflicts for social workers, and what to do when an ethical conflict arose.

Back in Montgomery County, I was teamed up with Veronica, an adult social worker, who gave me several client cases to read and learn about. We talked about each client's situation and how the social worker could work with the client, attorney, state's attorney, and the judge together to achieve a final outcome that would satisfy all parties involved. I quickly learned that an intern is given a lot of responsibility, and while we were always under the supervision of a licensed social worker, we were expected to perform the same tasks as a social worker. Over the course of my practicum, I learned that a social worker at OPD doesn't have one specific job to do; we do a little bit of everything. Sometimes we would help a client find housing, apply for Medicaid or food stamps, locate day care for their children, or get into a rehab or drug treatment program. We served as a contact person for the client's families, so they can keep up with court dates and find out about community resources available to them. Other times, we may have a longer, more in-depth relationship with the client, when we are asked to do a social history, assessment, and make a recommendation to the court. Generally, the goal of the assessment was to figure out why the client did what they did, and propose a way to help them that did not involve long-term incarceration. To complete the assessment, the social worker or intern would meet with the client several times (usually, at the local correctional facility) to get a social, medical, and mental health history; determine their current mental health status; determine what needs the client had; gain the client's perspective on their criminal case; and determine what programs or treatment approaches may be best for the client. The final report includes information from our client's medical records, conversations with their family or friends, and research from journal articles that support our final recommendation.

I found that the biggest challenge in my field practicum at OPD was balancing my work between what the attorney needed for court, and what my client needed for their own rehabilitation. I had several experiences where I did not feel that what the attorney and court wanted were in the client's best interest. For example, I had one client who was facing serious jail time and the attorney was able to get him into a drug treatment program as part of his probation. In this specific case, I felt like the program wasn't the best thing for him because the client still didn't believe he had a drug problem, and we were just setting him up to fail.

Before beginning my field practicum in forensic social work, I did not have a definitive career path in mind. I entered the MSW program thinking that perhaps I'd want to work with children who are in foster care or people who are struggling with addiction. In my 8 months at OPD, my eyes were opened to many more career paths that one can take as a social worker. I worked with men and women struggling with addiction, severe mental illness, unemployment, and homelessness. Some of them were facing a lifetime in jail or knew that their families or jobs would not be waiting for them upon their release. Going into my second year of the MSW program, I still don't have my career path decided, but my eyes have been opened to the possibility of continuing to work in forensic social work with the incarcerated population. I would recommend this field to someone who is interested in working with many different types of people and is able to listen to clients talk about their difficult lives and the hard situations that they have been involved in.

FORENSIC SOCIAL WORK IN JUVENILE JUSTICE

Public defenders offices in the juvenile justice system have been employing social workers to help them link clients to community-based services (e.g., substance abuse programs) as well as in preparing written psychosocial assessments and testifying in court. In recent years, communities across the United States have instituted specialized criminal courts for juvenile defendants with substance abuse disorders and mental illness. These specialized courts seek to prevent incarceration and facilitate community-based treatment for offenders, while at the same time providing for public safety. The purpose of forensic social work in this area is to develop successful sentencing plans in the court system based on the ultimate goal of rehabilitation. For more on information on other social work careers in juvenile justice, see chapter 10.

> ### Social Worker Spotlight: Joel T. Andrade, MSW, LICSW, Doctoral Candidate, Boston College Graduate School of Social Work, Bridgewater State Hospital, Bridgewater, Massachusetts, MHM Services, Inc.
>
> Going into the MSW program at Boston College Graduate School of Social Work, my career goal was to work with juvenile offenders. My first year internship was working with adolescents suspended from school due to a violent incident. Many of the youth I worked with were somehow involved with the criminal justice system in one form

or another—whether probation, parole, youth detention, or having a family member that was incarcerated. After this experience, I thought the best way to serve my clients in the future was to gain a better understanding of the criminal justice system. Therefore, I elected to do my second year internship in a correctional setting. Combining my interests in the criminal justice system and mental health, my second year internship was at Bridgewater State Hospital (BSH) in Massachusetts. BSH is the state's most secure forensic hospital and the staff is charged with evaluating and treating male forensic patients. I loved the forensic work, and when I completed my MSW, I worked for 1 year at a prison in Concord, Massachusetts, before returning to BSH.

Being a clinician in a forensic hospital has many challenges, particularly working with severe character disordered patients. I enjoyed the work and became very interested in the assessment and treatment of psychopathic inmates. In 2001, I decided to go back to the Boston College Graduate School of Social Work for my PhD to pursue this research interest. My dissertation is on the early-life experiences of psychopathic individuals.

While completing the doctoral requirements, I continued to work full-time at BSH in numerous capacities, including the director of the seclusion and restraint unit, the admission coordinator, and the clinical risk assessment coordinator. These positions have been extremely rewarding and continued to fuel my research interests. I became involved in numerous research groups presenting at national conferences in the areas of psychopathy, violence risk assessment, and sexual offending behavior. The combination of my forensic and research interest also led to the upcoming publication of a book I am editing in the area of violence risk assessment, treatment, and risk management for forensic practitioners. The goal of this volume is to provide the forensic practitioner with a hands-on guide to conducting violence risk assessments.

The field of social work, particularly forensic social work, has been an extremely rewarding career choice. Coupling this forensic work with academic pursuits of research has been particularly fulfilling for me. I strongly encourage social work students to consider an internship in a correctional or forensic setting—I considered it—and have never left!

Core Competencies and Skills

- Knowledge of the legal system and terminology.
- Strong assessment and interviewing skills.
- Ability to work with persons charged with criminal offenses.
- Knowledge of the appropriate treatment interventions for mentally ill inmates, substance abusing inmates, juvenile offenders, victims and perpetrators of family abuse and violence, and those returning to the community after incarceration.
- Strong mediation skills in high conflict situations.
- Knowledge of risk assessment and prevention.
- Ability to advocate for needed community resources.
- Demonstrate strong group facilitation skills.
- Work successfully as part of a multidisciplinary team.

Educational and Licensing Requirements

Forensic social work is an area of specialty practice and requires a master's degree. Many aspects of this job also require additional certifications and/or a license in clinical social work.

Working with a bachelor's degree in social work in the areas of foster care and adoptions, substance abuse prevention and treatment, juvenile and domestic relations courts, emergency shelters, group homes, case management, child and adult protective services, and disability and rehabilitation services is excellent preparation for gaining experience in this field and preparation for more advanced work in graduate school.

Many universities are beginning to offer specific courses in forensic social work. The National Organization of Forensic Social Workers was created to offer professional continuing education and certification in this growing area of practice.

Best Aspects of this Job

- Working to end disparities in the legal justice system is professionally rewarding.
- Being a valued member of a multidisciplinary team means you are not working alone in a difficult environment.
- Specializing in a new and growing area as well as developing expertise is a positive professional challenge.

- Much of this work can be fast paced and crisis oriented so you are never bored.
- There are many opportunities in this work to have positive outcomes from tragic circumstances.
- Bearing witness to the personal narratives of people, whose lives would never be known otherwise, offers personal satisfaction.
- The documentation of life stories is a contribution to the historical record so that others may benefit in preventing future tragedies.
- Working on behalf of a population (e.g., prisoners) who are typically underserved allows you to put social justice into action.

Challenging Aspects of this Job

- Working with difficult clients and families can be emotionally draining and it is very critical that you take care of yourself.
- Working with persons charged with criminal offenses may prove, too, challenging in balancing personal values and ethics.
- Negotiating with professional colleagues outside of the social work profession who may not respect your contributions can be frustrating at times.
- Working directly with victims and their families may contribute to your own traumatization if you do not provide for your own self-care.

Compensation and Employment Outlook

Most social workers in the area of forensics are working for publicly funded social service agencies, family courts, and state offices of the public defender. Master's level social workers (MSW) working in these places would receive the same salary as other workers in those occupational tiers; however, due to the need for highly experienced social workers in this field, compensation would most likely be higher than someone new to the organization with limited professional work.

Many social workers who are self-employed and work as independent licensed clinical social workers contract their services to the agencies mentioned above, or they are hired on behalf of clients. Social workers in private mental health practices typically earn between $40,000 and $60,000, with approximately 25% earning considerably more (NASW Workforce Survey, 2004).

Self-Assessment Checklist: Is this Job for Me?

☐ Would you be comfortable working with a group of professionals who hold different views and values than those of social workers?

☐ Can you be objective working on behalf of someone who is guilty of a crime?

☐ Would the nature of the crime impact your view of the client?

☐ Are you able to set personal limits and professional boundaries and stick to them?

☐ Can you deal with conflict or mediate between various parties?

☐ Can you tolerate your work being interrupted from time to time?

☐ Are you interested in the law and legal system?

☐ Would you be comfortable with public speaking and testifying in court?

☐ Would you be able to manage your own emotions in listening to a victim's story of abuse?

☐ Can you accept decisions that may be made in opposition to what you would decide?

If you answered "Yes" to seven or more of the above questions, then you may want to explore this area further!

RECOMMENDED READINGS/WEB SITES TO LEARN MORE

American Bar Association-Mitigation Project: www.aba.org

Barsky, A. E., & Gould, J. W. (2002). *Clinicians in court: A guide to subpoenas, depositions, testifying, and everything else you need to know.* New York: Columbia University Press.

Madden, R. G. (2003). *Essential law for social workers.* New York: Columbia University Press.

Maryland State Office of the Public Defender: www.opd.state.md.us

National Association of Social Workers—Law Notes: www.socialworkers.org

National Organization of Forensic Social Workers: www.nofsw.org

Reamer, F. G. (2003). *Criminal lessons: Case studies and commentary on crime and justice.* New York: Columbia University Press.

Schroeder, J., Guin, C. C., Pogue, R., & Bordelon, D. (2006). Mitigating circumstances in death penalty decisions: Using evidence-based research to inform social work practice in capital trials. *Social Work, 51*(4), 355–364.

Springer, D., & Roberts, A. (Eds.). (2007). *Handbook of forensic mental health with victims and offenders, assessment, treatment, and research.* New York: Springer Publications.

Forensic Social Work Exercise

Case Scenario

Shawna Cook is a 23-year-old female who has Down's Syndrome. Shawna lives in a group home of eight residents—four of them male and four of them female. Everyone in the group home is employed in a job that is within easy commuting distance. All of the residents are encouraged to lead independent lives and participate in community activities.

Shawna began dating Paul, a boy she met at her job, about 1 year ago. They are sexually active, and now, Shawna has learned that she is 2 months pregnant. The group home administrator notified Shawna's mother, who is her legal guardian. Mrs. Cook is very upset and has requested that the administrator make arrangements for the pregnancy to be terminated.

Shawna and Paul want to get married and keep the pregnancy. The Family Court Judge has asked the County Social Services to have a social worker evaluate Shawna for a competency hearing to be held in 2 weeks. You are the social worker given this task.

Questions

1. What is the ethical dilemma in this case?
2. As the social worker in this scenario what will you do first?
3. What kind of information do you need to gather?
4. If Mrs. Cook is Shawna's legal guardian, will you need her permission to interview Shawna?
5. Does the Group Home Administrator have a responsibility in this case? If so, what is it and to whom?
6. What do you think the outcome of this case should be?
7. What are your own personal values or biases, as you read this case?

REFERENCES

Barker, R. L. (2003). *The social work dictionary* (5th ed.). Washington, DC: NASW Press.

National Association of Social Workers. (2004). *National workforce survey*. Washington, DC: Author.

National Association of Social Workers. (2003). *Social workers as death penalty mitigation specialists*. Retrieved January 19, 2007, from http://www.socialworkers.org/ldf/legal_issue/200309.asp

Tyuse, S. W., & Linhorst, D. M. (2005). Drug courts and mental health courts: Implications for social work. *Social Work, 20*(2), 233–240.

Careers in International Social Work and Human Rights

In the news, we often see images of the war in Iraq and disasters, such as earthquakes and hurricanes, in various parts of the world. These tragedies leave in their wake individuals, families, and communities who require a variety of assistance, ranging from basic needs such as food, clothing, and shelter, to counseling and mental health services. If you are interested in helping in crisis situations around the globe, then international social work may be the career path for you.

Globalization; increased interdependency between cultures, geographic areas, and economies; and increased inequities between the haves and have-nots also warrants social work practice in an international context. The fact that a substantial percentage of people in third world countries live in extreme poverty—on less than $1.00 a day—is a major concern for the profession of social work. Social workers are called to contribute to knowledge, practice, and advocacy efforts that have global implications for people all over the world. Major organizations that have engaged in these international social work efforts include the United Nations, UNICEF, Save the Children, Amnesty International, Red Cross, Peace Corps, Human Rights Watch, International Association of Schools of Social Work, International Federation of Social Workers (IFSW), and the International Council on Social Welfare (ICSW). Within these organizations, social workers may be called on to provide leadership on a range of issues including combating poverty and hunger; social and economic development; assisting immigrants and refugees; helping those displaced by war, famine, or national disasters; providing healthcare and mental health services to those suffering from AIDS and other serious illnesses; human rights work; and combating illiteracy.

Social work is essentially an international/global profession. Although, historically, social work accompanied colonization in some countries, social workers today are needed in every country to help alleviate a host of social problems (Cox & Pawar, 2006). And even if you do not choose to work internationally, in the settings described above, there remains a high chance that you will serve individuals and families who have migrated from another country. For this reason, some would argue that *all* social work is international social work, even if one only works in the United States.

Social workers who engage in international social work must be culturally competent and well versed in international affairs, theories, and social and economic development. As such, many social work students complete elective courses in international social work or earn a dual/joint degree in international affairs.

This chapter will describe some of the many jobs available for those with social work education, training, and work experience who are interested in working in an international context.

U.S.-BASED IMMIGRANT, REFUGEE, AND ASYLEE RESETTLEMENT WORKER

As the number of immigrants arriving in the United States continues to grow, individuals with social work backgrounds will be needed to serve them. Social workers can contribute their expertise in multicultural practice and crisis intervention to provide services to families and communities in attaining social and economic independence and cultural adjustment. Bilingual social workers are in demand and will be very competitive in the job market. Services provided may include linking families to churches and communities of origin in the United States; helping immigrants locate cash assistance, medical assistance, employment, and housing; and also providing social services, including individual and family therapy, substance abuse treatment, English language courses and services in their native tongues, educational/vocational training, and other specialized mental health services.

Social Worker Spotlight: Marleine Bastien, BSW, MSW, LCSW, Founder, FANM Ayisyen Nan Miyami/Haitian Women of Miami

I grew up in a small village on the outskirt of Petite Riviere De L'artibonite called Pont Benoit, a town situated north of the capital of Haiti. The tradition of women partaking in all aspects of societal life yet excluded from the decision-making processes of the community is engrained in the village's consciousness. This tradition represents centuries of rigid rules and regulations that no one has ever dared challenging. I vowed, when I was young, to change this state one day, a day that hasn't arrived since I left Haiti, after completing secondary school. When the political situation became unbearable in Haiti, I left to come to the United States. I emigrated from Haiti in 1981.

Two days after I arrived in Miami, I started volunteering at the Haitian Refugee Center, thus starting a life of volunteering and strong advocacy on behalf of immigrant women and children. In 1994, I received a Volunteer of the Year Award from Miami-Dade County. I obtained an associate in arts degree from Miami Dade Community College, and a BSW and an MSW from Florida International University. As a licensed clinical social worker, I worked for 13 years at Jackson Memorial Hospital where I fought for AIDS, sickle cell, and breast cancer patients of all nationalities. Soon, my expertise, compassion, and strong advocacy for patients' rights became well known; my expertise in women's challenges to explain, for example, why a mother failed to bring her child for follow-up care or why an HIV-positive mom becomes pregnant again became widely known. I was consulted for all the specialty teams, and my opinion/authority in the domain of health access and women's struggle was respected. I was recognized as Social Worker of the Month by Jackson Memorial Hospital in 1996. In 2000, I received the Miami Dade County Social Worker of the Year Award.

In 1991, I founded Fanm Ayisyen Nan Miyami/Haitian Women of Miami, an organization whose mission is to empower Haitian women and their families and to facilitate their adjustment to life in South Florida. FANM was a volunteer organization for 9 years. I organized volunteers to keep it going, raising $5,000 a year through selling candies, coordinating yard sales, and selling cheap stuff at the flea market. FANM transitioned to a community-based organization in 2000. Now, FANM has a staff of 14 and a budget of $1.7 million, providing an array of services ranging from immigration, mental health, domestic violence, cancer prevention, counseling, crisis intervention, after school programming for disadvantaged children, a legal clinic, and a citizenship program. FANM was named Best Non-Profit of the Year by The Chamber of Commerce, Best Champion of the Powerless by the New Times, and Best Advocate by the Sun Post. I received the Human Rights Award from Amnesty International in 2000, among many other recognitions and accolades. In May 2005, *Essence Magazine* named me One of the 35 Most Powerful Women in the World.

Besides FANM, I'm also a founding member of the Haitian Coalition on Health. HCH (now defunct) was a pioneer organization that played a vital role in understanding the prevalence of HIV-AIDS in the Haitian-American community. I also instituted Miamians Working Together, which was a collaborative of Haitian and African American women to work together to combat AIDS. I found that there was too much friction between African Americans and Haitians. Miamians Working Together brought the two groups together, and they learned from each other's histories, traditions, and values through what I called "tea parties" (meetings held at members' houses where they eat, drink, and learn from each other). Once the groups were able to build a strong rapport, they got involved in a joint pilot project called AIDS Education and Prevention. The program was very successful in not only improving relationships among the two groups, but it was also instrumental in the fight against HIV/AIDS.

I have also used the media successfully to shed light on the plight of women with breast cancer. Through sheer resilience and determination, I developed a successful community outreach program that promotes prevention, education, mammograms, and the buddy system to educate the community about breast cancer. I instituted the buddy system called: "Fanm men nan men" (women hand in hand) where women provide support to others with breast cancer.

Domestic violence is a huge problem not only in the Haitian community, but also in the community at large. When I first implemented a domestic violence community education and intervention program in the early 80s targeting Haitian and Caribbean women, I received death threats. Even women admonished me for "trying to be an American woman who wants women to wear the pants in the families." Now, even men voluntarily come to FANM to seek help and learn how to control their anger. I fought to get domestic violence recognized as a "health issue." I strongly advocated for doctors to assess women who come to the emergency room at Jackson Hospital with serious and often strange injuries for domestic violence. I believe that health access is a human right, not a privilege, and women's health has always been a priority for me.

Since my arrival in the United States, I have advocated at the local, national, and international level on behalf of immigrant women and children. I fought to get women and their families out of detention, making a powerful case in their behalf on the streets, in boardrooms around the nation, and in the halls of Washington. Women from all around the world come to this country in search of a safe haven. They have oftentimes been traumatized, abused, maimed, jailed, and harassed in their native land. They come here in search of freedom and liberty. The least we can do is afford them the most basic right that is guaranteed under international laws—the right of due process.

As a social worker, I believe in women's rights. I strive daily to promote women's rights, social and economic justice, human rights, health education/prevention/access services, and treatment. I believe that world peace cannot be achieved without the full and complete emancipation of all women. Our country was built on the cherished principles of justice for all, and through my advocacy work, I wanted to show that women can be strong and compassionate, ambitious and nurturing, forceful but loving and caring.

Social Worker Spotlight: Juliane Ramic, MSW
Resettling Refugees

When I took my first job after college, I had no understanding of the field of social work. I was working at a refugee resettlement agency in St. Louis and fell in love with the work. My supervisor told me that there was little opportunity for advancement unless I got my master's in social work. Within a month, I had submitted my applications to local social work graduate programs. I was accepted at the George Warren Brown School of Social Work at Washington University. During my time there, I did everything I could to gain skills that could be transferred to working with refugees.

When a person is forced to leave their home, they often find relative safety in a refugee camp. Then, they may be deemed eligible for third country resettlement and, if so, are served by a local refugee resettlement agency. I wanted to understand the refugee experience and sought opportunities to work in refugee camps for national organizations that coordinated domestic refugee resettlement and then at local social service agencies serving newly arriving refugees. After graduate school, I had the honor of working in the Sudanese and Somali refugee camps in Ethiopia. Upon returning, I began working for the U.S. Committee for Refugees and Immigrants, an umbrella organization representing about 30 local refugee resettlement agencies. I loved connecting with the staff of these agencies and providing them with grant support and technical assistance, but I missed working with refugees! In 2004, I had the opportunity to join Nationalities Service Center in Philadelphia as the director of social services. It's been an incredible experience to gain inspiration from those we serve and use this to mold, modify, and design our programs to best serve the changing needs of refugees. I work with a dedicated team of incredible individuals, and together we try to ensure that our services are innovative, responsive, culturally appropriate, etc. Refugees now living in the United States are survivors, amazing advocates, and have so much to give. How can I not love what I do?

IMMIGRATION POLICY ADVOCATE

In addition to providing direct services to immigrants, social workers may help immigrant communities on a macro level by advocating for changes to immigration policies. This is especially true now, as anti-immigration policies in the wake of 9/11 have led to a rise in discriminatory practices against and treatment of many immigrants, both undocumented and otherwise. Social workers in organizations such as the American Civil Liberties Union (ACLU), Immigration Equality, the National Immigration Law Center, the National Council of La Raza (a Latino rights organization), the National Network for Arab American Communities, and many others are advocating for positive changes in national policies affecting the lives of immigrants, their families, and communities. In addition, there are many opportunities at state and city levels to advocate for local immigrant communities.

DISASTER RELIEF WORKER

Disaster relief workers with social work backgrounds are often employed by organizations, such as the Red Cross and other nongovernmental organizations (NGOs) to work in international settings. In these jobs, they contribute their specialized skills in crisis intervention, medicine, public health, and mental health to those recovering from a disaster. These workers also provide food and shelter.

Social Worker Spotlight: Susan Kosche Vallem, EdD, LISW Professor and Chair of the Social Work Department, Wartburg College, Waverly, IA

Although I teach undergraduate social work at Wartburg College, much of my social work practice was in medical social work. I received my undergraduate education from Wartburg College, my MSW from the University of Iowa, and my EdD from the University of Northern Iowa. As a practicing social worker, I particularly enjoyed working in the emergency room providing crisis intervention services. From that background, I became an American Red Cross disaster mental health volunteer.

I first became involved with Red Cross disaster mental health following the 9/11 attacks in New York City. Since then, the Red Cross has sent me all over the country to work with survivors of all sorts of natural disasters. I discovered how well my social work education and experience had prepared me for crisis intervention.

Two key values of social work are building on strengths and starting where the client is. Crisis intervention is not therapy in the clinical sense, but helping survivors of disasters to find their strengths and to begin to take control of a life that suddenly went out of control. For example, one of my duties in New York was to take families of victims into the Ground Zero area for some sense of closure. These people did not need therapy, but they did need help dealing with sudden death and grief. Through crisis intervention, I worked with them to help "normalize" an abnormal situation through understanding the grief process. I asked them to tell me about their loved-one who had died, to give value to that person's life. And then I thought about what to do next—what little act could they do to begin to take control of their loves and to move forward. The resiliency of people I work with is always amazing.

I believe in practicing what I teach. Working with people from all cultures and walks of life through the Red Cross is not only personally gratifying, but it also reinforces that social work education and practice is right on target. I work with many helping professions in the Red Cross, and social workers seem, to me, to be the best suited for crisis intervention. I base this opinion on watching social workers from around the country meet clients where they are at that moment, build on strengths, and use their creativity to develop, always with the client, positive intervention strategies. Volunteering with the American Red Cross fits with social work.

HUMAN RIGHTS WORKER

Human rights workers are advocates for human rights for all people. Those with social work training in policy issues and legislation are able to contribute positively to human rights work. They engage in report writing, monitoring and actively promoting compliance with international standards on human rights, working with intergovernmental organizations and NGOs, and the promotion of research and legal developments in relation to human rights.

INTERNATIONAL DEVELOPMENT WORKER

International development workers with social work backgrounds help meet the needs of individuals, families, and communities in developing countries in areas such as health, education, sanitation, businesses, agriculture, and community organization for the betterment of their economic and social conditions. Their work is framed by a collective and global perspective. For instance, Peace Corp Workers provide services in education, youth outreach, community development, business development, agriculture and environment, health and HIV/AIDS, and information technology. International development workers engage in a range of activities from counseling an adolescent in Tonga to teaching English in Spain.

CAREERS WITH UNITED NATIONS/UNICEF

Social workers who work for the United Nations/UNICEF work in a variety of programs to assist those in need. These workers protect children's rights and provide services to victims of war, disasters, exploitation, and poverty. They focus specifically on child survival and development, protection, education and gender equality, and HIV/AIDS prevention.

Social Worker Spotlight: Purnima Mane, MSW, PhD Deputy Executive Director (Program), UNFPA, the United Nations Population Fund

My professional life has been fueled by a deep belief in social justice and equity, and this drives me everyday. Throughout my career, I have championed sexual and reproductive health, with a particular focus on gender and AIDS. I was, therefore, particularly honored to be appointed Deputy Executive Director for Program at UNFPA, the United Nations Population Fund, and Assistant-Secretary-General of the United Nations.

As part of the United Nations, UNFPA promotes the right of every woman, man, and child to enjoy a life of health and equal opportunity. It supports countries in using population data for policies and programs to reduce poverty and promote universal access to reproductive health, gender equality, and women's empowerment.

My position allows me to bring my interests and expertise together to address social causes that are dear to my heart. As deputy executive director, I help shape global policies that have a direct impact on people's lives. I represent UNFPA at the highest level of policy dialogue with government officials, major international partners, and civil society representatives. I participate in many global gatherings and advocate for the goals and values of UNFPA. I also oversee UNFPA's programs and make sure that our activities are strategic, effectively managed, and benefit those who need them the most.

What I enjoy most about my work is that it gives me the opportunity to work with inspiring leaders and interact with some of the brightest and most committed people in the world. I am constantly in contact with interesting people and being confronted with complex and challenging situations.

Prior to joining UNFPA, I served in several international positions in UNAIDS; the Global Fund to Fight AIDS, Tuberculosis and Malaria; the World Health Organization; and the Population Council. I also worked for over a decade on public health and gender-related issues in my home country of India, and I was honored to teach at the prestigious Tata Institute of Social Sciences in Mumbai, which is Asia's first school of social work.

To prepare for my career, I completed an MSW, specializing in health along with a MPhil and a PhD in social work with a specialization in women's studies from the Tata Institute.

Guided by the principles of human rights and human dignity, I hope that my contribution to the work of the United Nations will make a difference in the lives of the most underprivileged and play a small but meaningful role in building a more humane and equitable world.

Core Competencies and Skills

- Embrace a global/international social and economic development and social welfare policy framework.
- Possess skills in critical analysis, understanding of the interdependency among nations, the inherently complex value and ethic

dilemmas that exist, theories and practices of international social work, and social and economic development.

- Demonstrate cultural and linguistic competencies appropriate for the populations being served.
- Demonstrate commitment to the protection of human rights and promotion of equality in an international context.
- Demonstrate sensitivity to the diversity of views on human rights issues.
- Possess skills in political advocacy, crisis intervention, immediate response to emergency situations, and brief therapy.
- Ability to assess needs, make decisions that ensure security and safety, and manage, monitor, and evaluate activities established for the betterment of international communities.
- Possess extensive knowledge and skills in community organizing, networking, teamwork, and relationship building among organizations providing services.
- Excellent verbal and written communication skills for an international audience.
- Skills in strategic planning for long-term development and/or disaster management.
- Demonstrate skills in research, policy assessment, legislative proposals, and response development appropriate to the respective country.
- Familiarity with the role of political structures, government, international organizations, and NGOs in international work.
- Possess technological skills that facilitate communication, accessibility, and availability of services to the international community.
- Possess specialized knowledge and skills in working with immigrants, refugees, and asylees.

Educational and Licensing Requirements

Educational and licensing qualifications for social workers working in an international context vary by country. Depending on the country, social workers can be employed in governmental agencies and NGOs including private, nonprofit, and faith-based agencies with a bachelor's (BSW), master's (MSW), or PhD degree in social work. Throughout the United States and its territories, many MSW programs have concentrations, specializations, emphasis, or certificates in international social work, which prepare students specifically for a career in international/global settings. Licensure in social work requires an individual to meet the respective country's standards for licensing, though many developing countries will not have such requirements.

Social workers in international/global settings provide services to vulnerable communities and their members through policy advocacy and practices on a micro, mezzo, and macro level. As a result, a high degree of knowledge, skills, and training are required to successfully meet the needs of these international communities.

Best Aspects of this Job

- Having the opportunity to live abroad and work with individuals, families, and communities from cultures worldwide.
- Gaining a better understanding of the interdependency of countries and contributing positively to strengthening those relationships.
- Expanding knowledge and experience with diverse cultures and developing cultural competency skills.
- Opportunity to advocate for equality, protection of human rights, and self-determination for all people globally.
- Opportunities for political advocacy on behalf of immigrants, refugees, and asylees.

Challenging Aspects of this Job

- Policy and practice changes on a global level may be difficult and slow.
- Working with victims of the immigration and refugee experience can be stressful, hazardous, and overwhelming.
- Knowing that sometimes domestic/U.S. policies are barriers to providing needed services to immigrants, refugees and asylees. The current political climate is punishing to undocumented immigrants.
- The heavy burden of being responsible for appropriate assessment and making decisions that affect children, youth, families, and communities.
- Being accepting of cultural practices that may be very different from your own.

- Difficulty in dealing with and seeing people who live without the basic necessities of life.

Compensation and Employment Outlook

War and conflict, economic issues, immigration, and refugee circumstances have contributed to the increased amount of international social work, both U.S. based and U.S. trained. The need for culturally and linguistically competent service providers in and out of the United States validates social work education and recruitment of social workers from diverse populations. The major shortage of social workers in the United States has led to a good employment outlook.

Salaries for individuals engaged in social work internationally/globally vary, depending on the country and organization that they are employed with. For instance, in the United States, the compensation for social workers who engage in U.S.-based international work may range from earning a median income of $38,000 annually (U.S. Department of Labor, Bureau of Labor Statistics, Occupational Outlook Handbook, 2008) to receiving only housing and a monthly allowance. In fact, a lot of international humanitarian work is done by volunteers.

Self-Assessment Checklist: Is this Job for Me?

- ☐ Do you have an interest in working on social issues that impact people internationally/globally?
- ☐ Do you think that you are able to work with people from diverse backgrounds, culturally and linguistically, and their communities?
- ☐ Are you passionate about political advocacy on behalf of immigrants, refugees, and asylees?
- ☐ Do you enjoy having a job where your work day is spent working with groups and organizations (e.g., governmental, NGOs) that embrace equality and protection of human rights?
- ☐ Would you be comfortable working under stressful and hazardous conditions?
- ☐ Do you have an assertive personality and are you comfortable dealing with conflict on an international/global level?
- ☐ Do you have an interest in living abroad and working with people to mobilize their communities?
- ☐ Are you interested in working with people suffering from disasters (e.g., earthquakes, hurricanes)?

☐ Are you willing to fight for marginalized families?

☐ Are you interested in the challenge of working with people from diverse backgrounds?

If you answered "yes" to seven or more of the above questions, then working in international/global settings might be the place for you!

RECOMMENDED READINGS/WEB SITES TO LEARN MORE

International Federation of Social Workers: www.ifsw.org/intro.html

International Social Work: www.isw.org/

Mapp, S. C. (2007). *Human rights and social justice in a global perspective: An introduction to international social work.* New York: Oxford University Press.

PayScale for Social Workers: www.payscale.com/research/US/Job=Social_Worker_(MSW)/Salary

Planet Social Work: www.planetsocialwork.com/

Reichert, E. (2007). *Challenges in human rights: A social work perspective.* New York: Columbia University Press.

Social Work Today magazine: www.socialworktoday.com/archive/swt_0105p14.htm

The New Social Worker online magazine: www.socialworker.com/home/Feature_Articles/Professional_Development_&_Advancement/How_to_Snag_a_Job_In_International_Social_Work/

International Social Work and Human Rights Exercise

One of the best ways to experience being a social worker in this setting is to travel. If you have never traveled to a foreign country, planning a trip is an exciting adventure. If the prospect of traveling alone is too intimidating, try going to a travel agency and explore the possibilities of joining a fixed tour to a country where you will be with a group of adventurers like yourself.

Participating in a Foreign Language Immersion Program will provide you with the experience of living with a host family while you are learning the language, culture, and history. This is an excellent way to actually be part of a community in a new country.

There are many programs that request help from volunteers to provide services to communities in need around the world. You may want to contact your own religious congregation to see if they have a program. Many social workers in this field had their own beginnings in volunteering for the Peace Corps (www.peacecorps.gov). If you visit the Peace Corps Web site, you will see all of the wonderful opportunities for international work available, with just a click of the mouse.

Happy traveling!

REFERENCES

Cox, D., & Pawar, M. (2006). *International social work: Issues, strategies, and programs.* Thousand Oaks, CA: Sage.

U.S. Department of Labor, Bureau of Labor Statistics. (2008). *Occupational Outlook Handbook 08–09.* [Online]. Retrieved April 17, 2008, from http://www.bls.gov/OCO/

13 Careers in Poverty and Homelessness

Americans in need are not strangers, they are citizens; not problems but priorities. —*Dr. Martin Luther King, Jr.*

The social work profession has a special dedication to assisting individuals and families who are living in poverty. This commitment is one of the features of the profession that sets us apart from other related disciplines. Other professions may charge fees for their services that many people cannot afford to pay, but social workers often work in agencies and organizations where the services are free or are offered on a sliding scale according to the client's ability to pay. People who are poor are often stigmatized and stereotyped as lazy or having no ambition. Many believe that poverty is due to a character defect in the individual. However, social workers understand, through research and work experience, that the causes of poverty are complex and multifaceted; that a combination of personal and environmental factors is often at play. Social workers believe that the desire to work and to contribute is universal. Social workers also believe in the power of government programs, such as social security, to lift millions of people (namely older adults) out of poverty.

When we refer to people living in poverty, we are talking about three groups:

1. The working poor (those making minimum wage).
2. The unemployed.
3. Those with deficits in human capital (lack of job skills and poor education).

Some people living in poverty might be homeless and others might be on welfare. Through research, we know that women, children, and people of color are overrepresented among the poor. We also know that there are a number of problems that contribute to an individual's ability to support themselves financially: lack of job skills and education; mental illness; poor health or disabilities; lack of affordable housing; substance abuse; women who are abused and battered; being a single mother; racial and gender discrimination; having a child who is ill; lack of child care and transportation; fluctuations in the economy and unemployment rate; and lack of jobs in the inner cities, rural areas, and various communities across this country. Thus, you will find social workers in every state working in various organizations and coalitions at the local, state, and federal levels to address these barriers and to create opportunities for people to be able to support themselves and their families.

INCOME ASSISTANCE CASEWORKER

In 1996, a major change in social welfare policy occurred when the Aid to Families with Dependent Children (AFDC) program was ended and replaced with a program called Temporary Assistance for Needy Families (TANF). Under TANF, welfare assistance is no longer an entitlement program and benefits are time limited and closely tied to work requirements. Since this new law was passed, a number of nonprofit and faith-based organizations started new programs and initiatives to focus on helping individuals leave the welfare system. These programs offer a variety of services such as job skills or vocational training; substance abuse treatment; educational programs focused on helping individuals complete high school, get their GED, or get into a community college; affordable housing programs; programs that focus on promoting marriage and preventing out-of-wedlock pregnancies; programs that offer help with transportation and child care; and new pilot programs that focus on helping low-income individuals accumulate assets or savings in order to purchase a home, start a business, or save for college. Individuals in these programs establish a savings account, which is then matched by public and private resources.

Social workers believe that a safety net is important so that, when individuals and families fall on hard times, they will at least have their basic needs met. You will find many social workers employed by the government who are charged with distributing cash assistance (e.g., TANF, supplemental security income [SSI]) and in-kind benefits (e.g., food stamps; public housing; supplemental food program for women, infants, and children, or WIC; Medicaid; State Children's Health Insurance Program, or S-CHIP) to eligible individuals and families. These social workers have various job titles such as eligibility service workers, income assistance social workers, human services caseworkers, and employment counselors. The following tasks are commonly performed by social workers to help people move out of poverty:

- Helping families in financial crisis receive benefits they are eligible for.
- Case planning and case management.
- Teaching clients about financial planning and budgeting.
- Providing job skills training.
- Providing opportunities for additional education and training that is required to compete in today's job market.
- Teaching clients the skills they need to get and keep a job (e.g., resume writing and cover letters, interviewing skills, dressing for interviews).
- Counseling and coaching skills (providing lots of encouragement).
- Facilitating support groups, mentoring programs, and/or workshops for participants.
- Providing services for children, such as childcare and early education programs (e.g., National Head Start Association and pre-k).
- Referring clients to other needed community services to address various barriers to employment (e.g., substance abuse treatment, housing assistance, vocational training programs, mental health treatment, battered women's shelter).

Core Competencies and Skills

- Financial planning skills and knowledge of the ever changing job market.

- Knowledge of interviewing techniques to obtain highly personal information.
- Understanding, compassionate, and nonjudgmental.
- Ability to perform basic arithmetic functions, including using decimals and computing percentages.
- Knowledge of the causes of poverty (both personal and environmental).
- Strong administrative and programmatic skills for those who want to run a program or become a program administrator.
- Ability to understand complex laws and policies to determine eligibility for various social welfare programs based on income.
- Strong coaching skills (need to be very encouraging).
- Crisis intervention skills.
- Knowledgeable about the many governmental and nongovernmental programs serving low income people.

Educational and Licensing Requirements

For most starting positions, in government and other settings, serving low income individuals and families, a master's degree is not required. A master's degree would be useful; however, if you would like to move into a supervisory or administrative position in the organization, or if you would like to work in public policy to advance sound economic policies that would be beneficial for this vulnerable population (e.g., ensuring the minimum wage is a livable wage and improved family leave policies).

Best Aspects of this Job

- Being there for a family who is experiencing a crisis of income in their life (e.g., loss of a job, mother fleeing domestic violence, major illness, having a child with a serious illness).
- Having the opportunity to provide or refer families to services that will enable them to gain skills or education so that they can live self-sufficiently.
- The satisfaction of serving people who are usually forgotten or marginalized.
- Having a job with predictable work hours.
- Good benefits, since this is typically a government job.

■ Having the opportunity to educate others about the causes of poverty and the importance of programs designed to increase opportunities for individuals and families living in poverty.

Challenging Aspects of this Job

■ Feeling that you are helping clients temporarily, but are not able to attack the root causes of poverty.

■ Dealing with the bureaucracy of the job and sorting through the many rules and regulations—lots of paperwork!

■ The lack of understanding and compassion for people who are poor in our society; blaming the victim mentality or feeling they are unworthy of help.

■ The politics of income: Legislators who pass laws that are meant to punish instead of assist people who are poor. The current political debate regarding whether undocumented immigrants should be eligible for public assistance.

■ Dealing with burnout.

■ Clients who are stressed and hopeless may see you as "the bad guy" or "part of the system" instead of as someone who is there to help them.

■ Seeing the effects of poverty on children and families.

Compensation and Employment Outlook

As shown in the Table 13.1, there are a wide range of salaries depending on the state or region of the country in which one resides, years of previous experience, and type of degree (undergraduate or graduate degree).

Self-Assessment Checklist: Is this Job for Me?

☐ Do you have a passion for helping individuals and families move out of poverty?

☐ Do you strongly believe in the value of economic justice for all people?

☐ Can you work with people who are living in poverty or on welfare and treat them with dignity and respect?

☐ Can you serve them without judgment?

☐ Do you believe that people have the right to basic needs such as food, shelter, and healthcare?

Table 13.1

SALARY RANGES FOR ELIGIBILITY CASEWORKERS IN SELECTED STATES, 2007

STATE	QUALIFICATIONS	SALARY RANGE FOR ELIGIBILITY CASEWORKERS (2007)
Texas	Education which demonstrates possession of the knowledge, skills, and abilities necessary for job performance. Professional experience in any of the following is helpful: social services, counseling, accounting, contracts, loan processing, tax preparation, and insurance.	$2,081.00 to $2,922.00 per month
Oregon	Bachelor's degree in behavioral or social science or closely related field, or relevant experience (1–3 years) in human services.	$2,530.00 to $3,672.00 per month
Illinois	Requires BA degree in psychology, sociology, anthropology, social welfare or a closely related field plus 1 year professional casework or crisis intervention experience in a social services agency.	$3,321.00 to $4,886 per month
Connecticut	Bachelor's or master's degree and 2 years experience providing social services to individuals and families in need. College training may be substituted for some years of general experience. Eligibility Services Worker (see #3 in the next column) requires 5 years of eligibility experience.	1. Social Services Trainee: $36,617 to $46,713 per year 2. Connecticut Careers Trainee: $38,371 to $48,813 per year 3. Eligibility Services Worker: $46,553 to $58,372 per year

Sources: 1. https://rm.accesshr.hhsc.state.tx.us/ENG/careerportal/default.cfm?
szUniqueCareerPortalID=fbc767e0-795a-412f-8897-431b08f314e8
2. http://oregon.gov/DHS/jobs/
3. http://work.illinois.gov/
4. http://www.das.state.ct.us/exam/bl_jobs_list.asp?F_Type_List=Exam

☐ Would you enjoy the challenge of helping a family leave welfare?
☐ Since change often takes some time, do you have the patience to work with this population?
☐ Are you a strong motivator, mentor, and coach?
☐ Can you work with people who are poor, and understand the causes of poverty, even if you have not experienced poverty yourself?
☐ Do you believe that the government has a role to play in combating poverty in our communities?

If you answered "yes" to seven or more of the above questions, then working in the field of income assistance might be for you!

RECOMMENDED READINGS/WEB SITES TO LEARN MORE

American Public Human Services Association: www.aphsa.org
Children's Defense Fund: www.childrensdefense.org
Economic Success Clearinghouse: www.financeproject.org/irc/win.asp
Ehrenreich, B. (2001). *Nickel and dimed: On not getting by in America*. London: Metropolitan Books.
The Institute for Research on Poverty: www.irp.wisc.edu
Joint Center for Poverty Research: www.jcpr.org
National Center on Children in Poverty: www.nccp.org
National Eligibility Workers Association: www.nationalnew.org
Rank, M. R. (2004). *One nation underprivileged: Why American poverty affects us all*. New York: Oxford University Press.
Shipler. D. (2005). *The working poor: Invisible in America*. New York: Vintage.

Income Assistance Caseworker Exercise

Test your knowledge

1. True or False
   The Unites States is the only industrialized country that does not have universal health care.
2. According to the U.S. Census Bureau, about ___% of the population were living in poverty in 2003.
3. True or False
   The poverty rate for children is higher than for any other age group.
4. True or False
   A worker making a minimum wage of $5.15 an hour would earn enough to be slightly above the poverty line.

5. Without social security, about ___% of elderly Americans would have incomes below the poverty line.
6. True or False
   Most families on welfare are large families, and mothers have more children in order to collect greater benefits.
7. In the typical or median state, TANF benefits in 2002 for a three person family totaled $___ per month.
8. True or False
   Poverty is more likely to happen to women than to men.
9. True or False
   Public assistance benefits provide a disincentive to work.
10. True or False
    The SSI program is set up primarily to provide cash assistance to people with disabilities.

Answers: 1. True; 2. 12%; 3. True; 4. False; 5. 50%; 6. False (average size of TANF family is 2.6 persons); 7. $355.00; 8. True; 9. False (since the benefits are too small for a family to live on, the majority of welfare recipients work); 10. True.

HOMELESS OUTREACH CASEWORKER

According to the National Coalition for the Homeless (2008), "It is a societal responsibility to provide safe, decent, accessible, affordable, and permanent housing for all people, including people experiencing homelessness, who are unable to secure such housing through their own means." When you work with the homeless, you are working with perhaps the poorest of the poor, those who have no home.

When most of us visualize someone who is homeless, the bag lady or disheveled man on the street begging for money usually comes to mind. However, the homeless population is extremely diverse, and the data may surprise you. In 2002, 41% of the homeless population included families, and 39% were children. Among the homeless you will find single-parent families, some escaping domestic violence; runaway youth; substance abusers; former foster youth; those with disabilities; the unemployed; individuals recently released from prison; the mentally ill; and veterans. Homelessness is not only a problem in the urban environment, but also in rural areas, where the majority of the homeless are families, single mothers, and children.

In recent years, there has been a move away from public housing projects which are often dilapidated and unsafe. Today, many homeless outreach caseworkers see the benefits of mixed income communities and are making efforts to help families establish a home in one of these communities (e.g., scattered site apartments).

Working with individuals and families who are homeless is very challenging and very rewarding. There are a variety of settings for social workers interested in this field. Perhaps the most common setting is the homeless shelter, where residents can stay temporarily while they are housed, fed, and provided with case management services. All shelters are different in terms of who they serve and the kinds of services they provide. For example, some shelters may serve only women and their children. The services provided on site may include anything from substance abuse treatment, parenting classes, GED or English as a second language classes, medical care, assistance finding employment, child care, and a variety of life skills classes. Clients will be referred to other services in the community that are not provided directly by the shelter, and the goal of many shelters is to assist residents in finding permanent housing. You are probably familiar with the domestic violence shelter and/or the Salvation Army shelter in your community. Another famous organization is Habitat for Humanity, which builds affordable homes for low-income individuals. Families must invest hundreds of hours building their home and the homes of others.

Many shelters and nonprofit organizations serving the homeless do outreach work by going where the clients are (on the streets), engaging them, and getting them into some form of temporary housing. More and more programs are using a "housing first" model, which centers on providing homeless people with housing quickly and *then* providing needed services. The idea is that people are more likely to participate in treatment when they feel safe and secure.

CAREERS IN RESEARCH

Some social workers with a strong interest in poverty and economic inequality choose to work at the macro level by conducting research. They enjoy doing research so that we can better understand the root causes of poverty and the best way to assist those who are poor or homeless. This is how we ensure that the interventions that we use with clients are "evidence based." A few of the many questions that can be answered through research include: What are the biggest risk factors for living in poverty? How many people are homeless in this country, and what are the demographics of homeless individuals? What are the barriers to people leaving welfare? What kinds of programs have been most successful in helping people leave poverty? What are the long-term outcomes of individuals who left the welfare rolls under the new welfare reform law? How many people experience hunger in the United States?

Social workers interested in conducting research typically work for universities, the government, nonprofit research organizations, and think tanks. Prominent organizations that conduct research in poverty include: National Poverty Research Center (University of Michigan at Ann Arbor); Institute for Research on Poverty (University of Wisconsin at Madison); University of Kentucky Poverty Research Center; West Coast Poverty Research Center; National Center for Children in Poverty (Columbia University); Economic Policy Institute; Institute for the Study of Homelessness and Poverty; Center of Hunger and Poverty (Brandeis University); Center for the Study of Urban Poverty (University of California, Los Angeles); American Public Human Services Association; Center on Urban Poverty and Social Change (Case Western Reserve University); Institute on Race and Poverty (University of Minnesota); Center on Budget and Policy Priorities; Rural Poverty Research Center; Urban Institute; and Poverty in America (University of Pennsylvania).

POVERTY ADVOCATE

After gaining a number of years of experience at the micro level, some social workers choose to move into an advocacy or policy making role. Social workers interested in advocacy are charged with educating the public about poverty and homelessness and influencing legislators to pass legislation at the local and national level that would help individuals and families in need. They would advocate for increased funding for community programs that serve the poor and homeless, particularly programs that focus on prevention. They would lobby legislators to strengthen important government programs for the poor such as Medicaid, SSI, WIC, and TANF. Social workers interested in this type of work might work for a legislator or an advocacy organization such as the National Alliance to End Homelessness, End Hunger Network, National Coalition for the Homeless, and the Coalition on Human Needs.

Social Worker Spotlight: Kristin Noel Ludwig, MSW
Community Action, Hillsboro, Oregon

My bachelor of arts degree in 1971 included concentrated study in French and Spanish. After working with people dealing with poverty in the social services world for 20 years, the urging of another social worker motivated me to combine theory and practice, and I returned to school in 1991. In 1994, received a master's degree in social work.

For the past 7 years, I have worked as the McKinney-Vento Student Advocate, a service partnership between Community Action, a nonprofit and the Hillsboro, Oregon, School District. I spend many of my days in the agency's family shelter (a 100-year-old house). The environment is sometimes chaotic and full of crisis, but it always offers a welcoming place for people to be listened to and accompanied as they reach goals for housing stability and renewed lives of self-sufficiency.

McKinney-Vento Homeless Education Act is a federal law mandating that all school districts identify and support students who are experiencing homelessness, high mobility, and housing insecurity to ensure school access and achievement. The best interests of children must be considered. In my role as advocate, I inform students, parents, and school staff of rights, expedite enrollment, and arrange transportation to the school of origin. The Act addresses best practices, which means dealing with students' emotional and health needs and linking to tutoring and resources for school success. I also find it crucial to dispel stereotypes of people in homeless situations; for example, when they are judged solely by their appearance. Students eligible for McKinney-Vento services are in temporary foster care; staying in family shelters, motels, cars, unheated garages; students who are doubled up with family and friends due to economic hardship; or students living in substandard housing, including many migrant camps. Some are unaccompanied youth who "sofa surf." Being in tenuous living situations weighs heavily on children and parents. The number of students dealing with the effects of poverty, including housing instability, is growing locally and nationally. Last year, school districts in Oregon counted more than 15,000 students who dealt with homelessness. The high cost of housing is an overarching theme and requires social policy solutions.

In practice, the transformational reality of the social work field acts on many levels.

Examples from my work include:

- **Individual.** Helping a student gain self-efficacy by making an agreement with her/him self to attend school regularly and complete homework.
- **Family.** Acknowledging a parent's walk toward recovery from substance abuse and the hard work of healing in the family.
- **Program.** Witnessing a teacher advocate for a student in foster care to not move schools again but be stable in their instruction, thus both teacher and student make strides.
- **Social Policy.** Organizing with others in my community of Washington County for our 10-Year Plan to End Homelessness, including financial support for emergency housing and more housing options that are sustainable and affordable.

What is valuable to me in this work? As social workers, we have a responsibility to impact change. In fact, that is our history, from participating in the tenement worker movement of the 19th century, to civil rights legislative action, and in solidarity with those who struggle for family wages, child care access, housing, and beyond. We build community and connections by our common values and actions.

I am inspired by the hope I see reflected in the eyes of students and families.

Core Competencies and Skills

- Knowledge of the housing market and housing options in your city or community.
- Understanding and compassionate.
- Nonjudgmental.
- Knowledge of the causes of poverty (both personal and environmental).
- Strong administrative and programmatic skills for those who want to run a program or become a program administrator.
- Knowledge of the laws and eligibility requirements for various federal housing programs.

- Strong coaching skills (need to be very encouraging).
- Crisis intervention skills.
- Knowledgeable about the many governmental and nongovernmental programs serving low-income people.
- Strong advocacy skills.

Educational and licensing requirements

For most starting positions in a homeless shelter, a Bachelor's degree is required. A master's degree would be useful if you would like to move into a supervisory or administrative position in the organization, or if you would like to work in public policy, to advance sound public policies that would be beneficial for this vulnerable population.

Best Aspects of this Job

- Helping a homeless family achieve stable housing that is safe and secure.
- Connecting people to available resources in the community where they can address various barriers to self-sufficiency.
- Working with individuals and families from diverse backgrounds, ages, and walks of life.
- Having the opportunity to advocate on behalf of homeless children and adults in your community and the need for affordable housing is rewarding.
- The satisfaction of serving a population that is often marginalized and misunderstood.
- Being able to work with a wide variety of individuals in the community to solve this problem, including city leaders and churches.
- You can specialize to some degree (e.g., work in a shelter for women and children, work in a program that does outreach for homeless or runaway teens).

Challenging Aspects of this Job

- Dealing with the myths and stereotypes that many people have about people who are homeless can be frustrating.
- Working to solve a problem that often seems very overwhelming on a large scale.
- Dealing with burnout.

- Trying to serve individuals who do not seem to want your assistance can be challenging (mentally ill, those who "choose to be homeless").
- Seeing the effects of homelessness on youth and adults can be really tough (e.g., witnessing what people need to do to survive such as prostitution, being without medical care, or being victims of crime and violence).

Compensation and Employment Outlook

Salaries for social workers working in homeless shelters, most of which are nonprofit organizations, will vary greatly from agency to agency and by state. Salaries will be higher for those who are in supervisory or administrative positions.

Self-Assessment Checklist: Is this Job for Me?

- ☐ Do you have a passion for helping homeless individuals and families find safe and affordable housing?
- ☐ Do you strongly believe in the value of economic justice for all people?
- ☐ Can you work with people who are living in extreme poverty and treat them with dignity and respect?
- ☐ Can you serve people living in poverty without judgment?
- ☐ Do you believe that people have the right to basic needs such as food, shelter, and healthcare?
- ☐ Are you comfortable working with individuals who are severely mentally ill or who are substance abusers?
- ☐ Since change often takes some time, do you have the patience to work with this population?
- ☐ Are you a strong motivator, mentor, and coach?
- ☐ Can you work with people who are poor, and understand the causes of poverty, even if you have not experienced this yourself?
- ☐ Do you believe that the government has a role to play in ensuring safe and affordable housing for low income people in our communities?

If you answered "yes" to seven or more of the above questions, then working with homeless individuals and families might be for you!

RECOMMENDED READINGS/WEB SITES TO LEARN MORE

Homelessness Resource Center: www.nrchmi.samhsa.org

National Alliance to End Homelessness: www.endhomelessness.org

National Association of the Education of Homeless Children and Youth: www.naehcy.org

National Center for Homeless Education: www.nche.org

National Coalition for the Homeless: www.nationalhomeless.org

National Low Income Housing Coalition: www.nlihc.org

Housing First, a year-long special reporting project from NPR News, which explores the housing dilemmas of Americans with special needs: www.npr.org/news/specials/housingfirst/

Kozol, J. (2006). *Rachel and her children: Homeless families in America.* New York: Three Rivers Press.

Vissing, Y. (2006). *Out of sight, out of mind: Homeless children and families in small town America.* Lexington, KY: University Press of Kentucky.

Homeless Outreach Caseworker Exercise

Case study

You are a social worker who has worked with the homeless for more than 10 years. Over the years, you have learned much about the struggles facing those who are homeless. For the past 2 years, you have been working with city officials and community leaders to build and develop a new homeless shelter for those with substance abuse problems, since this is a huge problem in your community. Countless hours have been spent designing this new program so that it is fresh and innovative and meets the unique needs of this population. The funding is also in place—a combination of grants, government funding, and private donations. However, a major problem arises when the city paper publishes a story about plans for this new shelter and it creates a firestorm of controversy. Many individuals and families who will be living near the new shelter are not happy and feel they were not consulted. They worry about the safety of their children because the individuals served by this shelter are drug addicts and alcoholics. They have started a petition and have been calling their government representatives protesting the development of this shelter. You quickly realize that the advocacy skills you learned in your social work program and on the job will be extremely useful, and you get ready to make a plan.

Questions

1. What thoughts and feelings come up for you as you read this case scenario?

2. Do you sympathize with the community members' concerns? Are their feelings valid? Why or why not?

3. What are your next steps? What can you do to overcome this obstacle at the community level?

4. In retrospect, what could have been done to avoid this problem?

5. One strategy would be to work with other concerned individuals and organizations to devise a media campaign to educate the public on this issue. What would your media campaign look like? What would be most effective? What message would you want to send? Be creative!

6. How could you address the stereotypes and misconceptions that many people have about homeless people and substance abusers?

7. How could you involve your clients in this effort?

REFERENCE

National Coalition to End Homelessness. *Core principles*. Retrieved June 4, 2008, from http://www.nationalhomeless.org/housing/index.html

14 Careers in Politics

Each time a person stands up for an ideal, or acts to improve the lot of others. . . . . she/he sends forth a tiny ripple of hope, and crossing each other from a million different centers of energy and daring, those ripples build a current that can sweep down the mightiest walls of oppression and resistance. —*Robert F. Kennedy (1925–1968)*

All social work is political. —**from book, *Affecting change: Social workers in the political arena* by *Haynes & Mickelson (2006)***

In chapter 1, we shared our observation that most people have a fairly limited view of exactly what social workers do. Many are surprised to learn that some social workers work in politics. In fact, there are a few members of Congress, such as Democratic Senators Barbara Mikulsky (Maryland) and Debbie Stabenow (Michigan), who have a degree in social work!

The social work profession has long recognized that to help people, change efforts must be directed at the individual, or micro level, as well as the macro level. An important part of macro social work is policy practice or political advocacy. Social workers who choose this career path work diligently to pass legislation at the local, state, or national level that benefits the individuals and families we serve and to defeat legislation that would be detrimental or harmful to our clients. Social workers in this field might work for an advocacy organization, a legislator as an aide or staffer, or a research organization, or "think tank," as a policy analyst. All social work programs accredited by the Council on Social Work Education are required to offer coursework in social welfare policy, which is a good place to begin learning about and preparing for this type of work.

Most people are surprised to learn that social workers have a rich history of working in a political context on behalf of various social causes and client populations. Since the profession's beginning, social workers have engaged in political advocacy in efforts to achieve social justice for the poor and disenfranchised in society. Some of the most politically active social workers were the settlement workers during the late 1800s and early 1900s. In their efforts to improve living conditions for the poor, they engaged in a number of political activities such as working to defeat corrupt ward bosses, campaigning for reform mayors, and influencing state and national legislation by collecting statistics and testifying before legislative committees.

During the Great Depression, social workers lobbied elected officials to adopt more humane policies for the millions thrown into poverty; these efforts contributed to the creation of the Social Security Act of 1935. During the 1960s, many social workers engaged in community organizing and worked to support the developing fight for welfare rights and civil rights. Today, social workers advocate on behalf of various issues in the political arena, including but not limited to, health care coverage for all children in the United States, better services for those in need of mental health treatment, poverty and homelessness, civil rights for gays and lesbians, and more federal funding for state children's protective services agencies.

Evidence of the social work profession's commitment to social change and political action on behalf of the poor and disenfranchised can be seen in the National Association of Social Worker's Code of Ethics, which states that:

> Social workers should engage in social and political action that seeks to ensure that all people have equal access to the resources, employment, services, and opportunities they require to meet their basic human needs and to develop fully. Social workers should be aware of the impact of the political arena on practice and should advocate for changes in policy and legislation to improve social conditions in order to meet basic human needs and promote social justice. (https://www.socialworkers.org/pubs/code/code.asp)

Many social workers would argue that "all social work is political," since our profession is so affected by the laws and policies that are passed at the local, state, and national levels. This chapter will look at a number of careers available to social workers who wish to work specifically in the political arena.

LOBBYIST

Many people have a negative reaction to the word "lobbyist;" immediately the image of a slick, high-powered professional who works for some corporate entity comes to mind. However, many nonprofit and human services organizations employ lobbyists to advocate for increased funding and other legislation to help the children, families, and adults that they serve. Lobbyists spend their days giving advice to the organization(s) they work for, regarding what is "politically feasible." Social workers are very idealistic and usually want big sweeping changes now! However, sometimes lobbyists must explain that smaller, incremental change is necessary, especially when an issue does not have widespread political support or when the bill includes a request for funding.

Lobbyists are experts at knowing how to draft legislation and how to get a bill passed into law. You may be surprised to learn that in Congress each year, only 5% to 10% of all bills that are introduced actually become law. As you can imagine, relationship building with legislators and key stakeholders is very important to being successful as a lobbyist. You must be able to engage in coalition building so that you can show legislators that there are a number of important people and organizations that support your bill. Lobbyists tend to be masters of persuasion. In other words, they are very skilled in determining which kinds of tactics will be most useful in getting various legislators to support this bill. Finally, lobbyists help support the organization in designing the overall legislative strategy which might include: letter writing campaigns, lining up people to testify at a congressional or public hearing, designing a creative media campaign (e.g, Web site content, informational flyers, radio/TV/newspaper ads, billboards), and guiding the grassroots work.

Examples of prominent advocacy organizations that employ lobbyists include the Children's Defense Fund, Child Welfare League of America, Human Rights Campaign, American Association of Retired Persons (AARP), National Alliance on Mental Illness (NAMI), Amnesty

International, National Alliance to End Homelessness, and the National Association of Social Workers (NASW) among many others.

CAMPAIGN WORKER

Sometimes social workers are hired (or volunteer) to work on a candidate's political campaign and are then offered a paid position if the candidate wins office (see "Legislative Aide" in this chapter). Campaign workers must be okay with doing a range of low-level (e.g., making copies and coffee) and high-level tasks. The fun part of working on a campaign includes working with other passionate political types and putting your all into getting your candidate elected. Campaign workers are responsible for making campaign materials, canvassing neighborhoods and talking to community members about your candidate, supervising a phone bank, organizing speaking events and rallies for your candidate, and fundraising.

Working on a political campaign is exciting work but involves long hours and entry-level pay. However, many young, idealistic individuals are willing to work under these conditions for the lure of a better and more prestigious position down the road.

Social Worker Spotlight: Greg Shufeldt, BSW, MSW
Political Social Worker, Missouri Pro-Vote Coalition, St. Louis, Missouri

I received both my BSW and MSW from St. Louis University (SLU). My time at SLU was rewarding, and I benefited from some nontraditional practicum opportunities that helped shape my practice. It was during my practicum opportunities as an organizer, advocate, and campaign worker that my love for political social work developed.

My first job after earning my MSW was working as a campaign manager for a local state representative campaign in Missouri. After this experience, I managed multiple campaigns for state legislature and helped organize St. Louis's city-wide and congressional campaigns. Ultimately, I became the political director for one of my old practicum placements, the Missouri Progressive Vote Coalition (Pro-Vote). Pro-Vote is a coalition of about 40 labor unions and community groups that work together to elect progressive candidates and advocate for progressive public policy solutions at the state and federal level. I am responsible for recruiting progressive candidates statewide and giving them the tools to run strong, successful campaigns.

People often assume that I have a background in political science, but I see the work that I'm doing as applying some of the central components of social work. I perform assessments on districts, neighborhoods, organizations, and candidates. I design intervention strategies and am constantly evaluating my own practice to improve. I work with consumers to speak up about injustices and am constantly working in coalitions with other community groups and individuals. I work in a small nonprofit setting, so I am grateful for the knowledge base about management, supervision, budgeting, and fundraising that allows Pro-Vote to thrive. Most importantly, I am doing political advocacy with the values and knowledge framework of a social worker.

What I really love most about my job is that it is not a job at all. It is a vocation and a passion of mine, and I get excited to go to work every morning to try to bring about change and social justice. My favorite part of my job is that I am a field instructor and get to train more political social workers. My own practicum experiences would have been strengthened by the presence and supervision of a social worker in the political realm. Some of my students have a passing interest in advocacy, whereas others have even thought about running for public office. Being a political social worker has been a great experience for me, and I am excited to share that experience and get more social workers involved in the political process.

LEGISLATIVE AIDE

Many legislators like to hire social workers to work as members of their staff since they are naturals at responding to constituent problems and concerns, which is very similar to casework. Social workers are also trained to be strong communicators and good listeners, which is important in this line of work. Legislative aides are vital to the work of a legislator.

During "session," they work extremely long hours to try to get important legislation passed and bad legislation defeated.

Typically, legislative aides are responsible for legislation in a specific area. For example, someone with a social work degree might be hired to be responsible for tracking/monitoring and working on any legislation dealing with health and human services. Aides spend their days meeting with individuals and organizations who are trying to influence your boss on a variety of bills or helping these same individuals and organizations draft legislation when your boss has agreed to sponsor a particular bill. Another important part of the job is called "constituent work." When people who live in your boss's district are having a problem, they sometimes call their legislator for help, and it will be your job to listen to their problem to see how you can assist them. Examples of problems might be an older adult who is being abused and not getting the help she needs from the state, or a family who lives in a housing project and cannot get their landlord to address the rat infestation in the building. Finally, you will be charged with writing speeches and testimony for your boss (who will get all of the glory!). This is a fun, fast-paced career for those with a passion for politics and a desire to be on "The Hill."

FIELD ORGANIZER

Many organizations employ field organizers to assist with building and organizing a grassroots movement around a particular issue (e.g., increasing the minimum wage, passing universal health care, legislation to address global warming). Field organizers must have excellent organizational skills and also be able to recruit and organize staff and volunteers in order to meet stated campaign goals.

Social Worker Spotlight: Elizabeth Alex, MSW
Lead Organizer/Manager, CASA of Maryland

I chose to pursue an MSW after serving as a Peace Corps volunteer in Mali, West Africa. I was searching for a profession that would build on the rewarding experience I had encountered as a Peace Corps volunteer, "helping people help themselves and each other" and addressing the systemic barriers faced by vulnerable communities in search of economic and social justice. A friend steered me in the direction of community organizing and suggested the MSW program at the University of MD, Baltimore. I graduated in 2002, and 6 years later (and another Peace Corps stint, this time in Ecuador, South America), I now manage a regional office serving, organizing, and advocating on behalf of low-income Latino and other immigrants. I spend about 40% of my time managing a day labor center, where recent immigrants (and some native Baltimoreans) are able to find dignified jobs at fair salaries, while also taking advantage of English classes, basic financial literacy, and legal assistance for unpaid wage cases.

But the other 60% of my work is what really motivates me— I coordinate a team of organizers and social work students to develop grassroots leadership, identify campaign priorities, and win real change for our members through advocacy and organizing efforts at the local, state, and national levels. One of my proudest moments has been watching an uneducated mother from Mexico in a lobby visit to Washington, DC—her powerful story, told proudly in broken English, had the entire room (including the congressman's chief of staff) in tears.

In just 1 year, I watched a group of four student leaders grow from innocent, frustrated high school students testifying in the state capitol to gain in-state tuition benefits for themselves and their peers, to mature professionals, able to articulate their position in front of U.S. senators and television cameras to rally a crowd of thousands in support of federal legislation to provide a pathway to citizenship for undocumented students. Some campaigns take years to win, but watching these leaders develop, grow, and show their inherent dignity and passion for justice continues to be a tremendously rewarding experience for me. This is what motivates me to continue advocating and organizing for social change. Si se puede!

POLICY ANALYST

Many research organizations and think tanks hire policy analysts to study various social problems and to evaluate the impact of legislation that has been passed. For example, in 1996, the Personal Responsibility and

Work Opportunity Act overhauled and changed the way the welfare system works in the United States. A policy analyst might conduct research several years later to see how this new policy affected families on welfare and whether it was helpful or harmful to the children and families served by this program. Social workers interested in this line of work must have strong research and statistical skills and an interest in working with large data sets. Some social workers might obtain a policy analyst position with a master's degree in social work (MSW), but a doctorate is often preferred.

LEGISLATOR OR PUBLIC OFFICIAL

There are a number of examples of social workers with a passion for politics and public service who run for public office at the local, state, or national level. Others get hired or appointed by presidents or governors to serve in important government positions within various state or federal agencies (e.g., health and human service agencies or important boards and commissions). Legislators come from many different walks of life and various educational backgrounds. There are social workers across the country who have won public office with a simple bachelor's degree in social work (BSW) or MSW degree. Others went down this path after getting an additional or joint degree in public policy or law, such as Elliott Naishtat (see his social worker spotlight below).

Social Worker Spotlight: Representative Elliott Naishtat, MSSW, JD., Attorney and Texas State Legislator

When I left New York City in 1967 to serve as a Volunteer In Service To America (VISTA) in Eagle Pass, Texas, I had no idea that I would wind up staying in Texas, pursuing graduate degrees in both social work and law at the University of Texas (UT) at Austin and, ultimately, serving as a long-standing member of the Texas House of Representatives. As I look back on my career, I realize that everything I've done is directly related to the community organizing and social work skills I developed fighting poverty in South Texas as a "front-line warrior" in Lyndon B. Johnson's War on Poverty.

Working at the grassroots level, trying to implement the policy of "eliminating the paradox of poverty in the midst of plenty in this nation," was always difficult and challenging. While we obviously didn't eliminate poverty, we did succeed in developing local leadership potential and maximizing the involvement of poor people in decision-making processes that directly affected their lives. Through community action programs, we gave people opportunities related to education, job training, and economic development. We helped people learn to negotiate the system. It was an exciting era in the history of this country, and it put me on a path to public service and advocacy for the needs of low-income families and vulnerable populations.

In the early 1970s, I studied community organizing at the UT School of Social Work, earning my MSW degree. My second-year field placement was with the Legislative Budget Board, which develops the proposed budget for all state agencies in Texas. This internship led to a 4-year stint as a member of the School of Social Work's field faculty, designing and running one of the nation's first legislative training programs for social work graduate students. The students worked on a full-time basis in the offices of state legislators serving on health and human services committees.

In the early 1980s, I attended the UT School of Law and earned my jurist doctor degree. Shortly thereafter, I accepted a position as staff counsel for a state senator who'd been one of my supervisors when I was a VISTA volunteer. I worked on legislation that enhanced protective services for elderly and disabled people, as well as for abused or neglected children. I drafted the Texas Anti-Hazing Act. I helped the senator become a champion for dropout prevention. I used my skills and training in social work and law to address at the state legislative level many of the same issues we'd focused on during the heyday of the war on poverty.

In 1990, while still working for the senator, I was approached by a group of people who thought I should run for a seat in the Texas House of Representatives, against a three-term incumbent from Austin who'd never lost. I told them that as a native New Yorker and ex-VISTA volunteer, I wouldn't have a chance. They convinced me that if I used my community organizing skills to put together an effective campaign, I might be able to win. I decided to give it a shot.

The incumbent had all the money. I had dedicated volunteers and a strong organization. We outworked the incumbent and I won by 10 percentage points. I took the oath of office in January 1991 and have been re-elected eight times. My focus in the Texas House of Representatives has always been on health, human services, housing, domestic violence, discrimination, and social justice. I work on issues that relate to the elderly, people with disabilities, children, minorities, women, and all vulnerable populations.

In 9 sessions, I've passed more than 150 bills, including the Braille Literacy Act, the Landlord-Tenant Security Devices Act, the Nursing Home Reform Act, the Newborn Hearing Screening Act, the Medicaid Simplification Act, and the Child Protective Services Reform Act. I've also passed bills that improved child labor law enforcement, enhanced crime victims' rights, and created a statewide guardianship program. In addition, I co-sponsored the Texas Anti-Stalking Act and Hate Crimes Act, as well as bills that increased protections for patients in health maintenance organizations and psychiatric, substance abuse, and rehabilitation facilities.

Although I never became a more traditional social worker, I've used my social work and legal training to carve out a career in the political realm. I work part-time as an attorney with a small law firm. And, every fall semester, I teach social policy and legislative advocacy as an adjunct professor at St. Edward's University. I am proud of what I do, face new challenges every day and sleep well at night knowing that I'm working in a meaningful way on behalf of people who occasionally need assistance from government or laws passed that will protect and enhance their rights.

If you would like to learn more about Representative Naishtat, visit: www.house.state.tx.us/members/dist49/naishtat.htm

Core Competencies and Skills

- Strong advocacy skills.
- Persuasive speaking skills which include the art of rhetoric, argumentation, and debate (e.g., testifying at a legislative or public hearing).
- Assertiveness and ability to stand your ground and fight for your cause.

- Knowledge of the legislative and political process (e.g., how a bill becomes a law).
- Strong writing skills (e.g., policy briefs, op-eds, talking points, written testimony, speeches).
- Knowledge of the research in your substantive area and how this informs the policy process.
- Ability to work with and build relationships with individuals and groups, including those with whom you have political differences.
- Ability to compromise when necessary.
- Skills in building coalitions around a particular issue.
- Patience—since legislative victories may take many years and the opposition is often better funded.
- Media skills (e.g., designing media campaigns and Web sites; writing press releases, brochures, informational handouts).

Educational and Licensing Requirements

Like any job, it helps to have connections, and this job can be fairly competitive because you will be competing with individuals from other backgrounds, such as law and public policy. However, there are a number of things you can do to get your foot in the door with political work such as:

1. Get your MSW from a school that has a concentration or specialty in macro or political social work.
2. During your social work program, do volunteer work or field work with an advocacy organization or in a legislator's office.
3. Find a MSW program where you can get a dual or joint degree and combine your social work degree with law or public policy.
4. Get political experience on your own time (e.g., volunteer for a political campaign, join a political organization, get involved in your community and network).
5. Do the front-line work before you move into lobbying or advocacy. For example, if you want to work to improve the child welfare system, it helps to begin working at Children's Protective Services so you have the requisite knowledge, experience, and credibility.

All of these things can get you a leg up on the competition!

Best Aspects of this Job

- Fast-paced and exciting environment; never boring.
- Working with smart, ambitious people from a variety of back-grounds, particularly law and public policy.
- The opportunity to work on an issue or for a legislator that you really believe in is very rewarding.
- Achieving a legislative victory that has the potential to benefit many people.
- Ability to hone your speaking and writing skills.
- Ability to move on to other exciting job opportunities in the political arena such as working for a legislator or national organization, or running for office yourself!
- Giving a voice to people in this country who are often marginalized and have little political power or clout.

Challenging Aspects of this Job

- Long hours and the work can be stressful, making it difficult to find a good balance between your work and personal life.
- Working in an environment that is often corrupt or unethical and does not always operate in the best interests of people.
- Doing the grunt work that is often involved in political or campaign work.
- Working with others who do not have the same values as social workers.
- Not getting too caught up in the power and glamour of the political world so that you lose your commitment to the issues you care about.
- Dealing with a loss after you have spent many hours fighting for an issue you are passionate about.
- Entry-level salaries, particularly when working in a legislator's office.

Compensation and Employment Outlook

Unfortunately, many jobs in the political arena have a reputation for being poorly compensated, having demanding long hours, and being a bit unstable. The common stereotype is a young person who is very smart, ambitious, and accomplished working on Capitol Hill or for a grassroots organization for low wages. To some degree, this is true, but not in all cases. It is true that some of these jobs are not as well compensated as they should be, because working for legislators and nonprofit organizations does not always pay a competitive salary. It is also true that when you have a job working for a political or issue campaign, the job can come to an end when the campaign ends or the legislator you work for leaves office.

However, what these jobs sometimes lack in salary, they more than make up for in exciting, invaluable experience. This is one career path where you often have to work hard and pay your dues until you are rewarded with a more lucrative or prestigious opportunity. Many social workers start out lobbying at the local and state level before working for a prominent national organization, where the salary (and pressure) is much higher. An entry-level job of $35,000 may lead, in 2 years or so, to a $60,000 to $70,000 yearly salary. Many of these jobs will require relocating to Washington, DC. Policy analyst positions often require a doctorate, and those salaries are typically commensurate with the higher level of education that is required.

Self-Assessment Checklist: Is this Job for Me?

- ☐ Would you describe yourself as a political junkie?
- ☐ Are there important political and social issues such as poverty, global warming, or healthcare that you are passionate about?
- ☐ Are you comfortable debating politics and issues with others?
- ☐ Do you follow current events closely and watch or listen to political or news shows (e.g., *Meet the Press*, National Public Radio, cable news, *The Daily Show with Jon Stewart*)?
- ☐ Are you politically active?
- ☐ Do you enjoy advocating for others?
- ☐ Are you passionate about legislation and the idea of creating social change on a larger scale?
- ☐ Do you believe in the power of government to improve conditions for various groups of people in this country and around the world?
- ☐ Do you have a strong and assertive personality?
- ☐ Would you be comfortable working in a setting with other professionals who were educated differently and may have different views and values than those of social workers?

If you answered "yes" to seven or more of the above questions, then working in the political arena might be for you!

RECOMMENDED READINGS/WEB SITES TO LEARN MORE

AlterNet: www.alternet.org

Center for Budget and Policy Priorities: www.cbpp.org

Child Welfare League of America: www.cwla.org

Children's Defense Fund: www.childrensdefense.org

The Daily Show with Jon Stewart: www.thedailyshow.com/

Haynes, K. S., & Mickelson, J. S. (2006). *Affecting change: Social workers in the political arena* (6th ed.). Boston: Allyn & Bacon.

Human Rights Campaign: www.hrc.org

Influencing State Policy: www.statepolicy.org

Karger, H. J., Midgley, J., Kindle, P. A., & Brown, C. B. (2007). *Controversial issues in social policy,* (3rd ed.). Boston: Allyn & Bacon.

Kush, C. (2004). *The one-hour activist: The 15 most powerful actions you can take to fight for the issues and candidates you care about.* San Francisco: Jossey-Bass.

NASW Pace—Building political power for social workers: www.socialworkers.org/pace/default.asp

National Alliance for Mental Illness: www.nami.org

National Association for Social Workers. (2006). *Social work speaks: National Association of Social Workers policy statements, 2006–2009,* (7th ed.). Washington, DC: NASW Press.

Shaw, R. (1996). *The activist's handbook: A primer.* Berkeley, CA: University of California Press.

Social Welfare Action Alliance—A National Organization of Progressive Workers in Social Welfare: www.socialwelfareactionalliance.org/

The Social Welfare Spot: http://socialwelfarespot.blogspot.com/

Careers in Politics Exercise

Test your Knowledge

1. True or False
   Part of the definition of social welfare policy includes anything a government chooses *not* to do which effects the quality of life of its people.

2. _____ is a framework of commonly held beliefs through which we view the world. How the world works? What has value? What is right?

3. True or False
   Politics is the process by which groups make decisions and can be observed in most organizations and institutions.

4. According to Social Work Professor Diana DiNitto, "Deciding what is to be decided" is the most important stage of the policy-making process. She is describing which of the following stages:

    a. agenda setting
    b. problem definition
    c. policy formulation
    d. legitimizing public policy
    e. policy implementation
5. Out of the tens of thousands of bills that get introduced in Congress, about ____ % become law.
    a. 75%
    b. 60%
    c. 20%
    d. 5%–10%
6. PAC's are an important player in the political process. What does this stand for? ____
7. True or False
    You cannot understand a current policy unless you understand the strategies used by policymakers in the past.
8. True or False
    Sometimes policy solutions change and evolve over time because of increasing knowledge about the causes of a social problem.
9. True or False
    Women have made sufficient progress in achieving equality with men in terms of government representation where almost half of U.S. lawmakers in Congress today are women.
10. True or False
    The United States does well compared to other countries when it comes to average voter turnout per year.
    How did you do?   My score: _____out of 10 points.

Answers: 1. True; 2. ideology; 3. True; 4. a; 5. d; 6. political action committee; 7. True; 8. True, a; 9. False; 10. False.

REFERENCE

Haynes, K. S., & Mickelson, J. S. (2006). *Affecting change: Social workers in the political arena* (6th ed.). Boston: Allyn & Bacon.

15 Careers in Community Practice

Although many social workers prefer to work with individuals and families, others choose to work at the community level. They use their social work training to revitalize and strengthen communities so that the individuals and families who reside there can be safe and thrive. Community social workers work to increase the social capital of a community. In communities with a substantial stock of social capital, you can see established and strong social networks, high levels of civic engagement, and community members who trust each other and help each other out. Participants' sense of self is less "I" and more "we."

Community work is integral to the social work profession because of its roots in community organization, planning, and development. The early social workers in the settlement house movement were strong community activists and saw firsthand how poverty and unsanitary conditions in urban ghettos affected the individual. Community practice has been an effective mechanism for resource accessibility and availability, particularly by marginalized, underserved, and underrepresented populations. Among indigenous cultures, the community has a personal meaning, in that it is a locus of control and the hook upon which individual identities hang. Social work promotes and embraces community practice in all its forms, shapes, and sizes as a way to bridge practice to both indigenous and contemporary cultures. It promotes the ideology and value that people are capable of organizing, uniting on a cause, and acting for themselves (Parachini & Covington, 2001). Curriculum of social work programs across the United States includes foundation content, courses, and concentrations in community practice. Indeed, community practice is central to social work education and professional practice.

This chapter will look at a few careers in community practice: planners, developers, organizers, and those who specialize in rural or urban communities.

COMMUNITY PLANNER

Community planners use a systems framework to examine the kinds of needs that exist in a community and devise plans to fill functions that are lacking. Community planners often conduct community needs assessments to determine gaps in services and then balance areas where there is inequity and a lack of resources. Community planners often work in city or county government.

Social Worker Spotlight: Odis Dolton, MSSW
Assistant Director for Finance, City of Abilene,
Abilene, Texas

My career in social work has covered a variety of fields of practice. I was a clinical social worker at the Abilene State School, a residential care facility for the mentally disabled and dual diagnosed adult males and females. I worked for Children's Protective Service (CPS) as a caseworker, supervisor, and program director. I also worked in day care licensing and foster care/adoptions during this time. I acquired my master's degree while working for CPS.

I have worked for the City of Abilene for 8 years now. I started as the assistant director for administrative services and now serve as the assistant director for finance.

As a professional, I always found ways to give back to the communities where I lived. I have served on boards and committees for the United Way, the American Red Cross, the Girl's Scouts, the Boy's Scouts, The National Children's Center for Illustrated Literature (NCCIL), the Juvenile Justice Board, The Fellowship of Christian Athletes, 100 Black Men of America Inc., and the African American

---

Leadership Committee. I have worked with the social work programs in my area, supervising social work student interns, in efforts to use the community as a learning lab for social work students.

I am one of the founding members and current vice chairman of a local nonprofit organization called Interested Citizens of Abilene North (I-CAN). Our goal is to revitalize communities and help community groups grow, develop, and serve their communities. We meet monthly and plan activities that include: community clean ups and health fairs; African American college workshops; tours to historically black colleges and universities; supporting youth groups and Juneteenth celebrations; work with local law enforcement to eradicate drug sales, prostitution, and crime; annually recognize neighborhood heroes and community leaders at luncheons; work with the local school district to solve problems; and much more!

I am also one of the founding directors and chairman of Neighborhoods in Progress (NIP). This is a local nonprofit with a mission to rebuild neighborhoods so low to moderate income citizens will have access to safe, decent, and affordable housing; to enhance quality of life for the elderly; to prevent and reduce homelessness; to revitalize neighborhoods; to enhance the physical environment of Abilene; and to enhance the economic well being of all citizens.

Finally, I am the chairman and founding member of Connecting Caring Communities (CCC). This is a community nonprofit that replicated the Shreveport-Bossier City Community Renewal program in Louisiana. Our mission is to systematically rebuild the human relationships needed to sustain community health using a neighborhood-based strategy.

I think I am a good example of a social worker who is committed to community-based social work through empowering communities and local grassroots efforts.

COMMUNITY DEVELOPER

Community developers use entrepreneurial skills to generate funding for needed community resources to enhance the social environment. There is a strong focus on urban renewal, asset building, community revitalization, and sustainability. The kinds of projects community developers typically focus on include affordable housing, schools, public transportation, health services, and recreational centers. Community social workers might also help to create a community development corporation (CDC), which is a community-based organization that serves low-income communities. CDCs are usually partnerships between business and government, though they are governed by a community board. There is a strong focus on citizen participation and keeping the profits from the CDC in the community it is serving.

Social Worker Spotlight: Amy Krings-Barnes, BSW, MSW
Community Police Partnering Center, Cincinnati, Ohio

I received my bachelor's degree in social work from Xavier University in Cincinnati, Ohio. I minored in peace studies and women and minority studies. I was attending Xavier when Cincinnati experienced civil unrest and riots in many communities, which were protesting the Cincinnati Police Department.

For my master's degree in social work, I attended the University of Michigan in Ann Arbor. There I concentrated in community organization and the management of human services.

After graduation, I returned to Cincinnati with the goal of working to improve race relations—particularly police/community relations. I took a job at a new nonprofit organization called the Community Police Partnering Center. The mission of the Partnering Center is, "In partnership with community stakeholders and members of the Cincinnati Police Department, the Community Police Partnering Center will develop and implement effective strategies to reduce crime and disorder while facilitating positive engagement and increased trust between the police and neighborhoods." In other words, community members and police officers are asked to come together as peers to problem-solve. Therefore, arrest was no longer the primary tool for police to reduce crime, and it gave citizens greater influence on how their neighborhoods are policed.

My work at the Partnering Center allows me to practice community building, training, and problem solving. I work in many neighborhoods with a broad range of demographics. This excites me. I deeply enjoy spending my time with many types of people as we work together on a common goal such as reducing drug sales, prostitution, domestic violence, or blighted buildings.

In 2006, reducing gun violence in Cincinnati became a priority for the Partnering Center, and therefore my work became more focused in fewer neighborhoods and on this one issue. In partnership with community groups and residents, we launched a campaign called "CeaseFire Cincinnati" in two pilot neighborhoods, and in 2008, we expanded to a third neighborhood. One unique aspect of this model is that it depends on peer-mentoring by outreach workers who in many cases have either been shot, or have shot someone else in the past. At some point in the outreach worker's life, they changed their lifestyle and now work to give back to the communities that they robbed from. They conduct conflict mediation and also have a caseload of people at the highest-risk to engage in gun violence.

My role is to engage the community and faith-based leaders to challenge the norms and expectations of the community as they relate to violence. One of the most visible aspects of my job is the organization of "shooting responses" to every shooting that results in injury in my three assigned neighborhoods within 72 hours. I believe in the efforts of this campaign, and the statistics suggest that it is having a positive effect. Still, although lives are being saved, there is still too much violence and at times this can feel overwhelming. I recognize the need for self-care and the maintenance of a supportive community in order to stay positive and focused.

My job does not require a social work background. Despite this fact, I believe that my social work education prepared me to do well in micro and macro practice. For example, my social work field internships allowed me to build relationships with many of the people who are involved in community building and police-community relations. I am able to facilitate a meeting or small group. I can listen to individuals and understand their self-interest and their needs. I understand how my daily work effects not just individuals and communities, but also impacts policy and culture on a broader scale. At the same time, I recognize that larger structural issues influence individuals and their choices.

Social work training has also opened doors for my future. This past year, I began adjunct teaching at Xavier University, and I love it. I now have an interest in pursuing a doctoral degree.

I am grateful for my social work degree and I believe that its combination of theory and practice has made me a better change agent, organizer, and leader.

COMMUNITY ORGANIZER

While community planners and developers use nonconflictual approaches, community organizers embrace a conflict model. Community organizing is based on the philosophy that powerful people and institutions often exploit the community for their own interests, and that those with power never surrender it voluntarily. Community organizers bring together coalitions of people in the community (e.g., citizens, neighborhood associations, churches) to address social problems in their community, assist them in developing their own solutions, and taking on the "powers that be." Examples of issues that can be addressed through community organizing include the following:

- Police brutality.
- Rights for immigrants.
- Improving substandard schools.
- The need for affordable housing.
- Preventing a big-box store from coming to town and threatening local businesses.
- Challenging predatory lending.
- Fighting a powerful developer whose project would harm the environment and the people living there.

Social Worker Spotlight: Trina Scordo, Senior Organizer, Change to Win Labor Federation, MSW student, Monmouth University, West Long Branch, NJ International and Community Development Concentration

My current work focuses on developing strategies with low-wage workers to build a worker controlled union and gain leverage at the collective bargaining table. This includes developing a supportive community movement which holds the employers and developers accountable for environmental issues, workplace health and safety, and issues such as workforce housing and transportation. In addition, many of the low-wage workers are immigrants. Therefore, working to eliminate the stigma of labels such as undocumented or illegal is central to this work. Every worker deserves a safe and healthy work environment, as well as a living wage and full health benefits. The formation of a worker organizing committee that builds solidarity among various groups and organizations shifts the balance of power to often marginalized groups.

Through this work, I have had the privilege to work with people from El Salvador, Mexico, and Ethiopia. Through the political struggles in their home countries, these workers taught me how to build solidarity and community. Social work is, in actuality, social justice work. Focusing on a framework of human rights and economic justice is what excites me most. More importantly, the opportunity to work with communities to make change is a revolutionary and transformative process. Communities work collectively to address legislative, policy, and regulatory issues in the areas of workplace health and safety, environment and land use, workforce housing, and transportation.

Through the master's degree in social work program at Monmouth University, I was afforded the opportunity to travel to Chile and live in a community called La Pincoya. This experience revolutionized me. I met trade unionists and community activists who had continued to organize during the vicious and violent Pinochet dictatorship. Many of the people whom I met and lived with had family members who were tortured and disappeared. This experience brought me back to my initial desire in life: to work in a global grassroots movement for social and economic justice.

I did not come to social work through a direct route. In 1996, I graduated from American University in Washington, DC with a bachelor of art in political science. By that time, I had had been part of several election campaigns, a legislative intern on capital hill and worked in a campaign finance office of a senior democratic senator. There was always something amiss for me in this work. I wanted to make change with people, not for people. I was struggling to find a model for change that engaged working class and poor communities as decision makers, not only recipients of services. Chile and the MSW International and Community Development track at Monmouth University have helped me to discover this work.

SOCIAL WORK IN URBAN COMMUNITIES

Unfortunately, for many Americans, community means living in an urban area with all the convenience of modern life as well as a high unemployment rate, substandard public schools, high rates of poverty, crime, gang violence, and less likelihood of strong social networks of neighbors caring for each other. Social workers who work in urban settings may focus on all of these areas of practice, or work with a particular racial or ethnic group within the community. Regardless of the social worker's interest, working in urban communities provide opportunities for growth and the sharpening of one's social work knowledge and skills.

RURAL SOCIAL WORKER

Rural social workers are central to communities in remote areas who struggle with issues of accessibility and availability of services. They commonly work with communities who are in poverty to improve infrastructure and service delivery. These social workers provide primary social services, including case management, referral, prevention and education, crisis intervention, specialized treatment (e.g., substance abuse), and others. Because of small populations and proximity of the living arrangements in rural areas, confidentiality may be an issue that rural social workers have to deal with on a continuous basis.

Core Competencies and Skills

- Ability to take risks and recognize the scarcity of resources and resistance of people to change.
- Value confidentiality and the dynamics of the community, particularly in rural communities.
- Strong entrepreneurial skills and knowledge of community development.
- Ability to work with people from diverse communities by age, gender, race/ethnicity, sexual orientation, rural versus urban areas, immigrants, and so forth.
- Knowledge and skills in conducting a community needs assessment.
- Understanding of the power patterns in the community and methods for motivating, empowering, and challenging people to act on their common interests.
- Understanding of any special needs or circumstances in rural communities.

- Ability to be creative in facilitating change, mediating conflict, and bringing coalitions of people together.
- Demonstrate cultural and linguistic competencies appropriate to the populations served, including immigrants and refugees.
- Ability to facilitate social action and change behind the scenes and allowing members of the community to be "the leaders."
- Possess technological skills that facilitate communication, accessibility, and availability of services to the community.

Educational and Licensing Requirements

Throughout the United States and its territories, many master's in social work education programs have concentrations, specializations, emphasis, or certificates in community social work practice which prepare students specifically for a career in community settings whether it is rural, urban, or suburban. There are usually no licensing requirements for social workers who work at the community level, though this varies by state.

Best Aspects of this Job

- Mobilizing an entire community to act on their own behalf to bring about social and economic change.
- Working with people from urban, suburban, and rural communities.
- Expanding knowledge about and experience with diverse cultures and developing cultural competency skills.
- Opportunity to advocate for equality, accessibility, and availability of services to remote communities.
- Opportunities for political advocacy for all community members, particularly those from underserved and underrepresented communities.

Challenging Aspects of this Job

- Motivating an entire community to act can be difficult and slow.
- Gaining the trust of the community (if you are an "outsider").
- Dealing with the political patterns of the community may be difficult.
- Uniting the community to pursue common goals may be difficult to achieve.

■ The heavy burden of being responsible for appropriate assessment and making decisions that affect community members.

Compensation and Employment Outlook

Diversity in community membership composition and locations (e.g., rural areas, inner cities) has contributed to the increased visibility of community organizers, planners, and developers. The need for culturally and linguistically competent service providers in communities validates social work education and recruitment of social workers from diverse populations. The major shortage of social workers in the United States results in a good employment outlook, especially in rural settings. Community social workers tend to be employed by the government and various non-profit community organizations.

Salaries for community social workers vary according to state and organization. For instance, community organizers may earn a median income of $31,000 annually (U.S. Department of Labor, Bureau of Labor Statistics, Occupational Outlook Handbook, 2008–09). However, there are also community organizers who are volunteers. Similarly, rural social workers most often make the lowest salaries by comparison.

Self-Assessment Checklist: Is this Job for Me?

☐ Do you have a strong interest in working on community issues?

☐ Do you think that you are able to work with people from diverse backgrounds, culturally and linguistically, in the context of their communities?

☐ Are you passionate about policy advocacy on behalf of communities?

☐ Do you enjoy having a job where your work day is spent facilitating community action?

☐ Would you be comfortable working under stressful and hazardous conditions?

☐ Do you have an assertive personality and are comfortable dealing with conflict on a community level?

☐ Can you be creative in building relationships, developing programs, and making services available and accessible?

☐ Do you embrace the perspective that people need to live in a strong and healthy community in order to reach their full potential?

☐ Do you have strong leadership skills?
☐ Can you train and empower others to be leaders?

If you answered "yes" to seven or more of the above questions, then working in a community setting might be for you!

RECOMMENDED READINGS/WEB SITES TO LEARN MORE

Community Based Social Work: www.scn.org/cmp/modules/adv-sw.htm
Alinsky, S. (1971). *Rules for radicals*. New York: Random House.
Association for Community Organization and Social Administration: www.acosa.org
COMM-ORG: http://comm-org.wisc.edu/The Community Organizing Toolbox: www.nfg.org/cotb/ or www.nfg.org/cotb/07whatisco.htm
Community Organizers Guide, Ability Maine: www.abilitymaine.org/rosc/cog.html
Community Practice: A Training Ground for Social Work Students: www.nova.edu/ssss/QR/QR6-1/jennings.html
Community Development Network: www.cdnportland.org
Homan, M. S. (2008). *Promoting community change: Making it happen in the real world* (4th ed.). Belmont, CA: Brooks/Cole.
Media and Process Educational Films & Chicago Video Project (Producer), Baldwin, A. (Narrator). (1999). *The democratic promise: Saul Alinsky and his legacy*. [Documentary Film]
National Public Radio story (3-11-08), "Community Organizer Fights for Immigrants.": www.npr.org/templates/story/story.php?storyID=88083529&sc=emaf
Putnam, R. D. (2001). *Bowling alone: The collapse and revival of American community*. New York: Simon & Schuster.
Salomon, L. R. (Ed.). (1998). *Roots of justice: Stories of organizing in communities of color*. San Francisco: Jossey-Bass.
Sen, R. (2003). *Stir it up: Lessons in community organizing and advocacy*. San Francisco: Jossey-Bass.

Community Practice Exercise

You are a social worker employed as the director of human services for the state of Vermont. There has been a recent influx of immigrants from the countries of Ethiopia and Somalia to several small towns in your state. The immigrants have been arriving by the busload; one to two buses a month for the past several months. The state of Vermont has very little experience with immigration issues and cultural diversity. The mayors of the small towns are very concerned about this rapid and large influx of "outsiders" and the pressures this puts on their local budgets and town services.

They have appealed to the Governor for assistance and the Governor asks you for a solution.

Questions

1. What additional information would you need before implementing an intervention plan?
2. With whom would you consult and why?
3. Briefly describe two possible approaches in addressing this problem: (1) one approach that could be implemented at the local level; and (2) another plan that could be implemented at the state level.
4. The Governor has told you to hire one full time staff person to assist you, however, whatever remedy you come up, no additional funding will be available to increase the budget of the local towns. Would this impact any of your recommendations, and if so, how?

REFERENCES

Parachini, L., & Covington, S. (2001). Community Organizing Toolbox: A Funder's Guide to Community Organizing. [Online]. Retrieved May 1, 2008, from http://www.nfg.org/cotb/

U.S. Department of Labor, Bureau of Labor Statistics, Occupational Outlook Handbook, 2008–2009.

16 Leadership in Human Service Organizations

Above all, we need leaders who will not accept that misery and deprivation are inevitable, for failure to act to ease suffering is a choice, and when we have the ability to choose, we have the power to change. *—Intrator & Scribner, LEADING from Within, 2007*

Some social workers are natural leaders and aspire to work in a leadership role, while others develop this expertise through experience, education, and training. Social workers perform leadership roles in various ways such as sitting on a board of directors, serving as a supervisor or executive director of a government or nonprofit organization, working as a community planner/organizer, being active in a professional organization (e.g., the National Association of Social Workers [NASW] or the Council on Social Work Education [CSWE]), or working in public policy. Being a good leader is hard to define, but we know it when we see it! However, strong leaders help define the mission and vision of an organization or cause, set high standards for strong performance and competence, and inspire others to strive for excellence. They set the tone and provide direction. They are politically savvy and have strong managerial skills. They persevere through good times and bad.

The traditional career path for many workers, in general, is that through the course of their experiences in various job settings, they have acquired a knowledge base and developed the skills eventually preparing them to assume a position of leadership within an organization. This path is no different for social workers. Working in various positions within social service delivery systems, over a period of time, is an excellent avenue to building a career path where you are eventually prepared to assume an administrative position (e.g., supervisor, program coordinator, division chief, executive director).

Many social workers prepare for a leadership role by pursuing a course of study in a master's in social work (MSW) program that specializes in administration, management, supervision, or organizational consulting. The MSW program approach to acquiring the knowledge and skills to be an effective leader is a more conscious choice of career goal.

ADMINISTRATOR

Administrators may work in government agencies, private companies, or for profit or nonprofit social service agencies. Administrators coordinate and direct the many support services that allow organizations to operate effectively, and as such they have a wide range of responsibilities. Administrators are responsible for the day-to-day operations of an organization and their duties may include:

- Developing services and programs.
- Hiring and supervising employees.
- Recruiting, training, and managing volunteers.
- Fundraising.
- Communicating with media.
- Overseeing community outreach.
- Maintaining budgets and payroll.
- Managing information and communication systems.
- Record keeping.
- Procurement of supplies and materials.
- Overseeing the secretarial and housekeeping staff.
- Security and parking.
- Contract negotiation with other service providers.

The exact role of an administrator will depend, in a large part, on the size and structure of the organization. In larger agencies (e.g., the department of social services for a city or county), a "first line" administrator typically would report to a "mid-level" manager, who in turn answers to the executive director of the department or organization.

In larger organizations, some of the roles described above (e.g., overseeing volunteers or fundraising) may be handled by separate individuals; read on for more about those specific functions.

EXECUTIVE DIRECTOR

In small organizations (e.g., a local nonprofit), executive directors may oversee all day-to-day support and operation services as described above. Executive directors often report to an organization's board of directors, who are responsible for creating the mission and goals of the organization. As such, executive directors are often concerned with making sure that the organization's programs and services are keeping with its mission and are responsive to the needs of the community.

Social Worker Spotlight: Laura Elmore Smith, LMSW Executive Director, Crime Prevention Institute, Austin, Texas

I have known since I was in the tenth grade that I wanted to be a social worker. The therapist my parents sent me to when they got divorced had a degree on her wall that said "MSW." My goal was to be a therapist and work with families in my own private practice. I decided to pursue my MSW, so I went to school and majored in psychology (I wasn't aware at the time that there was such a degree as a bachelor's degree in social work [BSW]) and went from there directly into the MSW program. Through some enlightening course and field work, and some great relationships with professional and academic mentors, my perspectives, worldview, and goals really shifted during that 2-year program. I entered the MSW program with every intent to graduate as a clinician who would go on to do private psychotherapy, and I graduated wanting nothing more than to dedicate my professional life to making changes in the criminal justice system and those affected by it.

My current position is executive director of the Crime Prevention Institute, a small nonprofit organization whose mission is to break the cycle of crime in those transitioning from incarceration to

---

communities. In short, we provide education, information, support, and job placement assistance to people leaving jail or prison and returning to Austin. Our goal is to help guide them toward law abiding productive lives again, sometimes for the first time in their lives. Our entire agency is located inside of a state jail so that we are closer to our clients and are able to work within the system in which they are incarcerated. I started out doing direct services work—I never saw myself as an ED, but now that I'm here, I am absolutely in love with it.

I believe so strongly in our mission and in our case management philosophy, part of which states: "We believe in the inherent worth and dignity of each individual client, no matter the crime or past behavior." That is not to say we always like their behavior, or even find some of our clients easy to be around. But, the successes. . . . while small to some of us. . . . are phenomenal. The client who gets his first job at age 35 because he's been dealing drugs his whole life—that kind of change in a person's life, and the bravery it takes to swim upstream like that astounds me. The client who gets sober and learns to be a father again once his daughters are grown, but can acknowledge that they don't know him anymore. . . . that kind of strength and self-honesty takes my breath away. I love working on behalf of those the rest of society has forgotten, or would like to forget. Working with these men and women in a direct services capacity was difficult and rewarding and challenging and wonderful. Being the executive director means it is my job to support those working in that capacity, to bring awareness to this important social issue, and to build effective community relationships that will help solve the complex problem of prisoner re-entry in Texas. It also allows me to set the values, tone, and environment for excellence in service and social work ethics. I am so very lucky to have a job I love so much.

PROGRAM MANAGER

The role of a program manager is an example of a "mid-level" management position within an organization. Program managers have oversight responsibility in very discrete areas of social service delivery. They may be responsible for the creation and development of a new program (e.g., initiating a crisis hotline for an agency) or be responsible for improving existing services (e.g., increasing an agency's evening and weekend hours of operation to improve client participation). At times, a program manager may even be the person who conducts the program.

Program managers or coordinators also often utilize skills in program assessment and evaluation. They examine if services are being delivered in the most cost efficient and cost effective manner, and they evaluate program outcomes to ensure that the goals and objectives of the services are being met. Programs that can prove their effectiveness and positive impact on a community in concrete, measurable terms are more likely to get funding; thus program assessment and evaluation is critical to the budget allocation and funding resources of an organization.

Social Worker Spotlight: Mary Kiernan-Stern, LCSW Arlington Hospital, Arlington, Virginia

After graduating with a liberal arts bachelor's degree, I worked as a crisis counselor for 4 years at a community teaching hospital. Over the course of time on the job, I had been given more responsibilities for supervising the work of the clinic that I always met successfully. I had received excellent training and mentoring in my direct service work, and was encouraged by my director, also a social worker, to pursue an MSW degree. I thought I would like to broaden my knowledge of social work practice and learn new skills in working with people. I specialized in community organization as my major focus, and took courses in a minor specializing in employee assistance programs.

This combination of course work prepared me to develop my supervisory and administrative skills giving me a depth of understanding on how organizations operate through various group processes, formal and informal communication structures, and effective and ethical leadership. I was prepared with information regarding grant writing, developing budgets, recruitment and retention of employees, conflict negotiation, mediation techniques, program development, and research and evaluation tools.

When I completed my MSW program, I relocated to another state and within a short time I interviewed for a director of social work position that became available at a local hospital. Not only did I land that job, but the hospital administration also gave me oversight of another department, the onsite Employee Day Care Center. Based on these additional responsibilities, I was able to negotiate a higher salary. Without a doubt, my previous hospital-based experience, and my specific course work and field experience in my MSW program certainly prepared me for this new administrative role within a health care organization.

ORGANIZATIONAL CONSULTANT

Many small and large agencies hire or "contract" a professional who has expertise in "growing" organizations. The executive board of an organization may decide in their strategic planning process, for example, that they need to pursue new directions of obtaining funding in order for their organization to continue to provide services to the community, or to expand the mission of the agency, and offer new or additional services. The executive board then seeks to hire, as a consultant or paid staff member, a person who specializes in fundraising and grant writing, or who may be an effective lobbyist in obtaining government contracts.

Another organization may be experiencing a high rate of staff turnover, which is disrupting the delivery of services to clients. To solve these types of organizational problems of the agency, the executive director will bring in an organizational consultant to assess and analyze the agency's strengths and weaknesses. These job roles are easily filled by social workers who have been trained in working with organizations and in organizational development.

PUBLIC RELATIONS/MEDIA RELATIONS

Social workers who have knowledge of public relations and working with various media outlets can help their organizations in communicating a message for specific agendas related to the organization's functioning. Social workers in public relations require skills in persuasive speech and in communicating a message with only three or four major points to a targeted audience. Media campaigns are coordinated efforts through multiple points of influence to communicate with and persuade people, e.g., to use or reuse a service or product, or to take action regarding a specific issue or need. Working in public and media relations requires skill in understanding what type of communication activity would give the best result in "getting the message out."

Some of the activities in this area could include writing and sending action alerts regarding an important issue up for vote in Congress or the State legislature; preparing written testimony, or an issue brief, to help educate government representatives on specific issues or funding needs regarding such areas as mental illness or child welfare; or holding a press conference to announce a new program or respond to a particular community concern.

Large health and human service organizations have internal public or community relations departments. Social workers in this role often assist in developing internal media campaigns during times of large scale transition and change in order to preserve organizational stability, resources for employees and clients, and as marketing tools to promote the organization's services and programs.

Media tools include direct marketing appeals through regular mail, E-advocacy, event sponsorship, television and radio, Web pages, word of mouth, and print media. Public relation skills require knowledge of how to work with news organizations and their communication outlets.

Social workers are perfect for this job because they focus on the issues and concerns of people. Social workers understand what people want to know and how to communicate with them because of their professional knowledge of human behavior and the social environment.

VOLUNTEER SERVICES DIRECTOR

This management position is often under the umbrella of an organization with an established administration hierarchy. An administrative role in the recruitment, retention, and professional development of volunteers is an essential and critical position for many organizations that rely on volunteers for a variety of activities, ranging from helping with day-to-day operations to the delivery of direct services to clients and communities. Social workers employed in this area must have skills in general management, budget development, grant writing, and fundraising.

Meals on Wheels programs are an excellent example of the crucial role of a volunteer services director. The volunteer services director may be paid by the local public social service agency to administer this program, and he or she may be given a budget for the kitchen materials and food supplies. However, without effective leadership in developing and maintaining a pool of quality volunteers who prepare the meals and pick up and deliver the meals to those in need, such programs could not exist.

Social workers employed in this area must have general management skills as well as skills in budget development, grant writing, and fundraising.

FUNDRAISER

As you can see from the employment opportunities listed above, raising money and writing grants for many different types of organizations is a primary responsibility for administrators in social work management. However, given that administrators have many tasks to attend to, and raising money requires specialized skills, this aspect of the job may be carved out for another person or team to manage. Grant writing and fundraising is, in many cases, the sole responsibility for a social worker who may work independently as a contractor, or who may be hired as salaried staff for this function.

There are several aspects to fundraising. Fundraisers may oversee annual letter- writing campaigns, charity events, or other programs designed to raise money for the organization. Others may spend most of their time cultivating people or organizations who share the same mission and interests as the organization's leadership and who would be willing to make a financial contribution. This is referred to as *donor development* or *special gifts fundraising* and is extremely important work in the sustainability of many human services organizations.

GRANT WRITER

Oftentimes, a fundraiser may also be in charge of writing grants. Grant writers must be aware of the many federal, state, and local organizations (e.g., governmental bodies such as the National Institutes of Health, foundations such as the Bill and Melinda Gates Foundation, and many large corporations) who are known to fund programs in certain areas. They must understand each funder's goals, application requirements, and deadlines. They must be able to write compelling grant applications that will persuade funders that any money granted to the organizations will be well spent. Competition for funding among social service and nonprofit organizations is intense, so grant writers must be able to raise funds in a highly competitive environment. As with fundraisers, grant writers must understand budgets and organizational needs.

Core Competencies and Skills

- Ability to pay attention to details.
- Good written and verbal communication skills.
- Ability to analyze and quickly solve problems.
- Demonstrate openness and flexibility.
- Ability to be decisive and follow through on a decision.
- Be able to establish effective relationships with diverse groups of people.
- Be able to coordinate several tasks at the same time.
- Cope with deadlines.
- Strong managerial skills.
- Understand budget systems and priorities.
- Knowledge of information and management systems.
- Knowledge of financial resources.

Educational and Licensing Requirements

Education and training requirements, as well as experience, vary widely depending on the size and complexity of the organization. In small social service agencies, experience and a bachelor's degree may be the only requirement for a management position, whereas, in larger organizations education at the graduate level and several years of experience and training may be needed.

Whatever the manager's educational background may be, it must be accompanied by relevant paid work experience reflecting their knowledge base and skills. Some top level administration positions require additional certification or training beyond a master's degree. As an illustration of this, if your master's in social work degree concentrated on direct practice or clinical social work skills, even though you have had work experience as a supervisor of a staff providing social services to clients, you may need evidence of other training or education to demonstrate your knowledge and ability to assume a higher level management position. This could be done through obtaining a certificate in nonprofit management or advanced training in human service management from a university or professional continuing education program.

Best Aspects of this Job

- The ability to initiate and plan social change.
- Independence.
- Higher salary.
- The ability to mentor others in professional development.
- Create innovative solutions to traditional problems.
- Serve large scale needs and achieve better outcomes.
- Improve the quality of life for workers and clients.
- Mediating conflict and growing consensus.
- Expand the delivery of social services to those in need.
- Empower persons in the workplace and in communities to lead the change in their lives.

Challenging Aspects of this Job

- Carry responsibility 24 hours a day and 7 days a week for an organization or department.
- Listening to employee problems.
- Negotiating with bureaucratic barriers to change.
- Managing transitions, change, and resistance.
- Operating under tight budgets and searching for funding alternatives.
- Firing employees or giving constructive feedback to employees who are not performing well.
- Attending to details.
- Multitasking often in a fast paced environment.

Compensation and Employment Outlook

Cost-cutting measures to improve profitability, streamline operations, and compete in various marketplaces will continue to be addressed by many public and private agencies during the next decade. This will result in a growing need to "out source" or contract with organizational consultants and managers to provide administration, supervision, and the provision of social services outside of the main agency. Job opportunities vary from year to year because the strength of the economy effects the demand for consulting, planning, and management services. Earnings of administrators greatly depend on the employer, the nature of the "business," and the geographic area. In general, for 2006, the median annual salary for sectors employing the largest numbers of managers was:

Management of companies and enterprises $77,040
General medical and surgical hospitals $72,210
State government $68,410
Local government $67,050
Colleges, universities, and professional schools $64,810

(U.S. Bureau of Labor Statistics, 2007)

Self-Assessment Checklist: Is this Job for Me?

☐ Are you politically savvy?
☐ Can you stick to a course of action once you make a decision?
☐ Do you enjoy working with different types of people?
☐ Do you thrive on getting the details "right?"
☐ Would you be flexible in the amount of time you may need to put into your workday?
☐ Are you able to handle a number of responsibilities at one time and still work on moving forward?
☐ Are you okay with making tough decisions that will not always be popular with your staff?
☐ Do you have the knowledge and skills to mentor and train others?
☐ Would you enjoy learning about organizations and how they work?
☐ Are you able to see "the bigger picture" of an issue and communicate this so others may understand?

If you were able to answer "Yes" to seven or more questions, get ready to assume a professional leadership role in some area of social work practice as you develop your career goals!

RECOMMENDED READINGS/WEB SITES TO LEARN MORE

Association for Community Organization and Social Administration: www.acosa.org
Houston, M. K., Nuehring, E. M., Daquio, E. R., National Association of Social Workers Insurance Trust (1997). *Prudent practice: A guide for managing malpractice risk.* Washington, DC: NASW Press.
Intrator, S. M., & Scribner, M. (2007). *Leading from within.* San Francisco: Jossey-Bass.
Kadushin, A., & Harkness, D. (2002). *Supervision in social work* (4th ed.). New York: Columbia University Press.
Munson, C. E. (2002). *Handbook of clinical social work supervision* (3rd ed.). Binghamton, NY: Haworth Press.

National Association of Social Worker: www.socialworkers.org
The National Center on Nonprofit Enterprise: www.nationalcne.org
The National Network of Grantmakers: www.nng.org
The National Network for Social Work Managers: www.socialworkmanager.org
The New Jersey Institute for Nonprofit and Social Work Management: www.kean.edu/~njswmgt/aboutus.html
Public Administration and Management: www.pamij.com
Westley, F., Zimmerman, B., & Patton, M. (2007). *Getting to maybe: How the world is changed.* Canada: Vintage Press.

Leadership in Human Service Organizations Exercise

John Nguyen is the executive director of the only HIV awareness and prevention program in a small county. Most of his agency's budget is received from the federal government with matching funds from the state. A small amount of revenue is generated from local donations. Mr. Nguyen has learned that in 3 months the federal government will no longer be funding prevention programs. This prevention program targets teens at risk and provides needed testing and counseling. He knows he will not have the money to pay his staff, office rent, or his own salary and fears he may have to close down his agency.

Questions

1. What is the first thing you would do if you were Mr. Nguyen?
2. Should this program continue and how will you evaluate this?
3. What are the available community assets or resources that could be helpful in the planning process here?

REFERENCE

U.S. Bureau of Labor Statistics. (2007). *Occupational outlook handbook* (2006–2007 ed.). [Online]. Retrieved April 30, 2008, from http://www.bls.gov/oco

17 Careers in Research and Academia

Life-long learning and continuing education beyond the bachelor's or master's social work (MSW) degree is embraced and promoted in social work education. After a number of years of experience, some practicing social workers with an MSW degree decide to return to graduate school to earn their doctorate and pursue a career in academia and/or research. An individual may earn a PhD or doctorate in social work (DWS), depending on the degree offered by a particular university. The process of earning a doctorate is a long and challenging road, but the rewards are great.

The specific requirements for earning a PhD or DSW vary by university. However, a person must have a passion for teaching and the research process. General requirements for earning the degree include earning a MSW degree, 2-years post-MSW experience (if one wants to teach social work practice courses), obtaining admission to a PhD or DSW program, completing the required course work, passing the comprehensive examinations, and completing a dissertation.

Generally, admission requirements include submission of a university and program application, letters of recommendations, a writing sample, results of the Graduate Record Examination (GRE) or other standardized tests, and other documents as requested by the respective university. These admission applications and supporting documents are reviewed and decided on by the PhD admission committee.

The process for earning the PhD/DSW may take 3 to 10 years, depending on the program and the length of time needed to complete the dissertation stage. The curriculum generally includes advanced courses in policy, research, statistics, and theory. Once a student successfully completes these courses, he/she must pass a comprehensive examination related to these courses. Following the comprehensive examination, the doctoral student moves to the dissertation stage. In the dissertation stage, students:

1. Select a topic of interest.
2. Select a committee with a chair.
3. Obtain committee approval of a dissertation proposal.
4. Carry out independent research, including data collection and analysis.
5. Write the dissertation.
6. Defend the dissertation.

Upon successful defense of the dissertation, a student earns a doctorate.

Those with a PhD/DSW earn the title of doctor and have the opportunity and responsibility of engaging in service to the community, molding minds, and contributing to the knowledge base in social work by engaging in innovative and cutting-edge research.

This chapter will highlight some common career tracks for those with a PhD or DSW.

SOCIAL WORK RESEARCHER

Researchers contribute extensively to the practice of social work by devoting their career to furthering knowledge in a given topic of interest. They have important questions that they would like to answer through research. They contribute to the knowledge base by publishing books and articles in peer-reviewed journals. Researchers are employed by governmental bodies including local, state, and federal government; and nongovernmental agencies, including private, nonprofit or for-profit organizations.

Some researchers are employed by universities as research faculty. The University of Hawaii/Manoa Social Welfare Evaluation, Research, and Training Unit, for example, provides evaluation, research, and training consultation and services to community agencies that provide social welfare services to the people of Hawaii and the Pacific/Asian region. The University of Texas at Austin, likewise, funds the Center for Social Work Research, which oversees dozens of research projects in any given year. The Institute for the Advancement of Social Work Research (IASWR) and the Society for Social Work and Research (SSWR) are organizations devoted to members whose interests include social work research.

SOCIAL WORK PROFESSOR

Professors are commonly employed by universities at both private and public institutions. An individual begins as an assistant professor, and after 6 to 7 years, he/she may apply for tenure and promotion to associate professor. Tenure gives one job security at that institution. To be tenured, one must demonstrate excellence in service, teaching, and research. The tenure earning years can be most stressful for a faculty member due to the pressure of "publish or perish"; however, once tenure is earned, job security is increased tremendously. These tenure-earning professors contribute to academia and the profession as a whole through research, teaching, and service.

The teaching load for social work university professors varies by university, but is usually somewhere between two and four courses a semester with summers off. If you choose to work for an institution that is research intensive, the teaching load is lighter due to the increasing demand to engage in research and publication. Those working in universities that emphasize teaching should expect a more demanding teaching schedule. Other than teaching, professors spend their time writing and finding ways to contribute to their community, often by serving on boards of directors or engaging in research and evaluation. Professors are also expected to provide service to their college by serving on various university committees.

ADJUNCT FACULTY/LECTURER

Teaching load and research expectations vary by university. For these reasons, other than the tenure-track positions, social work education programs also employ adjunct professors and/or lecturers to teach on a part-time, temporary basis in an area of specialty for the faculty member. The continuous growth of social work programs in terms of numbers and curriculum development have resulted in the demand for qualified adjunct professors and lecturers, particularly in social work practice and field education courses. This setting is an excellent choice for social workers who choose to practice social work in the community while also engaging in the education of future social workers. It is not necessary to have a PhD to work as an adjunct faculty member—you just need to have a demonstrated area of expertise as a social work practitioner.

FIELD EDUCATION DIRECTOR/COORDINATOR

Social work is unique among many other academic programs in that, as an applied science, it requires a substantial amount of student field education as a requisite for completing the BSW or MSW. Field education directors are dynamic individuals who have the exciting responsibility of overseeing the field program and coordinating the performance and progress of students, community agencies, and liaisons in the social work program. They establish critical relationships with social service agencies in the community, domestic and international, in which students may be placed to complete the field education requirement. These agencies vary in the services they provide, which could range from casework to individual therapy to political advocacy.

Large social work programs often employ field faculty whose job is to teach the field seminar and work with students as they progress through the field experience to assess their growth and to assist with any problems that may arise in their field placement. They also train the field instructors who work in the agencies and supervise students in the field to ensure that students have a meaningful learning experience. Field faculty members collaborate with students in planning and implementing their field experience(s) to ensure that they gain skills appropriate for practicing social work upon completion of the degree. The field experience is where the classroom knowledge and experiential learning all come together.

Depending on the academic institution, some field directors are on a tenure-track position and must fulfill the tenure and promotion requirements in order to continue employment; whereas, other institutions offer full-time employment with a contract renewal clause. Most field faculty members have their MSW and some an earned PhD.

Social Worker Spotlight: Jessica A. Ritter, BSW, MSSW, PhD Director of Field Education and Assistant Professor, Pacific University, Forest Grove, Oregon

I completed my PhD in social work at the University of Texas at Austin in 2006, and I am a "newbie" social work professor. I have to say, "I *love* my job." Every day, I have the rare opportunity to sit in front of a classroom and talk to undergraduate college students about important social problems in the United States and around the world. My favorite social work classes to teach are *Macro Social Work* and *Social Policy and Social Justice*, where my goal is to show social work students that work at the community level and in the political arena is exciting and interesting and not as scary or intimidating as they often imagine.

Since I have been a social work professor, I have published three journal articles, two of which report the results of my dissertation study focused on the political participation of social workers. However, my true passion is preparing social work students for the wonderfully challenging roles of social workers. This past year, my accomplishments as a professor include: applying and receiving funds to take three students with me to attend *Social Work Day at the United Nations* in New York City; taking another student with me to Durban, South Africa, to present at an international social work conference; helping students in my *Macro Social Work* class get a resolution passed by the Portland City Council; organizing a Legislative Advocacy Day for social work students in the greater Portland area; testifying before the Oregon state legislature on behalf of the rights of juvenile offenders; serving as the Chair of the Legislative Committee for National Association for Social Workers in Oregon; and completing this book!

I am also the director of field education in my small social work program that has only two social work professors. Last semester, I helped six students find their year long practicum placements for next year: two will be at Children's Protective Services, one will be in a community hospital, one is placed at the County Department on Aging, one will be working in an elementary school, and the final one will be doing a macro placement at the County Commission on Children and Families.

The best part of my job is teaching and mentoring social work students and serving as advisor of the social work club. Social work students inspire me every day because of their idealism and their desire to make a difference in the lives of individuals, families, and communities. I could not ask for a better job.

DIRECTOR OF SPECIAL PROGRAMS

Oftentimes, academic institutions will house interdisciplinary programs that specialize in research, teaching, or clinical work related to their disciplines. For example, the Fordham University Graduate School of Social Service promotes several research centers and institutes: The Bertram M. Beck Institute for Religion and Poverty, the Institute for Women and Girls, and the Ravazzin Center on Aging. Likewise, the various departments and schools of the Western Michigan University College of Health and Human Services provide state of the art clinical programs through its unified clinics to the community. Examples of the estimated dozen unified clinics include the Children's Trauma Assessment Center, Activities of Daily Living Clinic, and Comprehensive Women's Health Clinic. Many of these programs are directed or staffed by social work faculty. These settings offer further opportunities to increase the profile of the university and for faculty to continue conducting research and pursuing their professional interests.

PROGRAM DIRECTOR/DEPARTMENT CHAIR/DEAN

Some professors also choose to pursue administrative positions, such as BSW or MSW program director, department chair, dean, or even the provost/president of a university. These administrative positions involve a high level of involvement and leadership in areas such as student admission and registration, curriculum development, financial aid, student life, academic recruitment and retention, faculty life, campus facilities and development, budgeting and finances, and public relations. They are not only involved in overseeing the affairs of the program or university and governing policies and procedures, but also in taking a leadership role in deciding how the program or institution will develop and grow.

Core Competencies and Skills

- Excellent teaching skills in order to make the classroom an exciting, stimulating, and safe place for students to learn.
- Ability to craft and stay committed to a research agenda over the course of your career in academia.
- Strong research skills including ability to engage in data collection and statistical analysis.
- Expertise in writing grants and getting external funding for your research.
- Strong administrative skills and the ability to navigate the politics of academia.
- Superior writing skills because a large part of this job involves writing books and research articles.
- Good speaking skills, which are used in teaching and conference presentations.
- The ability to link research findings to the practice and theories of social work.
- Strong critical thinking skills.

Educational and Licensing Requirements

The educational requirements for earning and completing a DSW or PhD were explained in the beginning of this chapter. Earning a doctorate requires a lot of perseverance and determination because it takes a number of years to complete and you are being trained to be a scholar in your field. However, it is a wonderful career for anyone who loves teaching and research and wants to have a career with a lot of flexibility and independence. Licensing does not apply to those with a PhD in social work; however, many professors and researchers choose to keep up with their license as a social worker.

Best Aspects of this Job

- Enjoyment of academic freedom in relation to facilitation of critical thinking and thinking outside the box about social issues, among faculty and students.
- Enjoyment of flexible schedules (e.g., faculty are off on weekends, holidays, winter, spring, and summer breaks; faculty have control of their day's plan).

- Opportunity to attend exciting research conferences all over the country and even abroad.
- Enjoyment of the opportunity to teach future social workers, conduct research according to your interest, and provide services to your community and university.
- Once academic tenure is earned, your job security and academic freedom are protected.
- Opportunity to climb the ranks of assistant, associate, and full professor provides increase in esteem and salary.
- Opportunity to pursue administrative endeavors and learn the politics of the academy.

Challenging Aspects of this Job

- Many research and teaching jobs lack the structure and community feel of other jobs, which can feel lonely and isolating for some people.
- The heavy expectations to publish and to gather external funding can be very stressful.
- Balancing the teaching, research, and service expectations of professors can be challenging.
- Professors must be able to adapt to the changing needs of young people and their learning preferences because the current generation of students have grown up with technology.
- Social work professors must engage in gate-keeping, which involves weeding out students who are not a good fit for the social work profession.
- Not getting lost in the ivory tower; finding ways to stay connected to the field.
- The politics of academia can be challenging to deal with.

Compensation and Employment Outlook

Salaries for university professors vary according to state as well as private or public institutions. In 2008, the median expected annual salary for a social work professor in some parts of the United States is about $76,000. Other areas in the United States have median salary of $55,000 (Salary.com, 2008).

DSW or PhD education has positively impacted the employment outlook for social work educators. Current trends indicate that doctoral level social work faculty is in demand. Across the United States, there are more faculty vacancies than earned doctorates to fill these job vacancies.

Self-Assessment Checklist: Is this Job for Me?

- ☐ Are you extremely self-motivated (since you will be in charge of completing your own projects and meeting self-imposed deadlines)?
- ☐ Do you have a love of learning and a thirst for knowledge?
- ☐ Do you have a passion for teaching college students?
- ☐ Would you enjoy having access to cutting edge knowledge and working with experts in various fields?
- ☐ Can you handle criticism and rejection (e.g., teaching evaluations, submitting articles for publication)?
- ☐ Are you someone who often spends time thinking about important questions that you would like to address through research?
- ☐ Do you have strong writing skills and the ability to work on a draft and revise over and over again until it is acceptable for publication?
- ☐ Would you enjoy a job where you are extremely independent and do not have co-workers or supervisors in the traditional sense?
- ☐ Do you enjoy all phases of the research process from coming up with the question to coming up with the appropriate methodology to collecting and analyzing the data?
- ☐ Would you find it fulfilling to train/educate social work students and help them plan their careers?

If you answered "yes" to seven or more of the above questions, then getting a DSW or PhD in social work might be for you!

RECOMMENDED READINGS/WEB SITES TO LEARN MORE

Association of Baccalaureate Program Directors: www.bpdonline.org
Council on Social Work Education: www.cswe.org
Group for the Advancement of Doctoral Education in Social Work: www.gadephd.org
Institute for the Advancement of Social Work Research: www.iaswresearch.org
Journal of Social Work Education: www.cswe.org/CSWE/publications/journal/
National Institute of Mental Health: www.nimh.nih.gov
Society of Social Work and Research: www.sswr.org
Social Work (journal): www.naswpress.org/publications/journals/social_work/swintro.html

Research and Academia Exercise

Take a few minutes to think about and select a social problem that you are very passionate about and then answer the following:

1. What aspect of this problem would you most want to know or understand?
2. What would your research question(s) be?
3. How would you find out whether there has already been research conducted to answer this question? Where would you go to find out?
4. If you were going to devise a research project to answer this question, how would you gather your data (e.g., surveys, interviews, observation, review of existing data set or records)? What are the benefits and disadvantages of these various approaches?
5. Would this be a qualitative or quantitative study? (If you do not know the difference, do a Google search.)
6. Does your question pass the following test: *So what?*
7. What relevance does this question have for the social work profession?

REFERENCE

Salary.com. (2008). Salary wizard: Professor—social work. Retrieved June 13, 2008, from http://swz.salary.com/salarywizard/layouthtmls/swzl_compresult_national_ED03000244.html

18 Careers Beyond Social Work

Throughout this book, we have described an impressive array of options that are available for you when you choose a career in social work. Another aspect of the social work profession that is quite special is the opportunity to combine your social work degree with other degrees. Many social workers have multiple passions, and this is a great way to merge those interests. Joint programs have become very popular as universities respond to the appeals of social workers who wish to obtain an array of dual degrees such as—social work and law, social work and public policy, social work and public health, social work and business/nonprofit administration, etc.

So, in this final chapter focusing on careers in social work, we want to encourage you to think outside of the box when it comes to creating a career path that is exciting and tailored to your unique strengths, talents, and interests. There are countless numbers of social workers in this country, such as Dr. Murali Nair, who have done just that! Dr. Nair has written 10 books, has had several photography exhibits around the country and overseas, and has been involved in the production of six documentaries. Please read his profile later in the chapter. However, this is just one example of many.

NOVELIST/JOURNALIST

Social workers are in the unique position of seeing, firsthand, the vast array of social problems experienced by the most vulnerable people in our country, an exciting yet often daunting place to be. Since they see and experience life in a way that most people do not, they have a unique perspective to share with the world. Everyday they are dealing with fascinating, heartbreaking people and situations: child abuse, poverty and homelessness, drug abuse, mental illness, and sexual assault and violence, to name a few.

Social workers who enjoy writing can choose to use fiction writing or journalism as a way to share their unique viewpoints and outlooks with the world. We can very easily see social workers doing "human interest" stories for newspapers and television shows. An example of such a show is Lisa Ling's *Ultimate Explorer* on the National Geographic Channel. In this new age of reality television, there are ample opportunities for social workers to focus on important social problems in this country and around the world.

Social Worker Spotlight: Anne Driscoll, LCSW
Journalist and Author of the Girl to Girl guidebooks

As a girl, I dreamed of becoming a writer but as the oldest of four children from an Irish-Catholic, working-class family, that impractical dream seemed well beyond my reach. I didn't know any writers, and I didn't know anyone who knew any writers, so when I became the first of my family to pack off to college, I was practical and chose a career I hoped I could actually make a living from. Since I was always interested in what made people tick, I chose to pursue social work at a public college and the training, education, and internships I received there served me memorably well after I graduated, during the 3 years I worked with juvenile delinquent girls. But then it dawned on me—I wasn't really supporting myself all that well as a social worker—so I decided to pursue my dream and become a writer after all. Again, though, it seemed nearly just as impractical and unlikely a career choice as before since I didn't have any training at all—or so I thought. In the 25 years I've been working as a journalist, there isn't a day that goes by when I'm not thankful for the

skills I learned as a social worker: interviewing people from all kinds of circumstances, building a rapport with people from all types of backgrounds, getting them to trust you, open up, and tell you things.

I started out writing for the teeny *North Shore Sunday* and ended up writing for the colossal *New York Times*. It's been an amazing journey. I've been managing editor of *New England Bride Magazine*. I've written for the news wire services, ghostwritten three books on psychic skills and parapsychology, written a series of self-help books for tween-aged girls, covered a triple murder trial, and multiple alarm fires. I've interviewed both George Clooney on a red carpet for *People* magazine and a woman who is considered a living saint in India. And I now know that it's not only the skills that are the same in both social work and journalism, but it is also the function that is the same, as well. Remarkably, in both roles, you act as a witness for the other person, you validate their experience. That is the basis of the therapeutic social work relationship and it is also the foundation of a journalist's job. The difference is that as a social worker, it's you and that person in an office; as a reporter it's you and that person and, in the case of *People* magazine, 36 million other readers. My name, Anne, means grace or prayer and Driscoll means interpreter, intermediary, news bearer. I only hope I live up to my name.

For more information, visit annedriscoll.com or mastermediaspeakers.com.

DOCUMENTARY FILMMAKER

This is a great option for social workers who are attracted to filmmaking and work in the media. You have probably seen Michael Moore's *Sicko* and Al Gore's *An Inconvenient Truth*, which were both commercial and critical hits at the box office. Social workers who are trained as filmmakers have the ability to educate the general public and decision makers about the multitude of social problems that social workers confront daily.

The media can be a powerful tool for social change. We live in a media age, and filmmakers have the opportunity to tell important stories, reach millions of people, and educate others about important social problems in this country.

Social Worker Spotlight: Murali D. Nair, PhD
Communicating Beyond Print Media

I received my doctorate in social welfare from Columbia University and master's degree in computer science from New York Institute of Technology. I currently serve as Professor of Social Work at Cleveland State University. Cross-cultural and cross-national understanding of poverty, disaster management, and healing across cultures are some of the interests of mine.

Along with writing 10 social work related books, I was involved in the production of 6 documentaries, including a 30-minute documentary "Sri Lanka Experience," which documents my interactions with close to 100 poor families in tsunami affected areas. Photography is a childhood hobby of mine. Over the years, I have had several photo exhibits around the country and overseas.

Enriching our senses is an art. Observing, hearing, tasting, feeling, and smelling needs to be optimized for personal and others consumption. Compared to other senses, visual representation of things seems to stay with us for a long time. There is even a popular saying "a picture is worth a thousand words".

Though I have been teaching undergraduate and graduate social work students for the past 32 years and published 10 books, lately I am drawn more and more to producing documentaries. In the past 10 years, I have been involved in 6 documentaries in everything from camera work, editing, scripting, voice over, and cover design. To me self-fulfillment in the production of an audio visual work is much greater than writing a book or an article.

What is involved in making a documentary? Typically, I utilize video and still cameras in digital format. For a 30-minute video, I may tape up to 100 hours. Before going to the location, I create a mental image of what I intend to obtain on that particular day, then I write a script. Sometimes, I may not be able to collect all the information I need from the field, and at other times, there are new surprises that I should be able to capture spontaneously on my camera.

Subjects for three of my documentaries were from locations where the subjects spoke in local languages. Special attention is needed to make sure voice over is done properly.

Once all the video, audio, and still clippings are collected from the field, then the real task of editing begins. It can be an emotional issue. I try to save the 100s of hours of footage rather than discarding it. Every moment has sentimental value to me. However, it is not possible. At times, what I really like may not be the real theme of the documentary.

You get self-satisfaction when you see the end product being appreciated by others.

For more information about Professor Nair and his work, visit: http://facultyprofile.csuohio.edu/csufacultyprofile/detail.cfm?FacultyID=M_NAIR

ARTIST

Many social workers who are extremely talented artists in the areas of music, acting, painting, and dance have found creative ways to combine this with a career in social work. Some mental health professionals use art in a therapeutic context with their clients (e.g., music therapy, dance therapy). Others create nonprofit organizations and include art programs as an integral part of their service delivery system. Many organizations have learned that this can be a valuable intervention strategy with at-risk youth, older adults, and a variety of other client populations. For example, youth who have a difficult time expressing themselves by talking may find it safer and more therapeutic to express themselves through writing music, acting, or painting.

CORPORATE CONSULTANT

Increasingly, social workers are being hired by corporations to fill a variety of important roles, of which consultant may be one. Executives and managers hire consultants in order to help them analyze and improve the operations of the organization. For more on organizational consulting, see chapter 16.

CAREERS IN HUMAN RESOURCES

Because social workers are highly skilled in communication, group work, mediation, and crisis intervention, many corporations recognize that professional social workers have a unique contribution to make to the "human element" of their operations. Social workers who wish to work in corporate settings can make excellent human resource managers, where they can oversee recruitment, staff development and training, team building and team development, employee services and perks, organizational work/life balance programs, and much more.

CAREERS IN MEDIATION AND CONFLICT RESOLUTION

Mediation is a growing field in social work practice because social workers are natural mediators and are skilled in helping people resolve disputes. Mediation involves an impartial person who has the skills to empower others to resolve their conflicts in a constructive way. A mediator understands the "art of compromise." When a mediator has done his or her job well, the parties will reach an agreement and no one will feel like they "lost." Mediation has been traditionally used in legal settings as a way to help parties reach an agreement in child welfare, child custody, and divorce cases in order to avoid going to trial. However, this practice has been greatly expanded and is now being used in health care, the workplace, labor disputes, in neighborhoods and communities, in landlord/tenant disputes, in international affairs and peace keeping. Social work schools are responding to this growing demand by offering special coursework, joint degrees, and certificate programs in mediation.

OMBUDSMAN

A related job to mediation and conflict resolution is that of an *Ombudsman*. An Ombudsman can be found in many government agencies and businesses and is charged with responding to complaints from clients, customers, or members of the public.

SELF-EMPLOYMENT/CONSULTING CAREERS

Being "self-employed" as a social worker used to mean that you were an independently licensed mental health professional in your own private practice, or you worked as a consultant and trainer to organizations.

A large number of social workers have learned the business skills required for self-employment on their own, and have started their own business, non-profit organization or consulting group.

A growing opportunity in this area is the ability for social workers to work in primary care settings, where they consult with physicians, nurses, and other medical staff on mental health issues. These social workers are sometimes referred to as behavioral health consultants. However, social workers who have developed an expertise in a given area or field of practice may be hired by other organizations in the U.S. or abroad in help with developing a new agency or program.

Social Worker Spotlight: Richard B. Joelson, DSW, LCSW Private Practice, New York City

My decision to enter the field of social work was, I suppose, somewhat unusual. I became a Peace Corps Volunteer in Liberia, West Africa, immediately after graduation from college in 1965. In addition to my job as an elementary and high school teacher, I worked in a tribal mental hospital alongside a Canadian psychiatrist and several native healers (better known to us as "witch doctors"). The experience dazzled me and I decided to get trained as a social worker when I returned to the States. The profession seemed just right for me. Fortunately, Columbia University School of Social Work agreed and accepted me with a full-tuition scholarship for the first year of the 2-year master's program.

I have enjoyed a diversified professional life throughout my career, both before and after entering private practice. My first job was the proverbial trial by fire. I was a youth parole social worker with a caseload of 100 troubled adolescent boys living in a Brooklyn ghetto. After that, I worked as a psychiatric social worker and group therapist at a child and family guidance center. Subsequent employment: director of social work and then executive director at a mental health clinic in Greenwich Village and lastly, director of admissions and student affairs at New York University School of Social Work.

My entrance into private practice occurred sooner than I had planned. While at my second job—the child and family guidance center—many families who were on the clinic waiting list requested opportunities to see a staff member privately, rather than wait for weeks and months for service. Senior staff and administrators encouraged me (it didn't take much) to open my own practice so that I could accept referrals from the waiting list. And so my private practice was born!

The private practice of social work and I were a good fit from the start. As someone who always valued autonomy and was comfortable operating independently (perhaps traceable to the loss of my father at an early age), I liked the freedom of being what has been called "an agency of one." With good training and clinical and administrative background, and, I believe, many of the qualities associated with successful autonomous functioning, I enjoyed an active part-time practice for many years prior to making the leap into full-time practice after five years as an NYU administrator.

I have been in full-time practice since leaving that job in 1984 and have thoroughly enjoyed my experience and the many opportunities it has afforded me. I have taken pride in making full use of the social work principles and values I hold dear. After being in full-time practice for 7 years, and feeling the need to a new challenge, I entered the doctoral program at Hunter College School of Social Work in New York and graduated with my DSW 5 years later. I remain pleased that my particular degree indicates that my doctorate is in social work, as opposed to a PhD, which is silent on the matter of what subject area was studied.

Beginning in 1991, I taught a course entitled, "How to Develop A Private Practice: Essential Steps," which drew many new and seasoned social work practitioners who wanted to begin a private practice or strengthen an already existing one. The course gave me a wonderful opportunity to "preach what I practiced" to others, as well as an additional opportunity to be professionally active out of my office and not just inside; something I have always encouraged other private practitioners to do, as well.

Currently, in addition to a still full schedule of clients in my practice, I have developed a Web site. It is designed as a resource for people interested in understanding issues and topics in the field of mental health, as well as identifying services available if necessary. I am often contacted by people who read my articles or my monthly newsletter, asking for help in knowing more about what existing services and how to access them. This provision gives me a great deal of satisfaction. I have always believed that mental health professionals have an obligation to educate and enlighten the public on matters about which there is still too much mystery, distorted thinking, and negative beliefs. My Web site is one way that I try to help those unfamiliar with the field of mental health to become open to seeking the help they need.

For more information about Richard B. Joelson, DSW and his work, visit www.richardbjoelsondsw.com or www.psychotherapy-info.com

ENTREPRENEUR

The concepts behind social innovation and the skills of entrepreneurship have emerged as new areas for the growth of the social work profession. There are now dual and joint degree programs in social work that combine the master's degree in social work with a master's degree in business administration, which help social workers understand the technical business knowledge needed to run a successful operation. Entrepreneurship skills take the social work profession a step farther. Creating your own nonprofit agency with innovative service delivery to consumers or developing a business that promotes social and economic benefits for the community is an exciting venture for a "social work entrepreneur."

ATTORNEY

Many social workers have an interest in law and legal advocacy and go on to work in the following legal arenas: human rights work at the national or international level; children's advocacy, where they may serve as attorney ad litems for children in the foster care system or those in the middle of a custody dispute; family law; public defender's work, representing those accused of a crime; and the Legal Aid Society, to represent those with limited incomes.

As you can see, there is no "typical" social work career. You don't have to do what is traditional or expected. Don't be scared to create your own unique career as a social worker. Be a rebel. Blaze your own path—the options and opportunities are endless!

RECOMMENDED READINGS/WEB SITES TO LEARN MORE

Art as Healing: www.artashealing.org
Community for Creative Non-Violence: http://users.erols.com/ccnv/
Expressive Arts Institute: www.arts4change.com
Idealist.org: Action without Borders: www.idealist.org
Linda Grobman, Social Worker/Publisher: www.lindagrobman.com
Small Business Administration: www.sba.gov
Pipher, M. (2006). *Writing to change the world.* New York: Riverhead Books.

Social Worker and Beyond Exercise

Take a few minutes, and brainstorm your hobbies, interests, and passions (separate from social work). Think about what you most enjoy doing when you have some free time and what kinds of activities bring you joy. Write down each one that comes to mind on a piece of paper.

Questions

1. How might you combine these interests with a career in social work?
2. Who might be able to serve as a mentor(s) for you as you work towards creating a unique career of your own?
3. What will your next steps be?

Where Do We Go From Here?

Paying for Your Education

One of the realities of getting a college education is figuring out the best way to pay for this rather expensive investment. Some students are lucky enough to have their education financed by their parents; however, many more must rely on a combination of part-time or full-time work, scholarships, and financial aid, which can include grants and loans through the federal government.

More and more, students are taking an average of 6 to 7 years to complete a 4-year degree. Instead of saving money, many students are actually spending thousands more in tuition payments by extending their time in school when they work more than 15 hours a week. In addition, several studies have shown that there are negative consequences to a student's overall grade point average (GPA) with the greater the number of hours they work per week while enrolled full-time in school (Hawkins et al, 2005). If your plans include graduate studies later on in life, an unsatisfactory undergraduate GPA can be an extremely limiting factor in terms of which programs will admit you.

Working is a necessity for most of us, and a certain amount of part-time work is often helpful in keeping a balanced structure to the day and staying organized with studying and assignments. Looking at paying for college from a financial planning perspective, in addition to applying for financial aid, may help you reduce the number of hours you feel you must be employed and maximize the time you need to enjoy your education.

CONDUCTING A SCHOLARSHIP SEARCH

First, let's talk about the *free* money that's available. The scholarship search begins with learning the best strategy for conducting a search. There are many search engines that can help you navigate the thousands of scholarships available to undergraduate and graduate students.

One of the best *free* search engines is through the Sallie Mae Corporation at www.collegeanswer.com, where you can register and open an account. You will find very useful information regarding loans, grants, filling out the Federal Financial Aid for Student Assistance (FAFSA) form, and, of course, beginning your search for *free* scholarship money.

Many social work students become frustrated in their search because only a handful of small dollar amount scholarships are found in the field of social work. However, if you pay attention to certain key words as you fill out your *profile* for a scholarship search, you will find larger scholarships almost any student could apply for today.

- It is more helpful to look at your scholarship search as if it is a *job*, and not just a few minutes on Google to see what comes up when you plug in "social work." Dedicate a day every 2 months or so to review your profile and renew your search.
- Scholarship deadlines occur all year long, so you are bound to find something substantial to apply for just about any time you look.
- Fill out your scholarship profile on your Sallie Mae account by looking at every category and filling in what is relevant to you. You can change your profile often, so don't stick with the same information, because you will keep bringing up the same scholarships.
- For instance, if you look at the *Ethnicity* field at the beginning of the profile, and you happen to be of African American, Irish, and Native American heritage, *don't* select all three at one time because you will block out certain key words and "confuse" the system. Try one or two categories at a time. The same would be true for the *Athletics/Sports or Hobbies* category—try just two or three.
- Read what comes up in your search *very carefully*. First, look at the scholarships that have at least an 85% match to your profile and then look at the largest dollar amounts. Don't skim through this

information because you may miss out on applying for something you actually could be awarded.

■ *Spend time in crafting your application essay, and make sure it includes the key words that are spelled out in the guidelines.* For instance, if you have found a scholarship that is given to a student interested in *leadership* and *social justice* in the *community*, your essay should have these words somewhere in there. Many applications are submitted online and key words play a big part in this format.

■ In searching for scholarship money, it is important for social work students to keep in mind these key words: human services, public service, community service, advocacy, social justice, peace, leadership, innovation, communication, marketing, public relations, entrepreneurship, political advocacy, and government service, just to name a few. Many scholarships are focused on the *attributes* of student applicants and not necessarily what subject they are studying.

OTHER METHODS OF FINANCING YOUR EDUCATION

There are a few more items of information to think about regarding financial planning versus financial aid. Other ways to finance your education include:

■ Taking out money from your IRA or 401(k), if you have one. A person may pull out up to $10,000 from a retirement account for education purposes without paying a penalty fee.

■ Applying for a home equity line of credit or home equity loan to finance your education. You may also be able to itemize the interest rate on that loan on your income tax forms.

■ Looking at the tax benefits and allowable education expenses to deduct online at www.irs.gov through reading Publication 970. Some of your expenses might qualify as education expenses, business expenses, or professional expenses. The IRS offers free help to answer any questions you may have, and it could be worth the time and a little bit of money to pay for expert advice from a tax consultant.

■ If you are claimed as a dependent on your parents' tax forms, you may want to talk to them about speaking with a tax consultant.

You may qualify for more financial aid if you are not claimed as a dependent.

■ Lastly, many students do not take out enough in Financial Aid to begin with and do not know what education expenses they should be including in their package. Reviewing IRS Publication 970 should help you determine what your legitimate education expenses are.

■ Now, take a deep breath and try not to panic! Your education is an *investment*, so don't dwell on the amount of "debt" you are collecting right now. You will be able to have a good paying job once you have earned your bachelor's degree in social work (BSW) and/or master's degree in social work (MSW), and you will soon be on your way to a sound financial strategy for managing your repayment plan.

For more information, *Social Work Career Development—A Handbook for Job Hunting and Career Planning*, by Carol Nesslein Doelling, includes excellent resources on fellowships, internships, training, and loan forgiveness programs.

SOCIAL WORK SCHOLARSHIPS, FELLOWSHIPS, AND OTHER PROGRAMS

So, now you are ready to begin your search! You can start by researching the following scholarship information that may not readily surface in your results with a search engine:

National Association of Social Workers Foundation

The National Association of Social Workers (NASW) offers scholarships for MSW and doctoral level students, in addition to a research grant to individual NASW state chapters. Click on the "scholarship" link at www.naswfoundation.org

NASW Press

The journal *Social Work*, which is published for NASW by the NASW Press, offers a $500 award for a BSW or MSW level student. Submission guidelines may be found at www.naswpress.org

National Association of Black Social Workers

The National Association of Black Social Workers provides scholarships to qualified applicants every academic year. The scholarship amounts range from $250 to $2,000. Applications MUST be received by Friday, December 17th of the year before the scholarship is due. Any applications received after this date will not be accepted—No Exceptions. It is the responsibility of the applicant to ensure that all of his/her materials are received by the required date. Applicants should follow the scholarship criteria and procedure sheet exactly to ensure eligibility of their application. Separate applications must be submitted for each scholarship for which he/she will be considered. For more information, go to www.nabsw.org and click on the link *"contact us"* and call the office for scholarship information.

National Association of Puerto Rican and Hispanic Social Workers

The National Association of Puerto Rican and Hispanic Social Workers provides scholarships to full-time graduate social work students who can demonstrate interest in community organization and advocacy which impacts the Puerto Rican and Latino community. Financial need and academic proficiency should also be demonstrated. For more information visit www.naprhsw.org and click on the link *Provide Scholarship Monies*, that is embedded in the second paragraph of the home page.

Jack Kent Cooke Foundation Undergraduate Scholarship Program

The Jack Kent Cooke Foundation Undergraduate Scholarship Program is open to students who currently attend community college or 2-year institutions located in the United States, and who plan to transfer to a 4-year college or university. The award will provide funding for tuition, room and board, required fees, and books for the remainder of the recipients undergraduate degree. Award amounts will vary for each recipient based on the institution he or she attends. Scholarship monies not used during one academic year are not transferable to the next academic year. The scholarship is renewable for each year of the undergraduate study if the scholar continues to meet the program requirements. Application guidelines are found at: www.jackkentcookefoundation.org

National Merit Scholarships

National Merit Finalists in high school who are admitted to college may be eligible for the National Merit Scholarship. Students must apply for admission by January 15 of their senior year. All eligible admission applicants are considered; therefore, no separate application is required. National Merit Finalists are strongly considered for the Presidential Scholarships as well. For more information go to www.finaid. gmu.edu

National Science Foundation Graduate Research Fellowship

National Science Foundation Graduate Research Fellowships offer recognition and 3 years of support for *advanced study* to approximately 900 outstanding graduate students in the mathematical, physical, biological, engineering, and *behavioral and social sciences*, including the history of science and the philosophy of science, as well as to research-based PhD degrees in science education. Approximately 90 awards are in the women in engineering and women in computer and information science components. Awards made in March 2004 carried a stipend for each fellow of $30,000 for a 12-month tenure (prorated for lesser periods) and an annual cost-of-education allowance of $10,500, paid to the fellow's institution in lieu of tuition and fees. Information is available at www.nsf.org

Scholarships for Cancer Survivors

Some divisions of the American Cancer Society offer college scholarships for pediatric cancer survivors. The Young Cancer Survivor Scholarships are restricted to students within the states served by the division and details vary from division to division. Several hundred scholarships ranging from $1,000 to $10,000 are awarded each year. Information about these awards and the telephone number for your division can be obtained by calling the American Cancer Society at 1-800-ACS-2345 or visit www.cancer.org and put in the key word "scholarships" into the search bar on the top of the home page. Scholarships are also available for nursing studies, including doctoral level degrees.

Scholarship Information for Gay, Lesbian, Bisexual, Transgender, and Allies

The national association, Parents, Families and Friends of Lesbians and Gays (PFLAG) offers several scholarships to *high school seniors* who self-identify as gay, lesbian, bisexual, transgendered, or allies (students who have an interest in serving this community). For additional information visit: www.pflag.org and click on the link "education and programs" for specific information related to scholarships.

Minority and Corporate Scholarships

There are many scholarships in this category. To see all the listings and application information, please go to: http://www.menominee.edu/newcmn1/FinancialAid/Scholarships.htm
Scholarships in this category include:

- **Public Relations Society of America (PRSA) National Minority Scholarship Program:** Send your letter of inquiry with attention to Ms. Elaine Averick, 33 Irving Place, New York, NY 10003-2376. Scholarships are available to minority undergraduate students of junior standing or above; Public Relations Student Society of America member and major/minor in public relations preferred; minimum 3.0 GPA. Award amount: $1,500.
- **Coca-Cola Two-Year Colleges Scholarship Program:** For more information call 1-800-306-2653, or contact Norma Kent, nkent@aacc.nche.edu. Scholarships are offered for students who are attending 2-year degree-granting institutions throughout the United States, who have offered contributions to community service, and who have shown dedication to education. Scholarship awards must be used for educational expenses at a 2-year degree-granting institution. Please call 1-800-306-2653 for deadline information.

Scholarships are offered for students attending 2-year, degree-granting institutions throughout the United States, who have offered contributions to community service and have shown dedication to education. Scholarship awards must be used for educational expenses at a 2-year degree granting institution. Please call the 1-800 number for deadline information.

Scholarships for Foster Children and Adoptees

Many scholarships are found at the "scholarship" link of this national organization, *Onwards and Upwards*. For additional information, please visit: www.onwardsandupwards.org

The cost of getting a college education may seem astronomical at first. However, once you have made the decision to pursue that college degree, consider any money you spend on your education as a long-term investment that will pay big dividends. Getting a college degree is like putting money in the bank. Once you land your first professional social work job, you will be earning a good salary to repay any educational loans you may have needed as part of your financial aid package. With a little bit of sweat equity in searching for scholarships, you may not need to take out as much money in loans as you think!

REFERENCE

Hawkins, C. A., Smith, M. L., Hawkins, R. C., II, & Grant, D. (2005). The relationship among hours employed, perceived work interference, and grades as reported by undergraduate social work students. *Journal of Social Work Education, 41*(1), 13–27.

20 Job Hunting Tips

If you are reading this chapter, you are practically on your way to finding that perfect social work job!

Once you discover that you want to be a social worker, one of the most challenging next steps is deciding what you want to do exactly, due to the dizzying array of options. Many social work students report the feeling that they are interested in everything! Initially, you may be drawn to working with a number of client populations as you sit through your courses. Part of this process is discovering where you are most passionate, trying out a number of possibilities, and refining your interests through a process of elimination. All the while, you should keep in mind that the beauty of a social work degree is you can work with one client population for a number of years and then switch to do something different for an exciting new challenge. So, you really just need to figure out where you want to begin your career with the knowledge that you have no idea where this career may end up taking you.

One tip is to take advantage of your field opportunities while you are in school. All social work programs will offer a variety of courses that require spending a certain number of hours in a social service organization, which gives you the opportunity to talk to social workers in a particular field and to see if this feels like a good fit for you. During your senior year, you will do an intensive field practicum for one or two semesters (depending on the school) where you will have the opportunity to develop your professional social work skills and understand how the theory and research that you learned in school is connected to the practice of social work. Many students who have a wonderful experience in their practicum end up getting hired by the agency that is a win-win for everyone! Others will need to be prepared for all that is involved in going on the job market and landing a job as a social worker.

Excellent resources regarding resume preparation, cover letters, thank you letters, follow-up letters, interviewing, and conducting a job search, as well as linking to employers and job opportunities may be found through the following resources:

- Careerbuilders.com: www.careerbuilders.com
- The New Social Worker: www.socialworkjobs.com
- The Riley Guide: www.rileyguide.com
- ResumeEdge.com: www.resumeedge.com

BOOKS ON JOB HUNTING

Whether you are just starting out in your social work career, or a seasoned practitioner looking for a new direction, please read *Social Work Career Development—A Handbook for Job Hunting and Career Planning*, by Carol Nesslein Doelling. This is a 2005 publication of the NASW Press for $49.00 and well worth the expense. It includes a section on researching potential jobs, networking, resume writing, and more.

Another excellent resource, particularly for younger graduates, is Nicholas Aretakis' 2006 book, *No More Ramen—The 20-something's Real World Survival Guide* ($14.95). This book is very useful in helping you navigate through the minefield of job postings and the online application process. How you format a resume for an online application often differs from how you would prepare your more formal written resume. You can also find information from www.NoMoreRamenOnline.com.

One of the best and most affordable guides is *Knock 'em Dead—The Ultimate Job Seeker's Guide* ($14.95). This book has excellent advice on the interviewing process and negotiating better salaries and/or benefits, which many of us need assistance with when we are first looking for work right after graduation.

JOB-HUNTING WEB SITES

The Social Work Job Bank (www.socialworkjobs.com), as well as the national office of the National Association of Social Workers (NASW) (www.socialworkers.org) and the NASW state chapter associations have specific job listings for social workers.

Check out www.idealist.org for information about internships, fellowships, employment, and volunteer opportunities. Many internships and fellowships are also paid and some provide health benefits. They can be a good short-term solution to keeping you financially afloat and at the same time help you build your experience.

The following Web sites offer many excellent job opportunities:

- State employment offices provide information on the application process for state related jobs, in addition to information regarding starting a small business in the state.
- Federal employment: www.usajobs.opm.gov is the official Web site of the federal government. An additional Web resource is www.federaljobsearch.com.
- U.S. Department of State: There are several career opportunities here such as foreign service officer, civil service officer, and foreign service specialist, in addition to numerous student internships. More information may be obtained by going to www.state.gov/careers.
- In health and human services there is the Emerging Leaders program which accepts postgraduate students in a 2-year program, where they may rotate within the 12 agencies under the umbrella of HHS—http://www.hhs.gov/jobs/elp/ for information on the program as well as the application process to the program.
- There is a 2-year postgraduate fellowship, the Presidential Management Fellows Program at http://www.pmf.opm.gov that also involves rotational assignments throughout the federal government including Congress.
- Another program in leadership and service is the White House Fellows Program: http://www.whitehouse.gov/fellows/ and is known to be quite competitive.
- Other job opportunities for social workers may be found at the FBI, www.fbi.gov, and the Centers for Disease Control, www.cdc.gov, Web sites.

INTERNATIONAL SOCIAL WORK OPPORTUNITIES

If you have always dreamed of traveling or spending time in a foreign country, you may be interested in opportunities for international social work positions. The following organizations offer information as well as job postings:

- International Social Work: www.peacecorps.gov offers many overseas job opportunities with a typical 2-year commitment.
- London Qualified Social Workers: www.lqsw.com
- International Federation of Social Work: www.ifsw.org
- International Association of Schools of Social Work: www.iassw-aiets.org
- United Nations: www.UN.org

For a brief article on international social work, go to www.socialworkjobbank.com and click on the link "Resources" to get to articles.

ONLINE JOB HUNTING

Because most job searches these days are online, it is important to understand the function of key words in looking for employment opportunities in areas for which social workers are qualified. Start your search by exploring the types of jobs these key words find for you and see how your education and skills match up to the job descriptions. The better the match, the better the chance your resume will rise to the top of those resumes employers pull "out of the slush pile" to review.

Here are some keywords often found in social work jobs:

- Executive, director, coordinator, manager, supervisor, administrator, public administrator, development director, fundraising.
- Human resources, human services, social services, social work, family services, group services.
- Social justice, justice, peace and justice, advocacy, lobbying, social policy, policy, policy planning, policy analyst, public administration.
- Community planning, community development, development planner, regional planner, community organizer, tenant organizer, program planner, community outreach worker.

- Communications, media, public relations.
- Counseling, health, mental health, behavioral health, psychology, direct services, case management, community mental health worker.
- Research, education, and support services.

CREATING YOUR RESUME

As an exercise to get you started in applying for a professional social work job try formatting your education and experience using the following template:

A. **Name and full contact information, including cell number and e-mail address:** Create a nice heading and use at least a 14 pt. font in bold lettering. Employers need to be able to read your contact information in order to call you for that perfect job! Do not bother to write what your career goals or objectives are because everyone knows your main goal is to be employed.

B. **Education:** Put your most recent degree first and only the year you received the degree. If you have a master's degree, you no longer need to list high school information. If you have a bachelor's degree, continue to list high school. Make sure to include the name of the school, and the city and state where you attended.

C. **Certifications and Licenses:** Did you receive any special training or license such as Microsoft Office Certification, CPR or Red Cross training, or a social work license of any kind? If so, write it here.

D. **Languages:** If you have a language capability even at a basic level, enter that information in this section, including any proficiency you may have in American Sign Language.

E. **Professional Experience:** Include any paid work experience you had while attending college or after graduation. Start with your most recent job first, and then work your way back to your undergraduate days. Enter your job title, name of company, city and state, general time frame of employment, and briefly outline what you did in the job. For example:

> Medical Social Worker, Virginia Hospital, Arlington, Virginia, 2006–present. Responsibilities included conducting intakes and assessments of all emergency room patients, providing information

and referral resources, and attending multidisciplinary team meetings.

F. **Internships:** Use the same format as in the example above, and include the number of hours you completed.

G. **Service Activities:** Typically, this should encompass any volunteer or civic activities you perform. List your role, name of organization, city, state, and time served in that capacity.

H. **Awards and Honors:** This category includes any achievement you were recognized for in high school, college, or graduate school. You may have won an Outstanding Athlete Award or were inducted into the National Honor Society, and these are important items for employers to see if you have them. If not, leave this category out of your resume for the time being.

I. **Professional Memberships:** Even if you are a student member of an organization like a fraternity or NASW, those are professional memberships.

J. **Continuing Education Trainings Attended:** The section refers to professional formal programs you attended and not casual office trainings. Usually you will receive a Certificate of Attendance for this type of program. Please keep those for your records.

K. **References:** Actually, list three references with their name, title, *FULL* contact information, including telephone numbers and e-mail address.

Don't worry about making your resume look like something Donald Trump would expect to receive. Keep the font clean and simple, in a readable size, and on white or beige paper that is a step above multiuse paper for printers. Plain white linen paper with black or dark blue ink is always a winning combination.

Review your resume for typing errors and grammatical mistakes. One small error may be enough to put your resume below many others, and you could miss out on being called for an interview for the position you think would be a perfect fit for you.

NETWORKING

Now that you have a professional looking resume in order, finding your dream job is the next step. One of the most helpful hints all the career development and job hunting resources will give you, is to make use of the people you already know and the personal contacts through them; in other words—NETWORK! This is the number one source for most people finding a job. Networking is the basic foundation of information sharing, and the more you know about potential openings in different areas the better prepared you are to submit your resume and be called for an interview.

Give a copy of your resume to your parents, your friends' parents, minister, college professors, and the family you babysat for in high school. They all have networks and professional contacts, and one of them may be interested in you for that first social work job!

Best wishes to you as you move closer to having an extraordinary career as a professional social worker.

Epilogue

The authors of this book are in various stages of their own social work careers and firmly believe that social work is a career for an extraordinary life. It is challenging, rewarding, exciting, and demanding, all at the same time. It is a career that allows for tremendous professional and personal growth. It is never boring. It requires many skills and personal characteristics such as: compassion; patience; strong ethics; critical thinking; creativity; self-care; strong communication skills; and a passion for helping individuals, families, groups, organizations, and communities. It is a career that will continue to be in demand for years to come, providing job security for many aspiring social workers in this country.

The goal of this book has been fourfold:

- To answer the question: What is social work?
- To help readers assess whether they are well suited for a career in social work;
- To profile over 101 career options for social workers and assist readers in evaluating which of these might be a good fit for them; and
- To provide readers with the tools they need to creatively plan their social work career based on their unique skills and interests.

As we stated earlier in this book, social work is a wonderful career, but it is not for everyone. There are many misconceptions about social work, so we recommend taking an introductory social work course and talking to social workers in the field. Do some volunteer work where social workers are employed. Get to know yourself very well to assess whether you have the skills and personality needed to be an effective and competent social worker. Are you compassionate and nonjudgmental? Do you get upset by social injustice? Are you an effective communicator as well as a good listener? Do you have good problem solving skills? Do you believe that all individuals have dignity and worth? Is appreciating the differences among people something you celebrate?

One of the most exciting features of social work is that we get to work with a wide variety of client populations in a vast array of settings. Social workers are change agents who work to create positive change with individuals, families, groups, organizations, and communities. We work at the individual level as caseworkers and clinicians, and we also work at the macro level to create needed social and political change at the local, state, national, and international levels. And the best part is you can work in one area of practice for a period of time and then change your career focus to work with a new population or issue using new or different skills.

The social workers profiled in this book studied social work because it is a profession committed to social justice and helping those in our country who are often forgotten and marginalized. A social work education provides students with the knowledge, values, and skills to intervene with individuals and families in need. But social work students also study and learn to address social problems on a larger scale at the macro level—problems such as poverty and homelessness; violence in our families and communities; the millions of Americans who are without health insurance; discrimination; child abuse, neglect, and exploitation; human rights violations; inequalities in our public schools; and lack of mental health services. Social workers not only help individuals function better within their environment, but also work on changing the environment so it works better for individuals and families. This is one of the defining features of the social work profession.

If the six core values of the social work profession (service, social justice, competence, the importance of human relationships, integrity, and the dignity and worth of the person) speak to you, then you just might be a social worker!

For more information about the social work profession:

1. National Association of Social Workers: www.socialworkers.org
2. Council on Social Work Education: www.cswe.org
3. Edwards, Richard L. (Ed.). (2007). *Encyclopedia of social work* (20th ed.). Washington, DC: NASW Press.

4. Gibelman, M. (2005). *What social workers do* (2nd ed.). Washington, DC: NASW Press.
5. Glicken, M. D. (2007). *Social work in the 21st century: An introduction to social welfare, social issues, and the profession.* Thousand Oaks, CA: Sage Publications.
6. Grobman, L. M. (2004). *Days in the lives of social workers: 54 professionals tell real life stories from social work practice* (3rd ed.). Harrisburg, PA: White Hat Communications.
7. Information for Practice: www.nyu.edu/socialwork/ip
8. *Legacies of Social Change: 100 Years of Professional Social Work in the United States.* Video available from NASW Press at www.socialworkers.org
9. Morales, A. T., Sheafor, B. W., & Scott, M. E. (2006). *Social work: A profession of many faces* (11th ed.). Boston: Allyn & Bacon.
10. Payne, M. (2006). *What is professional social work?* Chicago, IL: Lyceum Books, Inc.
11. Segal, E. A., Gerdes, K. E., & Steiner, S. (2006). *An introduction to the profession of social work: Becoming a change agent.* Belmont, CA: Brooks/Cole.
12. Social Workers: Help Starts Here: www.helpstartshere.org

Index

Note: A *t* following a page number indicates tabular material.